A Fragment of a Sociological Autobiography

A Fragment of a Sociological Autobiography

The History of
My Pursuit of
a Few Ideas

Edward Shils

Steven Grosby
editor

Transaction Publishers
New Brunswick (U.S.A.) and London (U.K.)

Library of Congress Catalog Number: 2006044477
ISBN: 0-7658-0336-4
Printed in the United States of America

Library of Congress Cataloging-in-Publication Data

Shils, Edward, 1910-1995.
    A fragment of a sociological autobiography : the history of my pursuit
of a few ideas / Edward Shils ; edited by Steven Grosby ; with an introd.
by Steven Grosby.
       p. cm.
    Includes bibliographical references and index.
    ISBN 0-7658-0336-4 (alk. paper)
    1. Sociology. 2. Sociology—Philosophy. 3. Social values. 4. Civil
society. 5. Shils, Edward, 1910-1995. I. Grosby, Steven Elliott, 1951-
II. Title.

HM585.S5165   2006
301.092—dc22   2006044477

Contents

Acknowledgements

I began efforts to publish *A Fragment of a Sociological Autobiography* with accompanying manuscripts in 2000. However, shortly thereafter, I put the proposal aside because of pressing obligations to finish two books of my own, *Biblical Ideas of Nationality: Ancient and Modern* (2002) and *Nationalism: A Very Short Introduction* (2005). It was in August 2004 when Professor S. N. Eisenstadt, over dinner at his home in Jerusalem, strongly urged me to take up again the idea of the publication of this volume. I thank him for reminding me of what I should not have had to be reminded, namely, the significance of these manuscripts for theoretical sociology. I also thank Mr. Joseph Epstein, good friend of Edward Shils and co-executor of his estate, for joining Professor Eisenstadt in urging me to proceed. Finally, I thank Edward Shils' friend and my wife Professor Naomi Farber and our son Samuel for making certain that I had the time to prepare this volume for publication.

Introduction

Edward Shils wrote *A Fragment of a Sociological Autobiography: The History of My Pursuit of a Few Ideas* during the years of 1991 and 1992, when he was eighty-one years old. He was in full command of his considerable intellectual abilities, and remained so until only a few months before his death in January 1995. I was in a position to judge firsthand how intellectually powerful he remained during even the last six months of his life; for, in July 1994, I accompanied him to the meeting of the Academic Advisory Board of the Institut für die Wissenschaften vom Menschen held at the summer residence, Castelgandolfo, of Pope John Paul II. Cancer had spread throughout his body, and the treatments of chemotherapy had physically exhausted him to the point where he could not travel alone, which is why I was with him in Italy and, later, England. Nonetheless, his comments during the discussions at Castelgandolfo were in full accord with the intellectual insight and bravery that were characteristic of him throughout his life. I remember one evening at Castelgandolfo Paul Ricoeur saying to me that, while he did not always agree with Shils' views, he had always admired Shils' intellectual and personal bravery, and never more so than at that time in Italy.

At the time of the composition of the three manuscripts that comprise this volume, Shils, even at eighty-one, maintained his demanding pace of activities, traveling regularly between his two homes—Chicago and Cambridge, England—with frequent visits to Italy, Austria, and Germany. His capacity for work remained prodigious: writing many important papers; continuing to edit *Minerva: A Review of Science, Learning, and Policy;* teaching seminars during the Autumn and Spring semesters at The University of Chicago; and organizing the conference "The University of the 21st Century" as the central event of the centennial celebration of The University of Chicago in 1991.[1] To mark further the centenary of that university, at which he had spent more than sixty years, Shils had edited *Remem-*

1

bering The University of Chicago, consisting of forty-seven chapters of recollections of those teachers, scientists, and scholars who had made that university famous.[2] During this period he also began, in collaboration with his friend Carmen Blacker, the volume *Cambridge Women*.[3]

Many of the papers that Shils wrote during this period, including the previously unpublished two that accompany the *Fragment* in this volume—"Society, Collective Self-Consciousness and Collective Self-Consciousnesses" and "Collective Self-Consciousness and Rational Choice"—are important theoretical contributions. The same may be said of those other papers written by him during this time on civility and civil society. Among these, especially three merit careful attention: "Civility and Civil Society: Good Manners Between Persons and Concern for the Common Good in Public Affairs"; "Nation, Nationality, Nationalism and Civil Society"; and "The Virtue of Civility." These latter three papers are to be found in the posthumously published volume, *The Virtue of Civility*.[4]

More should be said about the place of the manuscripts of this volume in the history of Shils' thought. Shils had delivered in 1974 the T.S. Eliot Memorial Lectures at the University of Kent at Canterbury. The revision of those lectures appeared in 1981, when Shils was seventy-one, as *Tradition*, published by Faber and Faber and The University of Chicago Press. *Tradition* was the last book-length monograph by Shils to have been published during his life. It had been preceded by the publication of three volumes of his selected papers, published by The University of Chicago: *The Intellectuals and the Powers* (1972), *Center and Periphery* (1975), and *The Calling of Sociology* (1980). However, as I have stressed, from 1981 to 1994, Shils continued his work; he deepened his theoretical understanding and pushed out into new directions. The manuscript *Movements of Knowledge*, about which more below, represented the new direction of his work. As to those problems that he had worked on previously but now returned to with a deeper understanding, his writings during the late 1980s and early 1990s on civility and civil society are considerably richer than his earlier, important essays on these subjects.[5] The other area that received his renewed attention was the problem of "consensus," or as he referred to it during the last fifteen years of his life and in the manuscripts of this volume, "collective self-consciousness." The problem of collective self-consciousness brings us to this book.

The largest part of this book, from which it takes its title, is *A Fragment of a Sociological Autobiography*. As indicated by the title, there is a wealth of autobiographical detail in the *Fragment*. Here, Shils, the son of Jewish immigrants, describes his boyhood in Philadelphia, where his father worked as a cigar maker; his discovery of the work of Mencken; his undergraduate years at The University of Pennsylvania; the years of 1931-32, when he worked as a social worker first in New York City and then in Chicago; and how, during 1932 and 1933, he became associated with The University of Chicago. The reader will also find Shils' fascinating reflections on the numerous individuals whom he knew well and who were significant to the social sciences in the twentieth century, among them Louis Wirth, Frank Knight, Karl Mannheim, Talcott Parsons, R.H. Tawney, Michael Polanyi, Audrey Richards, Friedrich Hayek, and Raymond Aron. We learn of other individuals and their place in Shils' life: Howard Becker, Salo Baron, Hebert Bulmer, Robert Hutchins, Nathan Leites, Everett Hughes, Karl Popper, Alexander von Shelting, and many more. There are discussions of Shils' appointments at the London School of Economics, Cambridge University, and, of course, the University of Chicago; his time in India; his relation with the Tavistock Institute; the pivotal role he played in the Congress for Cultural Freedom; and the founding of *Minerva*, which he edited for almost twenty-five years. Interspersed among such autobiographical reflections are references to many interesting details on the development of the social sciences, for example, the seminar held by Frank Knight in 1936 on the work of Max Weber, attended by, in addition to Edward Shils, Milton Friedman and George Stigler. Obviously, the *Fragment* represents an important contribution to the history of the social sciences in the twentieth century.

It would, however, be grossly inaccurate to view the *Fragment* as primarily a personal memoir. This clearly was not Shils' intention. First, there are many penetrating theoretical evaluations: of the work of Mannheim; of *Toward a General Theory of Action*, and of the work of Talcott Parsons subsequent to his collaboration with Shils; and of the works of Tönnies, Simmel, Durkheim, Sorel, and Weber. There are extended analyses of the concepts of status and deference, of the "primary group" and its place in the evolution of Shils' understanding of *gemeinschaftliche* relations, of ideology, and of civility. Above all, reflecting on his life's work, Shils' concluded that, despite the wide range of areas on which he wrote (the constitution of society, primary groups, the "new" states, secrecy, privacy, intellectuals, tradition, higher education), there was, in fact, a thematic unity of concern: the moral order of a society. The history of the development and the nature of the theoretical refinement of this concern are the real subjects of the *Fragment*.

In the 1930s and subsequently, this theoretical preoccupation with the character of the order of society was expressed by Shils through the category of "consensus," both its structure (as a "primary group," or as a relation between "center and periphery," or as the place of deference in its constitution, or as a vehicle for an attenuated charisma) and its moral pattern (through an ideological orientation that would inevitably lead to tyranny, or through that component necessary for and constitutive of a democratic society of ordered liberty, namely civility). What Shils was concerned with throughout his life's work was the fact of the existence of a "we," whether as a friendship, as the result of love, as a religious organization, or as a national society. Near the end of the *Fragment*, Shils himself is clear about this thematic unity of concern throughout his life: "I have really been chipping away on the same rock. The rock is a single problem. What is that problem? It is the problem of all of classical sociology and political theory, namely, the nature and conditions of consensus, or of social solidarity, or loyalty." It is the problem posed by Simmel, "How is society possible?"

It was shortly before and especially several years after Shils' collaboration with Talcott Parsons in the formulation of *Toward a General Theory of Action* that Shils set to work to present systematically his views on this problem.[6] The result of this work was the over 800 page-long manuscript *Love, Belief, and Civility*. Several of Shils' important papers during the 1950s arose out of this manuscript, specifically, "Primordial, Personal, Sacred and Civil Ties," "Ideology and Civility," "The Concentration and Dispersion of Charisma," and "Center and Periphery."[7] As Shils discusses in some detail the manuscript *Love, Belief, and Civility* in the *Fragment*, it is unnecessary for me to describe it further here. The manuscript is today located in the collection of Shils' papers at the Regenstein Library of the University of Chicago, so that those who wish to examine it today can do so.

It should be emphasized that Shils explicitly understood human relations, during this period and subsequently, as being pluralistic in their orientations. This recognition of the character of human conduct must be kept front and center if one wishes to understand properly Shils' work. While it is obviously the case that Shils was always preoccupied with the character of solidarity, to characterize that preoccupation as being "structural-functionalist" is not only to engage thoughtlessly in the obfuscating and simplistic formulations that unfortunately infuse social science discourse (formulations that Shils both never used and, in fact, despised), but also to avoid the complications posed by a plurality of orientations to any solidarity—complications that were always on Shils' mind.

Shils' reflections on tradition during the 1970s, culminating in the publication of *Tradition*, led him to refine his understanding of social relations and the constitution of society. This further development of his thought resulted in the reformulation of "consensus" as "collective self-consciousness." Here, again, there is no need to repeat what the reader will find in this book regarding Shils' understanding of "collective self-consciousness" and how it differs from "collective consciousness"; and certainly so as Shils always accepted the obligation to convey his thoughts in the clearest possible manner (*Toward a General Theory of Action* being the only exception to this obligation throughout his long career). I wish only to stress that in Shils' deliberations on the existence of a "we" of various kinds—of qualitatively heterogeneous collective self-consciousnesses—he always accepted, as factually necessary, the principle of methodological individualism; that is, that all action could only be the action of individuals. Nonetheless, the very existence of a "we" (or the reality to which the wide use of such terms as "identity" or "shared" refer) forced Shils to conclude that one must qualify the principle of methodological individualism. He rejected a hyper-individualism that refused to recognize a reality outside the mind of the individual. It was the recognition of the necessity for such a qualification and to understand better the nature of that reality that led to Shils' warm reception of the idea of "World Three" of Karl Popper's "Epistemology Without a Knowing Subject" (1968) and "On the Theory of Objective Mind" (1970).[8] Shils had certainly already held these views for some time; for they account for his insistence, twenty years earlier in *Toward a General Theory of Action*, on the *relative* independence of the realm of culture. Moreover, intimations of these views are to be found in Frank Knight's writings; and there should be no doubt that anyone could have read Knight's writings with more care than Shils had in the 1930s and subsequently.

As my own views on these matters became clearer to me around 1988, Shils suggested to me that I might benefit from reading Hans Freyer's *Theorie des objektiven Geistes: eine Einleitung in die Kulturphilosophie*. Being impressed with this work, I subsequently translated it.[9] Shils told me that he had reread this work by Freyer during his collaboration with Parsons. I mention this conversation between Shils and me to indicate that he had been aware for many years, probably since the late 1930s but assuredly by the late 1940s during his seminar with Karl Popper at the London School of Economics, of those complications in human conduct that require qualifying one's understanding of methodological individualism. It is this theoretical background of the relative independence of culture that was, I think, the precondition for Shils' evaluation and extension of Weber's concept of charisma during the 1960s and 1970s, and, as explained by him in the *Fragment*, his renewed, but critical, interest during the 1980s in Durkheim.

Concurrent with the writing of the *Fragment*, Shils conducted a several semesters-long seminar at The University of Chicago with S. N. Eisenstadt and James Coleman. The primary reading for that seminar was Coleman's *The Foundations of Social Theory*.[10] Over the course of the seminar, Shils wrote two papers in which he presented his views, and the ways they differed from those of Coleman. Those papers, "Society, Collective Self-Consciousness and Collective Self-Consciousnesses" and "Collective Self-Consciousness and Rational Choice," have been included in this book because their theme is one with the theoretical concern of the *Fragment*. Thus, this book is an important contribution not only to the history of the social sciences in the twentieth century, but also to theoretical sociology.

These latter two papers represent Shils' final elaboration of his views on "collective self-consciousness." In evaluating the merit of these views, the interested reader would do well also to consider the following four additional articles written during the last several years of Shils' life. As I have mentioned, the first two, "Civility and Civil Society: Good Manners Between Persons and Concern for the Common Good" and "Nation, Nationality, Nationalism and Civil Society" are to be found in *The Virtue of Civility*. The third, "Reflections on Tradition, Center and Periphery, and the Universal Validity of Science: The Significance of the life of S. Ramanujan" appeared in *Minerva* Winter 1991. The final paper, "Henry Sumner Maine in the Tradition of Analysis of Society" appeared in *The Victorian Achieve-*

ment, edited by Alan Diamond and published by Cambridge University Press in 1991.

In addition to the unfinished manuscript from the 1950s, *Love, Belief, and Civility*, one will also find among Shils' papers at the Regenstein Library the work that preoccupied most of his attention during the 1980s, *Movements of Knowledge*. The emphasis of this work, as described by Shils, was "to arrive at an understanding of how collectivities that are formed around the collective possession of knowledge are constituted, how they expand and contract, and what are the limits of their expansion." The breadth of this manuscript—in both its current state and its aim—is encyclopaedic, covering different areas of knowledge (scientific, humanistic, religious, wisdom, technological, self-knowledge, and knowledge of society) and their institutional and cultural settings. Of course, to have knowledge of one's own society is to participate in a collective self-consciousness. As Shils discusses at length *Movements of Knowledge* near the end of the *Fragment*, I will in this introduction limit myself to only a few additional observations about that manuscript.

Although Shils published several papers from his work on *Movements of Knowledge* and although a few of the manuscript's unpublished sections are polished, for example, the section on wisdom, most of the manuscript—taking up ten full boxes of his papers—is regrettably in the form of extensive, detailed outlines and notes. Secondly, I believe that Shils' long and close friendship with Arnaldo Momigliano had an influence on Shils' conception of *Movements of Knowledge*, even though Momigliano is not mentioned in the *Fragment*. Anyone familiar with Momigliano's work will see clearly the thematic overlap. It is obvious from Momigliano's writings on: alien wisdom; on the relation of one culture to another (specifically, the influence, or lack thereof, of Roman, Greek, and Jewish cultures on one another); and on the methodological problems of the knowledge of one's society that confront that society's historians (and, for that matter, the historian of those historians). I cannot account for why there is no mention of Momigliano in the *Fragment*. But then there is so much about Shils' intellectual interests that does not appear in the *Fragment*. He was a careful student of all periods of history; a voracious reader of literature; a close friend to many writers (for example, it was Shils, despite the misgivings of Edward Levi (so Edward Levi told me in a conversation in his office), who brought Saul Bellow to the University of Chicago); knowledgeable about art

and architecture; and, of course, intimately familiar with philosophy, especially social and political. He was equally at home with the
works of Ernest Renan, E. H. Gombrich, and Michael Oakeshott.

The *Fragment* and these two papers on collective self-consciousness were unpublished. It has never been the desire of Mr. Joseph
Epstein and myself, as co-executors of the estate of Edward Shils, to
seek to publish everything written by Shils. We have thought, rightly
I believe, that we should not bring into print those manuscripts (for
example, *Love, Belief, and Civility*) that Shils himself did not seek to
publish. We have made an exception with the manuscripts in this
volume because we thought that they were of considerable theoretical importance and, although not revised for publication by Shils,
were nevertheless polished enough for us to publish. It is possibly
the case that had he lived longer, Shils might have published revisions of them. We also knew from those published papers written
during the early 1990s, for example, on Ramanujan and on Henry
Sumner Maine, that Shils continued to refine in important ways his
theoretical understanding of society and human conduct.

A few more words on the editing of the manuscripts of this volume are in order. First, there is a small amount of repetition among
the sections of the *Fragment* and the two papers. I have let that repetition remain, largely because, where it occurs, it is often related to
points of pressing importance. For example, the reader will find discussions of Shils' understanding of methodological individualism
and its bearing on collective self-consciousness near the end of the
Fragment and also in "Collective Self-Consciousness and Rational
Choice." Second, I have not translated into English Shils' frequent
use of numerous German and French terms; nor have I supplied
extensive bibliographical references to the many books referred to
by Shils. I have not done this because I have assumed a familiarity
with much of this material by the readers who are likely to take an
interest in this book. Finally, I have, for the most part, confined the
endnotes to references to Shils' work. All endnotes are by the editor.

I wish to conclude this introduction with my own, most partial
and brief recollection of Shils as I knew him—first, as a student,
then as his friend—from 1982 to 1995.[11] In preparing this volume
for publication, I was struck by how well the following excerpt from
the *Fragment* opened up for examination the intellectual character
of Edward Shils. In 1931, Shils had left Philadelphia for New York
City, where he was employed as a social worker. In describing that

time in his life, he relates the impression that The New York Public Library had left on him—no doubt, a description that says more about the man he had become than who he was then at the age of twenty-one.

> The ecclesiastical atmosphere of the great reading rooms of the New York Library, particularly the South Reading Room awed me by the spiritual atmosphere in which so many individuals, probably very few of whom were professional intellectuals, spent their evenings and weekends in reading books in the library. I remember having the impression that there was a lofty communion of spirits occurring in that grand room, with its small circles of light on the polished tables, with the darkness in the upper atmosphere and the walls up to about seven feet, lined by more reference works then I had ever imagined. Many of the encyclopaedias, learned books and dictionaries were greasy from long and frequent consultation over many years. Obscure lives in which the flame of the love of knowledge flickered and sometimes burned steadily were part of the allure of the great city. That residue of the eagerness for knowledge has left an enduring imprint on my sociological reflections.

Three parts of this excerpt especially reminded me of the Edward Shils whom I knew.

In this description of the New York Public Library, Shils assumes that many of the individuals who spent their evenings and weekends reading books in that library were not professional intellectuals. As I think about that assumption, I am reminded of how democratic Shils was in both his understanding of other individuals and his relations to them. I am reminded of those times during the 1980s when I would take Shils shopping (he did not have a car). Having finished purchasing various items for myself, I invariably could not find Shils. He would, time and again, be in some isolated corner of the store, engaged in a lengthy conversation with some clerk about the details of his or her life. He was fascinated with such details—the knowledge of the goods that the person was selling, the other person's hopes and disappointments, and their struggle to make their way in this world. He continually sought out and established relations with such people, not as a famous professor but as a fellow human being. And we would talk at great length about these people during our drive home from those stores.

Shils also refers to "the lofty communion of spirits." When Shils uses such language, he is, of course, aware of its unsatisfactory metaphysical imprecision. His work is to be understood as a continual attempt to describe the reality of that communion, but freed from any metaphysical obfuscation. But the point here is to observe Shils' abiding love for the life of the mind, one expression of which was the obligation he accepted to clarify, and by so doing defend, the purpose of the university.[12] He would not tolerate deviations from that purpose; and, as anyone within the academy knows, those deviations are a daily occurrence. As a doctoral student writing a dissertation under Shils' supervision, I knew that, even though the dissertation had been thoroughly revised three times in response to Shils' extensive, sentence by sentence, criticisms, the dissertation would be sent out to an external examiner with whom I had had no contact. (It was sent to Professor E.W. Nicholson, provost of Oriel College, Oxford.) It did not matter in the least to Shils that his colleagues may not have insisted upon a rigorous, thoroughly impartial external examination for the acceptance of a dissertation. I was sitting next to Shils when he read the external report of a 600 page-long dissertation on pre-Han China written by a favored pupil of his. The report recommended that the dissertation be rejected. Shils was saddened by the conclusion of the report; but, for him, that external verdict was final; there was nothing more to be done.

Shils was a man who loved knowledge for its own sake. To pursue knowledge for its own sake was, for him, the expression, *par excellence*, of the freedom of the mind. This love, and the freedom and character that it requires, was everywhere in his life. For example, from 1982 until just a few months before he died, *every* conversation between us began with Shils asking me what book I was currently reading. Even when we lived in different cities, when we would speak on the phone usually twice a week, the conversation would always begin the same way. In *every* private conversation between us, both before and after I was his pupil, on some substantive, theoretical subject, I was always asked by him to state clearly my views first on that subject. He wanted to know what I thought; he never was interested in having his views repeated to him. He demanded an independence of thought; he could not have been less interested in establishing a "school." To cultivate "followers"—so easy a temptation among professors—was abhorrent to him.

Finally, there was Shils' own library, about 15,000 volumes, mostly in Chicago, the rest in Cambridge, England. To enter his home in Chicago was to be surrounded by those books. In every room and hallway, in every direction one turned, there were books, including on the dining room table on which he served so many delicious meals prepared by him. In the living room, every wall of which was lined from the floor up to the ceiling with books, there were three large bronze busts: of Max Weber, of Joseph Conrad, and of Jacob Epstein.

Over the years I have occasionally heard it said that Edward Shils was "difficult." I have wondered just what was meant by such a characterization. He was a man who accepted and lived by the academic ethic. He embodied the standards of what the life of the university should be. If this is what is meant by "difficult," then Edward Shils was indeed difficult; although obviously it is a characterization by those who are unfaithful to those standards. It is true that, for those close to him, the expectations were high. I remember one day while Shils was staying in our home in Philadelphia, my wife found him looking around my desk. My wife said, "Edward, is there something I can get for you? Do you want a writing pad, or a cup of tea?" He responded by saying, "No, my dear, I am trying to see what books *in foreign languages* your husband has been reading." Such were his expectations; but would that more academics today had such expectations!

The scene of Shils glancing over my desk depicts, of course, his attempt to judge the development of a former pupil. It, however, also represents something more about Shils: his desire for intellectual engagement with others for the purpose of clarifying his own thoughts, arising out of his own intellectual uncertainty. That uncertainty, while acknowledged in the *Fragment*, should not be underestimated. After my first article had been accepted for publication in the *Zeitschrift für die alttestamentliche Wissenschaft*, I regularly received from Shils the rough drafts of his manuscripts. They were most certainly not sent to me for my instruction or approval; rather, he wanted hard criticisms from me—criticisms that at that stage of my development I was too often not able to provide.

He was a kind man, always sensitive to the difficulties of life. But he was a man with uncompromising standards. He detested what he often called "wire-pulling," the too often academic behavior of pursuing one's self-interest at the expense of those standards; the attempt to appoint or promote one's own students or only those who mimic one's own views is an egregious example. It seems to me that now more than ever our times call out for such "difficult" individu-

als. As I have come to understand what is meant by this characterization, it, in fact, refers to "character." As I think about my teacher
and friend, he was a man of the highest and finest character.

Steven Grosby

Notes

1. The proceedings of that remarkable conference appeared in *Minerva* Summer 1992.
2. Edward Shils, ed., *Remembering The University of Chicago* (Chicago: The Univer-
    sity of Chicago Press, 1991).
3. Carmen Blacker and Edward Shils, eds., *Cambridge Women: Twelve Portraits*
    (Cambridge: Cambridge University Press, 1996).
4. Edward Shils, *The Virtue of Civility: Selected Essays on Liberalism, Tradition, and
    Civil Society*, ed., Steven Grosby with an introduction by Steven Grosby (India-
    napolis: Liberty Fund, 1997).
5. See "Ideology and Civility" (1958), "Tradition and Liberty" (1958) and "The Anti-
    nomies of Liberalism" (1978), all of which appear in *The Virtue of Civility*. See also
    "Primordial, Personal, Sacred and Civil Ties" (1957), reprinted in *Center and Pe-
    riphery* (Chicago: The University of Chicago Press, 1975) and *The Torment of
    Secrecy*, published originally in 1956, but reissued by Ivan R. Dee in 1996.
6. *Toward a General Theory of Action* has been brought back into print by Transaction.
7. All of these papers were reprinted in *Center and Periphery*.
8. See Karl Popper, *Objective Knowledge* (Oxford: Oxford University Press, 1972).
9. Hans Freyer, *Theory of Objective Mind: An Introduction to the Philosophy of
    Culture*, translated, and with an introduction, by Steven Grosby, *Series in Continen-
    tal Thought* 25 (Athens: Ohio University Press, 1998).
10. James Coleman, *The Foundations of Social Theory* (Cambridge, MA: Harvard
    University Press, 1990).
11. For Joseph Epstein's recollection of Shils, see "My Friend Edward" in Edward
    Shils, *Portraits: A Gallery of Intellectuals*, ed., Joseph Epstein (Chicago: The Uni-
    versity of Chicago Press, 1997).
12. See Edward Shils, *The Calling of Education: The Academic Ethic and Other Es-
    says on Higher Education*, ed., Steven Grosby (Chicago: The University of Chi-
    cago Press, 1997); *The Order of Learning: Essays on the Contemporary Univer-
    sity*, ed., Philip Altback (New Brunswick, NJ: Transaction Publishers, 1997).

A Fragment of a Sociological Autobiography

The History of My Pursuit of a Few Ideas

Preliminary Note

This is an autobiography of one strand of my life, namely, the development of an idea about society. It does not in the main attempt to describe the societies in which I have lived or the persons I have known. It is not even an autobiographical account of my intellectual interests or experiences. It is not even an account of my education except where it has to refer to particular persons from whom I have acquired certain ideas.

It is true that in the early pages I do refer to my parents and their friends; and I refer to a few teachers when those references are pertinent to understanding why I initially moved in a certain direction. I have, on the whole, avoided saying whether I liked or disliked anyone. I have certainly tried to do so, and especially to avoid the latter. It is very much my desire to cause no discomfiture to anyone living. I have said very little about the institutions in which I have been a participant. I have done that elsewhere. In short, this essay would be better classified as an "ideography" if that word had not already been preempted for another meaning.

Despite all these efforts to confine the essay to a quite impersonal narrative, it might nevertheless have some interest. For one thing, I think that I have journeyed in the right direction, although the destination is still not discerned. I think that it might make my ideas more intelligible when I trace their history showing how they emerged from earlier ideas that were once current enough for some readers to recall them.

At each stage, I discovered something I had not known before I drew out a potentiality of the earlier idea. This has not been done simply by excogitation. It has been done by pondering on events observed by me or by others. It seems however to have shown the fruitfulness of the idea. The fact that it could be enlarged or differentiated sufficiently to be applied to the elucidation of events for which it would not have been adequate in its earlier form seems to me still to give evidence that it was the product of a groping in the right direction. What it means perhaps is that some of those older ideas cannot be regarded as superseded. Words like "consensus" and "primary groups" and "fusions of selves," etc., are still used by me but when they are used, I use them in a new sense which is a refinement and differentiation of the older sense and hence an advance over it. That is the main justification for this long and unspectacular journey.

I

I never had a course in sociology at the University of Pennsylvania where I was an undergraduate from the autumn of 1927 to the end of the first semester of the session of 1930-1931. I studied several languages and primarily French literature, and to a lesser extent the German, Swedish and Italian languages and literatures. I also studied English literature with which I was already moderately familiar as the result of an excellent education at Philadelphia Central High School. I also studied Christian theology.

I had never heard of sociology at Central High School. After I came to the University, I heard a certain amount about it from several friends of mine who attended courses in it. At that time, the department of sociology at the University of Pennsylvania was a quite respectable affair. Professors Bossard, Lichtenberger, Donald Young, Thorsten Sellin, Rex Crawford, Howard Becker, Ray Abrams were not great figures intellectually but looking back at them, they leave an impression of sobriety and diligence. They wrote mostly textbooks if they wrote at all. Of the entire department I knew personally and only very slightly, Howard Becker. Many years later, I met Donald Young, Sellin, and Crawford; but I never became close to any of them. I must also have heard of sociology through a review of *Middletown* by the Lynds. It appeared in 1929 and must have been reviewed in the *Nation* and the *New Republic*, which I used to read. I read the book and thought it rather dreary. I first heard the names of William Graham Sumner and Charles Cooley from my friends in the department of sociology. I probably heard of the "Chicago School of Sociology" from them also, but I cannot say this with certainty.

I was a great browser in the stacks of the University Library, having been given a "stack permit" when I was a freshman, because the librarians decided that they could not cope with my incessant requests for books. Books about cities, Jews, Negroes, the rich and the poor interested me, and that is what the Chicago Sociological Series was about.

I first heard of Max Weber's work from references to it in R. H. Tawney's *Religion and the Rise of Capitalism* which I discovered by accident on a table in the main branch of the Philadelphia Public Library and from Bukharin's which I discovered also by accident, on a small set of shelves of recently returned books placed at the end of the circulation desk of the University of Pennsylvania Library. I wonder who their readers were; I never met anyone in Philadelphia, except Howard Becker, who knew about Tawney, and I never knew anyone who had heard of Bukharin. I was very fascinated by the references to *Gesammelte Aufsätze zur Religionssoziologie* in both these books. In my freshman year, I knew just enough German to know what the title meant. I did not know what the sociology of religion was but I was convinced that it was important. My surmise turned out to be right. It was that awareness of Max Weber that made me determined to learn German. In my second year, I took the first half of a one-year two-semester course. I never took the second semester. That is the reason why I am now so weak in German grammar, particularly in subjunctives since the subjunctives came toward the end of the course.

On the basis of this half course of German, I took out of the University of Pennsylvania Library the *Wirtschaftsgeschichte* of Max Weber and the first volume of Sombart's *Der moderne Kapitalismus*. I read a good part of those volumes on hot nights in the summer of 1929 in Philadelphia. My mind was excited by Sombart's various categories, particularly by the distinction between *Bedarfsdeckunqswirtschaft* and *Tauschwirtschaft*. The *Wirtschaftsgeschichte* of Max Weber was much harder going. Sombart had a rather good style for a German academic of his time; Max Weber was more resistant to my efforts. In both cases I would read a page or paragraph, write down all the German words I did not know (which were very numerous), look them up in the Muret-Saunders dictionary, write down alongside the German word its English equivalent on a sheet of paper, re-read the two columns and then go back and re-read the page or the paragraph. This way I acquired a moderately competent knowledge of German although I was and still am occasionally perplexed by complicated grammatical constructions such as were undoubtedly dealt with at the latter chapters of the grammar book which I studied only on my own and not under the supervision of the teacher whose teachings I had deserted.

I also borrowed from the University Library Sombart's *Das Proletariat*, the first volume in the series *Die Gesellschaft* edited by Martin Buber. That was a marvelous series. (Buber must have been no older than twenty-five when he persuaded a famous German publisher to bring out the series in an original format, with typography, binding and endpapers very much in the *neuer Stil*). I still remember Sombart's description of the sparrows twittering among the *Mietskaserne*. I have not re-read the book since then, but I have some fairly sharp recollections of it. I recall particularly Sombart's sympathy with the children playing in the streets or on bare ground and the hopping, twittering sparrows, lively in dismal circumstances. I also recall my pleasure in reading through a whole German book; it was probably only about eighty pages long.

Another incident in this story of my sociological interest arose through another friend, who was studying philosophy; he was especially interested in German philosophy. From him I learned of the existence of Max Scheler. Although I did not try to read Max Scheler while I was an undergraduate, I was, however, fascinated by the title *Wesen und Formen der Sympathie*. (When I went to live in New York in the autumn of 1931, I bought a copy of that volume from Stechert, a wonderful large bookshop at 39 East 11th Street, a building of about four or five stories, containing books, thousands and thousands, new and second-hand, in all European languages and probably even in Oriental languages, although I did not yet venture in that direction.) It was only later that I learned about Scheler's *Wissensformen und die Gesellschaft*. I did not see the book until I came to Chicago in September 1932.

The library of the University of Chicago, after the library of the University of Pennsylvania, dazzled me. It made my heart beat faster when I thumbed for the first time the cards in the catalogue and then the books on the shelves. These libraries were the best part of my education. I already knew about Karl Mannheim's writings but I had not studied them.

II

In Philadelphia, I had lived at home and had a small circle of friends at the University all of whom were Philadelphians. Having gone to a very distinguished secondary school, I felt no great disjunction between secondary school and university. I also retained a number of my secondary school friends, so I never experienced in those years the great city in which an individual is lost. I was very well acquainted with Philadelphia, having lived, as a result of the frequent moving of my parents, in many different parts of the city. Through long walks from about the age of ten until practically the time of my departure from Philadelphia in the autumn of 1931 for New York, I extended that acquaintance to many areas of the city in which we had not lived. Nearly every Sunday, I left home at about 10:30 in the morning and returned home at about six o'clock. It is interesting to observe in view what now exists in big American cities that as far as I know, my dear mother, who was as anxious about her two children as any mother could be, never seemed to worry about what would happen to me on those jaunts throughout the city. I cannot recall her ever cautioning me against speaking to "strangers," "evil-looking persons," etc. Perhaps I looked more evil than they did; but I was never accosted by such persons if I did cross their path, and I was never asked for money or endangered by my sometimes pugnacious Irish coevals or the Italian boys' hypersensitivity to the dangers of the evil eye. There were some moments when it was "touch and go." Sometimes they demanded to know what I was "looking at." Somehow I always got away with my skin whole and my honor unscathed.

As I result of this, I gained a good sense of Philadelphia and had an affectionate intimacy with it. My father's fellow-cigarmakers used to visit our home sometimes for dinner on Saturday evening or Sunday noon; they were very interesting men of mainly Anglo-American, Irish, or German stock, sometimes relatively recent immigrants; there were also Cubans and Portuguese who came to see us. Mr. Hickman, Tom Collins who had wooden leg and who was connected in a very humble way with the "Vare machine" and Mr. Finzelberger, who gave my father a walking stick beautifully carved by a convict in a German prison at the end of the last century. I still possess that stick. All this gave me a sense of membership in a heterogeneous urban community that was a community despite all the differences.

There were no Negroes living on the street where we lived, but there were all the others: Scots, English, Irish, Germans, Italians, "old Americans," and of course, lots of Eastern European Jews.

The Negroes were of course segregated and we had no family contact with them. In my elementary school, however, about 20 percent (calculated from the photograph of my graduating class picture of 1923) of the children were Negroes. I do not recall any instance of an untoward reference to the Negroes as "niggers" or any other then current derogation. In the main, the white children did not walk home with the Negro children, partly because they lived in different directions. They were always as tidy and as well dressed as the white children; they were poor but probably not much poorer than some of the Irish and the Jewish children were in our school. The Negro children were just as well behaved and as polite as all the other children; I myself was perhaps more friendly with them than the other white children in the school, particularly with two of them. They were twins named Tate, one's first name was Pinkney and the first name of the other I cannot recall. They were both excellent runners in the fifty-yard dash—and I fancied myself also to be a good runner—so at least on my side, I thought that we were part of the elite of the school by virtue of our prowess as runners and hence belonged in a distinctive category which seemed more important than color and race. Perhaps I was pretty good compared with the worst runners in the school. On occasion I would see one of the Negro children after school or on Saturday morning pulling a little "express wagon" with freshly ironed laundry on it; the child's mother was a laundress at home and he was delivering the finished laundry. How she collected and brought it to her house, I do not know; they had no motorcars. Perhaps the children collected soiled linen in bags and brought it home on the same "express wagons."

All these experiences of the numerous neighborhoods in which we lived, the heterogeneity of my school classes, my Sunday walks and then my year of wandering around in New York in 1931 and 1932 made me into an eager proto-sociologist.

III

To return to my pre-career as proto-sociologist, I must have heard of Park and Burgess while I was still an undergraduate. Whether I heard about them from friends who had taken courses in sociology or from the late Howard P. Becker, who at that time was an instructor in sociology at the University of Pennsylvania and who had studied at the University of Chicago under Park, I do not recall. Becker was esteemed by me—from a distance—because I was told that he had studied in Germany. Becker, I learned later, was at war with the sociology department at Chicago and probably would not have referred to Park and Burgess sympathetically.

During my junior year, I took the initiative to form a sociology club and invited my friends to join it. It was a registered club of the University; we met about once a month. I cannot recall very much about the meetings. On one occasion I delivered a paper on "Protestantism and Capitalism." It was a fiasco! On another occasion, Howard Becker, whom I had not known but only heard of, was invited by me, to speak. My friends who were studying sociology told me that Becker had written a dissertation at Chicago on the "sacred and secular" in the Ionian cities. Since from my childhood I had been an eager reader of Greek history, having read Charles Oman's school textbook *The History of Greece*, which I had bought for five or ten cents at Leary's Bookstore, and Grote, in the Everyman's edition borrowed from the Kensington branch of the Philadelphia Public Library. Becker, a sociologist who dealt with Greece, aroused my interest. He was a nervous, tense, not at all a pleasant sort of man. There was a rasping truculence about him; I thought that he had staring angry eyes. Nevertheless, he was the first person I ever met who appeared to be connected with the great, solvent secrets of sociology. I thought that he knew all about German sociology about which I knew very little; and he had some connections with Park, about whom I had only a very vague notion. That disposed me in his favor. In those days, I was a Germanophile in academic matters. I thought that German professors knew all that was to be known. I thought that when a German professor took any problem in hand, the definitive solution was assured. (I have since learned better.)

Becker was not at all like the one teacher at the University of Pennsylvania for whom I felt affection, namely, Émile Caillet who was a member of the French department and perhaps also the philosophy or anthropology departments; I am not sure of this. Caillet was a broad-shouldered and thick-bodied, red-cheeked Frenchman; he was rumored to have been a student of Lévy-Bruhl, and adherent of what my friends referred to as "the French School of Sociology" and had done field work in Madagascar. He aroused our wonderment. I had a course of French thought in the nineteenth century with him; I wrote a relatively short paper (I had a penchant for submitting papers of seventy to eighty pages in length, written by hand on closely ruled foolscap) on which Caillet wrote, "Travail trop riche d'idées." He wrote a number of comments in a kindly and amused way about some of my hyperbolic statements about romanticism, about individualism, etc.; the message was, "stay close to the earth." On a few occasions he sat at my table at the Horn and Hardart cafeteria across from College Hall on Woodland Avenue where I ate most of my dinners of baked beans and fried potatoes at the cost of about fifteen cents a day. Those meetings with Émile Caillet at Horn and Hardart were the only times of my years as an undergraduate that I had an opportunity to sit alone with a teacher in the University. He was a very benevolent man. He must have been very amused by my oddities, my adventurous reading, relatively wide for an undergraduate, and the somewhat grandiose expression of my ideas such as they were; he certainly was indulgent towards them.

It was in about my junior year that I played a special role in a seminar given by Caillet in the anthropology department. The seminar was called "The French School of Sociology." I did not register for this course. When the seminar assembled for its first meeting, it turned out that I was the only student there who could read French. In those days *Les formes élémentaires de la vie religieuse* was the only book of Durkheim that had been translated into English. Professor Caillet thought that we should begin with the *Les règles de la méthode sociologigue*. I was therefore assigned the task of presenting a summary of the *Les règles* at the second meeting. Being contrary by nature, I read the *De la division du travail social*. He was somewhat vexed and he ordered me to prepare the summary of the *Les règles* for the next class. The course met once weekly for two hours. Again, contrary to my instructions, I prepared a report on *The Elementary Forms*. Again the presentation of *Les règles* was put off until the following week. I was strictly enjoined to present a summary of the *Les règles*. Again, I came prepared only to report on *Le suicide*. Finally, after these three miscarriages that could be attributed only to my mischievousness or antinomianism, I finally gave the report on the *Les règles*. By this time, Professor Caillet was quite exasperated but he never ceased his kindliness when we met on our white glass-topped tables of Horn and Hardart. I should emphasize what must be obvious, namely, that none of my reports was a scintillating performance. Quite apart from my poor exposition and imperfect grasp of the subject, I was not moved to enthusiasm by Durkheim in the way Sombart and Weber had moved me. I wrote out my analysis in my unpleasing handwriting and undoubtedly on the closely ruled foolscap that I then used. Although I could barely make out what I had written, I read the paper because I was too nervous and too lacking in self-confidence to speak freely, as I have learned to do since then. My indifference to the ideas of Durkheim over all the years up until about fifteen years ago was a result of this initial and intense immersion into Durkheim's writings. Many years after, my friend, Raymond Aron, told me that Durkheim bored him while Weber excited him intellectually. I was completely in agreement with him. Since then, my views about Durkheim have changed. I think that he was on to something important; but he could not reach the point of an adequate formulation about collective consciousness.

I am not sure when I first encountered the book *The City* edited by Park and Burgess with a bibliography by Louis Wirth. I certainly became acutely and excitedly aware of it in the year 1931-1932, which I spent as apprentice student social worker in New York. I lived on Morningside Heights part of that year and had access to The Seth Low Library, where I read Roman history and some parts of Simmel's sociology. It was then that I read Simmel's *Die Grossstadt und das Geistesleben*. That fitted perfectly with my experience of New York—scarcely at all with my experience of Philadelphia— and it whetted my appetite for Chicago and its sociology.

It was at Columbia that I attended my first course in sociology— with Theodore Abel—on "Social Conflict." Abel was a handsome elegant man of charming manners. Harry Alpert was clearly the favorite student of the department and he bore himself accordingly. I do not recall anything of the substance of the course; but I do recall Theodore Abel's pleasant voice, his refined foreign accent. I do not recall any of the books he recommended.

I do recall Professor Salo Baron much more vividly. He made a great impression on me through his course on "The History of the Jews." He was then a quite young man with bright blue eyes, blondish hair, a broad face and a kindly smile. Unlike Abel, he was fairly short in height and fairly broad. Like Abel, he was always elegantly dressed. He was a dramatic lecturer with a deep resonant voice and a gift for very evocative similes. I recall his description of the life of Baghdad in the tenth and eleventh century, "a city with the vitality of New York City." (New York was at that time a truly marvelous city for me after the placidity of Philadelphia.) I wrote an immense paper on the Jews in the Roman Empire for Professor Baron—more than a hundred pages, handwritten! The book that I recall best was Jean Juster's great work, *Les Juifs dans l'Empire romain*. On one occasion, I asked Professor Baron's opinion of Weber's *Das antike Judentum*. He said, "Very good for a gentile scholar." In the years that followed, I have repeatedly regretted that such a brilliant and learned lecturer was so humdrum in his books. Nevertheless, he was a man of great erudition and he was a warmhearted person whom I still appreciate.

When he said that Baghdad had "the vitality of New York City," I knew what he meant. I was dazzled by urban life of which New York seemed to me to be the epitome. I have a clear recollection of the excitement aroused in me by some of the numerous titles in Wirth's bibliography. My wandering around in the great city in the course of my work and on weekends, the essays of Park and Burgess, and the numerous references in Wirth's bibliography were fused in that one exhilarating year.

The ecclesiastical atmosphere of the great reading rooms of the New York Library, particularly the South Reading Room awed me by the spiritual atmosphere in which so many individuals, probably very few of whom were professional intellectuals, spent their evenings and weekends in reading books in the library. I remember having the impression that there was a lofty communion of spirits occurring in that grand room, with its small circles of light on the polished tables, with the darkness in the upper atmosphere and the walls up to about seven feet, lined by more reference works then I had ever imagined. Many of the encyclopaedias, learned books and dictionaries were greasy from long and frequent consultation over many years. Obscure lives in which the flame of the love of knowledge flickered and sometimes burned steadily were part of the allure of the great city. That residue of the eagerness for knowledge has left an enduring imprint on my sociological reflections.

All these I saw as part of the substance of city life. It was the desire to expand a cognitive pleasure, the pleasure of apprehending the daily life of ordinary people like those I used to see in my parental home and in the streets of Philadelphia or in the subway in New York that led me to wish to extend what little I knew of the Parkian sociology. I was at the time less aware of the economic function of cities; that was something that I learned later from my studies in Chicago.

I began to read Simmel in the autumn of 1931. I must have learned about him during my inspection of the *Introduction of the Science of Sociology* by Park and Burgess in which some passages of Simmel were translated, but particularly from the reference to *Die Grossstadt und das Geistesleben* in Wirth's bibliography. In the spring of 1932, I purchased a handsome edition of Simmel's *Soziologie* for $2.50 at Stecherts. I read the sections on the stranger and on written communication. I thought that Simmel was a dazzler but not what I thought a German professor should be; he was a bubbling fountain, not a broad powerful, irresistible river like Max Weber.

Simmel exhilarated me by the profusion and novelty of his *aperçus.* Yet, I thought that a proper German professor should proceed more systematically and should make it possible to learn from his writings what he regarded as most fundamental, as distinct from what was of secondary or derivative importance. Over the years, I have concluded that Simmel had no conception of society; that meant that his revelatory insights into particular situations were too self-contained. They were by their nature fragmentary. They lacked an essential element, namely, an understanding of the significance for individuals of being parts of society. (Simmel's defect in this regard is evident in his programmatic answer to the question: *Wie ist Gesellschaft überhaupt möglich?* The answer was, "through interaction." That is like saying that a building is made up of bricks; that might be true but it does not say what a building is.)

I should add that I never found any author, sociological or otherwise, who answered the question satisfactorily to me. Of course, all these questions were in the future. They were certainly not clear to me when I first read Simmel; indeed I never confronted the question until the end of the 1950s when I saw through the poverty of the theories of national character. Indeed, of my main interests over the past fifty years, the problem of the nature of society emerged rather late.

No less enduring an imprint has been the awareness that much of social life is lived in "aimless camaraderie," as Frank Knight called it. I also appreciated the qualities of the various ethnic groups through whose districts I loved to walk. I was moved by the sight of old Europe living in the so different American cities like grass growing between cobblestones. I had another interest, that of French literature from the early nineteenth century to the present, i.e., about 1925. I knew the prose literature quite well. I was interested, too, in the religious, social and political attitudes of the main writers; I was interested in the predominance of certain ideas, particularly the ideas writers had about themselves and the society in which they lived. I was interested not only in the ideas of particular writers on particular topics; I was interested in the patterns formed of the various ideas of the same individual on particular topics. I was also interested in the inter-individual patterns of the ideas of different individuals. It was simple enough to say that some ideas are "statistically representative" of the ideas of many persons. That did not satisfy me. I wanted to discern the inter-individual pattern of ideas (or beliefs) in a collectivity. I wanted to be able to delineate the inter-individual pattern and to see how the individual fitted into or "participated" in the pattern. During the last years of the 1920s, the idea of a *Zeitgeist* was still common but I do not recall any analysis of what it was.

During my undergraduate years, perhaps during my second year, I read a good part of George Brandes' *Main Currents of European Literature*. I did not read all six volumes, but I read several of them in full and some of them in part. I was attracted and troubled by the idea of "main currents." How does one define and discern a "main current"? How does one distinguish a "main current" from "minor currents"? How does one distinguish these from a "counter-current"? I was bothered by the terms used by George Brandes in his lectures on European literature in the first half of the nineteenth century. Apart for my admiration for the European breadth of Brandes' intellectual culture, I was convinced that the term "main current" meant something worth knowing, but what it meant was not clear from *Main Currents of European Literature*. It is one thing to say that certain writers were the best writers of a particular period, but it is quite another thing to say that the works or the works of others formed a "main current." Of which larger whole were the main currents parts? This was one of my problems. That is why I was interested in studying Dilthey's *Einleitung in die Geisteswissenschaften*. Meanwhile, I thought that once I was able to get into Mannheim's works, I would be on the right track. But at this stage, I had not done more than look at Mannheim's essays in the *Archiv für Sozialwissenschaft* (1925), *Das Problem einer Soziologie des Wissens*, and in the *Jahrbuch für Soziologie*(1926), *Ideologische und Soziologische Interpretation geistiger Gebilde.*

IV

The criticism made much later by Ernst Gombrich in his *In Search for Cultural History* of the idea that there was a pervasive "spirit of the age" or "*Zeitgeist*," was already evident to me. I was aware enough of the multiplicity of voices in any particular period, not only in the United States of the late 1920s but in France in the eighteenth and nineteenth centuries which was the country and period which I knew best. But the simple rejection of the idea of a *Zeitgeist* did not resolve my difficulties because I already saw that there were inter-individual patterns which were both received and rejected by succeeding generations. Somehow there arose in my mind an idea that if I were to study Dilthey's *Einleitung in die Geisteswissenschaften* I would get a notion as how to describe these inter-individual patterns of beliefs, these "currents," "main currents" and "minor currents," the "spirit of an age," etc. I was wrong. I did not obtain this from Dilthey. In fact, I got nothing from Dilthey, although I have not given up the hope. The idea of *Ideenzusammenhänge* that Mannheim made familiar to me, and the notions of *geistige Gebilde* and of *geistige Objektivationen* that I adapted from Hans Freyer intermittently occurred to me. It took me some time to put behind me Mannheim's effort to abolish the boundary between the intellectual and the social.

What I wanted to do was to combine the study of the history of "ideas" contained in intellectual works with the sociological study of intellectuals, intellectuals' attitudes, intellectual institutions and intellectual collectivities. But I could not find the way to do so.

I thought that if I mastered sociology, I would find the answer to this question. I was not confident of myself because I knew that my grasp of the problem was too nebulous. I kept slipping back into overly individualistic interpretations. Had I paid more attention to Durkheim's ideas about "conscience collective" with which I was already acquainted, I might have developed at that time the ideas which much later appeared to me to become very urgent when I began to work out my ideas in connection with my manuscript *Move-*

ments of Knowledge.[1] In any case, I did not do so. Still, in 1931 and 1932, I thought that if I could only arrange to study Dilthey and, of course, Max Weber I would find my way forward.

This interest was closely connected with another interest in what I later called "consensus."[2] It received no encouragement from anyone I met except for an occasional remark dropped by Frank Knight in his seminars and writings. I caught a glimpse of it in phrases like "the autonomy of the cultural sphere," or "the super-organic." From time to time it appeared in my efforts to establish a proper understanding of social stratification. I wanted to get rid of the misleading idea of "socio-economic status" as a constellation of "objective factors" like occupation, income, entrepreneurial or managerial power, etc. I wanted to establish that status was a "matter of opinion," of evaluation of those "objective factors." I also saw that the "socio-economic classification" postulated a single distribution of status, while I was aiming at showing that, being a matter of "opinion," it might be consensual but only rarely; the stratification "system" was vague, dissensual and not continuously salient.

I did not succeed for a long time in formulating my views of social status or deference as kinds of collective self-consciousness. I contented myself with trying to learn more about intellectuals who were constituted as intellectuals by their participation in "the cultural sphere" through the production and interpretation of intellectual works about all the different subjects which engage the human mind. As a result of this failure to pursue the phenomenon of the constitution of the cosmos of knowledge and evaluations (values), the political and moral attitudes of intellectuals remained as the object of my attention.

These three major substantive interests and my pleasure in contemplating the moral order of urban society emerged very early. It is with their development, elaboration, and fusion that I am concerned in this set of recollections.

It was this fragmentation of my thought that I did not overcome. Indeed, I did not even see the obligation to overcome it. As a result, although my interest in intellectuals in order to reach a higher level (or to go more deeply) needed to be brought together with my then inchoate ideas about consensus as an internally connected objectivation made up of the emissions of individual minds and with my dim perception of the city as a moral order, I did not do so (anymore than I brought my interest in the integration of primary groups and the fusion of selves with the *Abstand* of the intellectuals from the rest of their society).

The same is to be said of my approach to tradition. It is not a matter of "how societies remember." It is rather of how the act of acceptance of a tradition is a participation in a contemporal collective self-consciousness. It is not an act of memory that constitutes the society; it is rather the society, i.e., the collective self-consciousness, which constitutes the memory. The collective self-consciousness is there; the incoming individual participates in it. Then he learns what it refers to. One knows about the Battle of Gettysburg because the collective self-consciousness has incorporated into itself the union and hence the Union Army and the actions of the Union Army.

V

The date of my arrival in Chicago was, I think, 22 September 1932. I went to Chicago with the expectation that sooner or later I would study sociology. I had no means except for the generosity of my dear friend, Sidney Sufrin, who had been a classmate of mine in Pennsylvania and who had been a research assistant in the economics department the preceding year. I had no plans to become a professional sociologist. In fact, I had no professional plan or ambitions at all; I did not think about the future. I assumed that I could always find employment and I did not worry about what kind of employment it was. I was interested in pursuing my intellectual interests and this involved learning about the things that I thought sociology knew about and was capable of discovering. My ideas about why I should study sociology were not clear; but they did not need to be clear since I was in no hurry.

I went to Chicago for a number of inchoate reasons. For one thing, the University of Chicago already stood out in my mind as a famous university and its sociological study of urban life was especially attractive to me. Sidney Sufrin was extremely enthusiastic about Chicago after his first year there; and in the summer of 1932, he urged me to go to Chicago. He told me about Frank Knight of whom he was a great admirer; I had read already one essay by Knight on the methodology of economics that I discovered in a book edited by Rexford Tugwell, *The Trend of Economics*, which I bought in the alley that separated Gimbel's from Leary's off 9th Street for nineteen cents.

Knight's trenchancy and intellectual honesty that did not spare himself or anyone else was evident even in that one essay and it made Chicago more attractive. I doubt whether I understood what Knight was saying but I knew even from that essay that Knight was a man who took the world seriously, who grappled with it and who struggled to understand it. I was already aware that Knight had translated Max Weber's *Wirtschaftsgeschichte* which I had struggled to read in German several years earlier.

Then, too, Chicago was a city made famous to me by Frank Norris, Theodore Dreiser, Sherwood Anderson, Upton Sinclair, and Jane Addams. I wanted to go on with my intellectual interests; and Chicago seemed to be the best place because Park's, Burgess' and Wirth's books had made me think that at Chicago they understood what big cities are, and that drew me to it. Then, too, I had read cursorily, again by accident, Harold Lasswell's *Psychopatholoqy and Politics*, in which Weber, Mosca and Pareto were mentioned. I was not entirely on the side of psychoanalysis of which at that time, I must admit, I knew rather little; but Lasswell's adventurous coupling of it with European sociology strengthened my conviction that there would be boundless intellectual delights in Chicago. I was not entirely wrong.

I also knew about Robert Hutchins having read about him in the *New York Times* and his misadventures with the philosophy department over the recommendation of Mortimer Adler for an appointment in that department. But I did not know anything about him and did not think about it. Later I was to have views (mixed—admiring and critical) about Hutchins, and still after I became acquainted with him and enjoyed his presence, wit and melancholy. In those early years, university presidents where of no importance to me. I did not understand what they were about.

I did not go to Chicago with the intention of preparing myself for a career as a sociologist or any other sort of academic career. In the great depression, my best coevals did not think of a career. We were pleased to remain alive and to live from day to day or year to year. The notion of a career, moving steadily on a foreseen straight path, was not thought about during these years, as much as it has since then. (Permanent tenure became an obsession of young academics only after the Second World War.) In those years, it was not uncommon for young persons to be indifferent about considerations of a career. I had intellectual ambitions; but at that time, they were not linked to professional or social or economic ambitions. In any case, I did not associate studying a subject with doing so in preparation for a profession. Although I ignorantly admired German professors, I did not think that learning need be pursued professionally or academically. Perhaps it was the example of H. C. Lea, the Philadelphian historian of the Inquisition who wrote his erudite works as an amateur, or of George Brandes who was never a professor, although he was invited to lecture in universities, or of a man whom I never met named Philip Minassian whose copies of the classics of Marxism, Marx, Engels, Labriola, Kautsky, Plekhanov, I bought in Leary's, heavily underscored and annotated, for from ten to twenty-five cents. I had about a half dozen copies of Minassian's books with his firm and clear signature and occasional marginal comment. I tried to find out who he was. All I could discover was that he was a machinist. I thought if a machinist could carry on a studious life, so could I.

VI

It was in the spring of 1931, when I think that I saw an announcement in the *Archiv für Sozialwissenschaft und Sozialpolitik* of a competition for a prize on the history of the sociology of knowledge to be awarded by the Wiener Soziologische Gesellschaft. I thought for a short time that I should enter the competition but lack of self-confidence and particularly lack of confidence in my German, deterred me from entering the competition. It might have been a good thing had I done so. I probably would not have done it much more poorly than it was done by the prize-winner. (Ernst Grünwald, was a very young man who died at a very early age—in a mountain-climbing accident. There is a photograph of him as the frontispiece. Very young looking, very shy-looking, very much a nice Jewish boy with an open collar, folded down over his jacket collar like F. R. Leavis. His essay was published by Braumüller in Vienna in about 1934; I still have it. His work was rather pedestrian as far as I can recall, although I doubt very much whether my own entry would have been as good.) I would have been in a much better position in a few years. But by that time, I had read all the literature of the problematical subject of the sociology of knowledge. Much of it, on looking back at it, was nonsensical, although I was not forthrightly aware of it at the time. I already knew in 1931 the names of the main writers whom I should read, namely Max Scheler, Wilhelm Jerusalem, Paul Szende,

Karl Mannheim, and of course, Durkheim. Durkheim was the only one I had read. The term "sociology of knowledge" was quite thrilling to me. I saw some affinity between my interests combining intellectual history with sociological studies that seemed to correspond with the sociology of knowledge. That is why I gravitated in that direction. It took me some time to see through it.

I had already read a good deal of Marx and Engels giving particular attention to the very brief introduction to the *Critique of Political Economy* in which the theses about the *Überbau* and the *Unterbau* was set forth. It seemed to me very daring but also very crude.

VII

Some days after I arrived at the University of Chicago, I went to see Louis Wirth. I am not sure why I went to him. Perhaps it was because Park was away or because I knew his name from the bibliography and from his book *The Ghetto*, which was a sympathetic little book. I knew that he knew German although I did not know that he had been born in Germany. I visited Wirth in room 314 of the Social Science Research Building. I remember his desk being against the West wall. He had a very soft voice; he did not speak much but when he did speak, he spoke fluently but dispassionately, as if he were not very interested. Perhaps he was not interested in me; that would have been very justified. I told him that I intended to study sociology and that I was interested in learning about German sociology and particularly about Max Weber. He asked me if I had heard of Karl Mannheim. I told him that I had, that he was on the list of authors that I wanted to know about. I also told him of my abandoned plan to enter the competition about the sociology of knowledge; he made no comment on that. He told me that he had spoken with Mannheim in Frankfurt during his year as a fellow of the Social Science Research Council in Germany; he told me of Mannheim's forthcoming review of Stuart Rice's book on the social sciences. He told me that Mannheim was eager to have *Ideologie und Utopie* translated into English. He spoke in a very detached way about Mannheim, not indifferently, but without strong feeling.

Our interview could not have lasted more than fifteen minutes at the most. He did not seem to find much of interest in me. Perhaps he had other more important things on his mind. The threat of National Socialism was certainly already apparent to him; and he must have been preoccupied with the fate of his elderly parents and his numerous brothers and sisters in Germany. This is only a surmise. In any case, he was certainly amiable.

I later attended Wirth's course on the History of "European Sociology," perhaps it was "German Sociology," at 8:00 AM in the morning before going to work. (I am not entirely certain but I think that it might have been in the spring of 1933.) The text was the three little green volumes *Soziologische Lesestücke*, edited by Franz Oppenheimer and Gottfried Salomon. They were excellent little books containing long excerpts or passages from Lorenz von Stein, Albert Schäffle, Moritz Lazarus, Heymann Steinthal, et al. All the students were expected to acquire these books that were kept in stock at the University of Chicago bookshop. Although it was as long ago as the 1930s, the requirement of knowledge of foreign languages as a condition for admission to candidacy for the doctorate had already become a mockery; practically none of the students could read German.

Wirth's pedagogical procedure consisted in reading aloud, in German, whole pages at a time from the textbook. Occasionally he interspersed a comment, seldom of any considerable length. I think that I was the only member of the class of about twelve or fifteen who could read German; and I was also the only one who followed his reading from the volume that I kept open before me. The other students did not complain. Perhaps they got enough from his occasional comments, which were in fact sometimes quite penetrating, even though brief and infrequent. As I remember, they dealt mainly with how human beings became to act in concert, understanding each other's expectations and conforming with them. Indeed, not only did the students in the class not complain about this method of teaching through a foreign language that they did not understand, but they even admired him for it. Whether the prestige that accrued to him from knowing German was so great that it compensated them for his unintelligibility or whether Wirth's prestige among the students for his presumed learning and high intelligence was so high that even that very ineffective method of teaching could not lower that prestige, I cannot say. I can, however, say that in the period of the student agitation about thirty-five years later, when students in sociology complained about everything and regarded themselves as connoisseurs of pedagogical techniques, I often thought of those patient, often admiring students in Louis Wirth's course on German sociology.

Wirth himself was certainly a quick-witted person and sometimes beautifully fluent. He had a rhythmic soft voice; he spoke without hems or haws, he also seemed to say what he intended to say, unlike Park, who always seemed to be struggling to say what he wished to say and who sometimes admitted that his words did not adequately express his ideas. Burgess was a very shy speaker; there were times when he would stop for what seemed to be a half minute while waiting for the arrival of the next word.

Wirth was the hope of the department. Everyone including Park and Burgess apparently (except probably Ogburn who disapproved of Wirth as belonging to the unscientific, unquantitative branch of sociology and Faris who was probably, in his indolently clever and ingenious way, anti-Semitic) thought Wirth was destined to carry on the tradition of the Chicago School of Sociology. It was thought that he was a master of German sociological analysis and he was the heir of what was richest and most fruitful in the tradition of Park's and Burgess' urban sociology. Although he was known to have a sharp tongue on occasion, he was much liked by the students for his sympathetic manner. He was certainly kind to me.

There was also Herbert Blumer, combining the appearance of a Red Indian and a football fullback. He spoke very gravely and deliberately, looking down at the table at which he was seated, playing with a piece of chalk—like George Herbert Mead, so I was told by the older students who had attended Mead's courses. Blumer did not strike me as having any contact with any intellectual achievements aside from Mead's; he reiterated Mead's opaque statements about the "I" and the "me" with no more references to concrete things other than an occasional invocation of dogs—again very much like Mead. Nevertheless, in the spring of 1933, he gave a seminar on "the French School of Sociology" based on his studies during a year in Europe on a fellowship of the Social Science Research Council; it seemed to me then to be based on rather careful reading. It was not very fruitful because he laid so much emphasis on Simiand, certainly the least interesting of Durkheim's protégés. Still, occasionally in his exposition of Halbwachs on the "social framework of memory" or of Durkheim on "collective representations," he seemed to catch a glimpse of what intermittently and dimly concerned me already at that time and which now concerns me more than anything else, namely, "collective self-consciousness." Blumer, in later years, forgot, and even denied, that he had ever given such a seminar. About ten years ago, I told Professor Horst Helle of this seminar; but when he asked Blumer about it, he drew only a blank. My own recollection is that he tried to make Durkheim, Halbwachs, etc., sound like copies of Georg Herbert Mead; but that he did it with an occasional moment of going beyond Mead.

That was the Chicago School of Sociology; it really was only Park, a bit of Burgess, who was under Park's domination, and Louis Wirth, who was a promise rather than a fulfillment.

I read a good bit of Chicago sociology—articles from the *American Journal of Sociology* and doctoral dissertations. During the winter of 1933, in my alternately overheated and freezing little room (11 Snell Hall) I read Mannheim's *Ideologie und Utopie*. It caused my blood to flow more quickly; but when I tried to reformulate it in more prosaic terms, it disappeared. I was certainly not persuaded by his attempted improvement on Marxism by the replacement of "class positions," as a determinant of the content and form of intellectual works, by "social position." I am not sure of what it was that impressed me so much, whether it was Mannheim's apparent mastery of Thomas Münzer's ideas, his apparent grasp of the fundamental variants of attitudes towards any existing social order or whether it was the melodramatic portentiousness of Mannheim's rhetoric. I cannot say for certain. But I must admit that I was exhilarated by that book.

In later years, I came to be at a loss to account for that enchantment. When on several occasions I undertook to re-read that book, it was difficult to find anything there. Yet, I have also been from time to time troubled by the thought that I have done an injustice to a powerful and penetrating mind. Sometimes I charge myself with having absorbed into my thought what was best in Mannheim and only judged the worst. When I do that and ask myself what it was that I have taken into myself, I find myself at a loss. At the same time, I must confess my excitement by his ideas, such as they might be. (It seems to have been the same with his pupils at the London School of Economics where he was an immensely popular lecturer; but when I have tried to extract from such of his auditors like Mrs. Jean Floud and Herbert Goldhamer what ideas they got from him, they have been at a loss to say what they were.)

Of course, I did not read only Mannheim that winter. I read or tried to read *Gemeinschaft und Gesellschaft, Wirtschaft und Gesellschaft*, and Pareto's *Traité de Sociologie générale*. I also became very familiar with the *Archiv für Sozialwissenschaft und Sozialpolitik*, to a lesser extent with the *Zeitschrift für die gesamte Staatswissenschaft* and Schmoller's *Jahrbuch für Gesetzgebung*. Also in connection with my reading of Mannheim, I read widely in Grünbergs *Archiv für die Geschichte des Sozialismus und der Arbeiterbewegung* (the predecessor of the *Zeitschrift für Sozialforschung*). In the latter I studied especially Paul Szende's *Enthüllung und Verhüllung*.

I was still pursuing my undergraduate interest in intellectuals and my efforts to place and describe "main currents." I was also perplexed by Mannheim's way of discussing ideology. It took me years to cut away that thicket of confusion.

What was wrong with Karl Mannheim? Why did this brilliant and imaginative man say so little from which one can still learn? I think that provincial or peripheral parochiality had something to do with it. Mannheim was a Hungarian at a time when German culture was the center for so many intellectuals of the lesser countries of Central and Eastern Europe. Germany seemed to be the center of Western culture and that meant of world culture in the period when Mannheim was growing up. Mannheim, like another intellectual of his youth Georg Lukacs, made his career in Germany. Being at what he thought was the center of the world, he thought it unnecessary to study the periphery. What happened at the center was a microcosm of the macrocosm. This was the reason why Mannheim generalized the situation of the Weimar republic so that it came to stand for all of Western liberal democratic societies. But this was clearly not the case.

Another reason, in my view, for Mannheim's inability to see the world as it was, was a Marxist view that he inherited from some of his masters (Lukacs, Szabo, etc.) and from which he tried to escape. Quite apart from the failures of the economic policies of the successive Weimar governments, he did not see that German nationalism was a response to the absence of German nationality. He did not see that one of the sources of German National Socialism was the persistent tradition of *Kleinstaaten* that had prevented the formation of a German civility. Nationalism exacerbated by the lost war was partly a response to the very weakness of the German sense of German nationality. (This is more complicated!)

Mannheim's belief in "situational determinism" obscured for him the functioning of tradition, although he did not invariably think that way. He did speak about the *Schollengebundenheit der Menschen*; but he thought that was something that had long been abolished (in this respect sharing the views of Tönnies, et al). But as far as "modern man" is concerned, "functional rationalization" has made man a victim of his own irrational impulse.

Why did Mannheim think that a mixture of market economy and institutional autonomy was, if placed along side of a regime of "democratic planning" (whatever that was), was bound to cause a severe crisis? He was optimistic that the crisis would pass once the regime of planning replaced the pluralistic market economy that he called laissez faire.

It is difficult to formulate exactly what Mannheim believed. In *Ideologie und Utopie*, he was very preoccupied with revolution and counter-revolution, with progress and reaction. Although revolution and counter-revolution are very important, I think that they must not be allowed to supersede the analysis of society, always changing, not drastically, only by small increments. That would permit the revolutions and counter-revolutions to be placed in the more realistic perspective which shows what revolutions accomplish and what they do not accomplish. In *Ideologie und Utopie*, there was far too much concern about the theories of the relations of theory and practice of various revolutionary doctrines. This was a gem of ingenuity but it was only a very marginal phenomenon with which it dealt.

I think that it is a mistake to speak of crisis without thinking first of the normal situation. If one places crisis in the foreground, the normal case usually is described so unrealistically that the crisis itself becomes the normal case. I think that this was what was wrong in Mannheim's sociology.

Now I must speak of him personally. I must do so because he was so generous to me. It is true that he had reason to be grateful because, by my translation, I had made him known beyond the precincts of the London School of Economics. He also thought that I was more important than I really was. But the fact is that he was a kind person, particularly to younger persons. Although he was only seventeen years older than I was, seventeen years makes a big difference when it is between thirty-two and forty-nine.

I never presumed to be equal to him. Maybe he thought that I was very influential. After all, I had helped Hans Gerth to find a post and the same was true of my role in the case of Nathan Leites. So perhaps he had heard some exaggerated version and that I should be treated as an equal. (It is possible that he still thought of emigrating to the United States; after all, he was very unhappy at the London School of Economics; his unhappiness centered on Morris Ginsberg. He felt uncertain whether he could continue at the School. There had been a misunderstanding from the very beginning about the duration of his first appointment in 1933).

One thing is certain and that he was very elusive about his standing in the United States. In fact, the very first thing he said to me when we entered his study, after his servant had taken my hat and coat, was, "what do they think of me in America?" That did not seem to me then or now a question that a famous man ought to ask a younger person. Self-respect should have forbidden it.

We always got on very amicably. I think he felt affectionately towards me; I, too, towards him. Sometimes, I fear that my criticisms were too sharp; but he never spoke sharply to me, nor I to him. When he showed me that manuscript which he had written for Chatham House about "Freedom, Power and Democratic Planning," I returned it to him with many criticisms of the ambiguities, omissions, etc. He said it was too late to take my corrections into the manuscript but that he promised to do so when he wrote his next book. (There was no next book except one that appeared posthumously.) I do not know what he worked on between the end of the war and January 1947 when he died. He had accepted the professorship of the sociology of education at the Institute of Education of the University of London and he went regularly to Nottingham where the Institute had been evacuated for the duration of the war; he had also been going regularly to Cambridge to which the London School of Economics had been evacuated. He was, I think, a conscientious as well as a very stimulating teacher and teaching at two institutions in quite different places in England while residing in London must have taken most of his time and energy. He was not robust; he had a weak heart and he caught colds easily. He died of the latter.

I was to have had dinner with him on the Saturday evening before he died; but either on Friday or Saturday, he telephoned me and asked to agree to the postponement of our dinner until the next Monday or Tuesday evening. It was probably Tuesday because on

Monday afternoon, not knowing that he had died on Sunday, I was not thinking of going out to his home in Hampstead that evening. Late in the afternoon, I was in a taxicab with Michael Polanyi, going from the School to Euston Station (Polanyi was returning to Manchester). I had not had time to look into my *Times* that day, so I did so in the taxi. As we neared the station, I read in the obituaries that Mannheim had died the preceding day (i.e., Sunday). I could not resist allowing my grief to escape me. I said, "Karl Mannheim died yesterday." Polanyi did not say a word. They must have known each other since they were youths in Budapest before the First World War. I am sure that they had some correspondence in the 1930s, but something must have happened. Polanyi often did not hear what he did not want to hear. In any case, he said not a word.

As soon as I deposited Polanyi at the Station, I went directly to Golders Green where Mannheim lived. First Julia, the faithful servant, came to the door, weeping as she admitted me. Mrs. Mannheim embraced me and said, "Ginsberg killed him."

Some of my awareness of the objectivity of knowledge, I owe paradoxically enough to my early struggles to see if there was anything I could salvage from Mannheim's writings. My conclusions were negative, more negative than I would have liked them to be because I had and still have, after 45 years, very affectionate sentiments about Mannheim. I tried several times to reconsider my views about him. First immediately after his death, then some years later when I wrote twice about him, once in the *International Enyclopaedia of the Social Sciences* and at another occasion when I contributed an essay on *Ideology and Utopia* to a symposium on influential books of the twentieth century commissioned by the editor of *Daedalus*. I still feel uneasy; yet, whenever I set myself to think about his work once more, I find that I have no alternative.

Mannheim's sociology of knowledge was not really dealing with knowledge. It was dealing with political desires, political aspirations rather than with knowledge although some references to cognitive things. His theory of society was not a theory of how society functions; it is an image of how human beings should behave. The sociological analysis of such theories might make those initiated dependent on or to grow out of the interests or desires of their exponents for such an order of society. The exponents of such theories of a desirable order might proffer them to others aiming intentionally to realize the kind of society which they desire or which they anticipate will be. On the other hand, a theory of the workings of the market, or a theory of the coherence of the family, or a proposition about the distribution of different types of families in a particular society in a particular year, decade, or century are cognitive propositions that can be adjudged to be true or false or to contain elements of truth and elements of falsity. A scholar, a sociologist in this case, might assert such propositions because he has observed the events to which they refer or has used governmentally gathered statistics of families to construct such a proposition. The fact that the sociologist was born in a particular "class" or ethnic group might be interesting in a study of the social origins of the profession of sociologists; but a sociology of knowledge could not explain the sociologists putting forth that proposition by stating that he came form such a particular social class or ethnic group. It might explain why he chose to study the distribution of types of families rather than to study, let us say, behavior of school children during their holidays or their behavior in the school yard during "recesses"; but it could not explain the proposition itself or why he puts forward one proposition about families or school children rather than some alternative proposition about the families, etc. The sociologist's capacity for observation, his capacity for imagining what he does not see, first reasoning about and weighing the evidence that he has assembled in the course of his investigation of families or school children or whatever are intellectual capacities. These capacities might be strong, disciplined and focused or they might be feeble, dispersed in the objects on which they focus; but they are intellectual capacities.

Mannheim never made this clear to himself when he promulgated his sociology of knowledge or when he attempted to apply his sociology of knowledge to the study of German conservative thought. That was I think a major omission and a major defect of his sociology of knowledge. Max Scheler at least allowed an appreciation of the empirical truthfulness of a proposition when he gave a prominent position to *Idealfaktoren*. There was no comparable category in Mannheim's sociology of knowledge. In this respect von Schelting's criticism of the postulates of Mannheim's sociology of knowledge was right.

Mannheim did not like von Schelting. Whether he disliked him because he found during their years in Heidelberg certain features of von Schelting's conduct distasteful or whether it was because von Schelting had criticized him, I do not know. But he did once say to me that he regarded von Schelting as a proponent of an antiquated "idealism."

But I never discussed the sociology of knowledge with Mannheim. I saw no point in raising a question that would have given rise to a disagreement. Furthermore Mannheim had ceased to practice the sociology of knowledge that he had put forward in his essay of 1924 in the *Archiv*. I never asked him why he did not pursue his old interest. I was of the opinion that he had given it up because he realized that he had been in the wrong. No less likely was the possibility that he had moved in his intellectual interests to subjects that he thought would be more interesting to Englishmen, such as the place of religion in society. I cannot say why he changed; but it is perfectly clear that once he settled in England and found friends—outside the London School of Economics—he tried to deal with subjects that they would find interesting. He was very proud of his new friends, especially T. S. Eliot. He was proud, too, to be a friend of E. H. Carr, Hubert Read, A. D. Lindsay and others. He was faithful in his attendance at the Moot and he went quite regularly to its meetings in Haslemere. He was, as I have said, not in robust health; he caught colds easily and the travel to the railway station and then the journey in the British railway carriages, dirty and unhealthy, was a danger to him; but he would not be deterred.

He loved England and he would have loved the London School of Economics if Ginsberg had been friendlier to him, if Hayek had shown greater appreciation for him. I think he liked Laski, who, with all his faults, was a generous and affectionate person.

His death grieved me, not only for the loss of a person whom I esteemed and liked despite our intellectual disagreements. I grieve for him because of those disagreements. I did not like to disagree with him because disagreements pained him. But I grieved also because I thought that I perhaps was doing him an injustice. But I could not do anything else.

VIII

Returning to my first years in Chicago, I earned my livelihood there as a social worker for the Cook County Bureau of Public Welfare. I worked in the Black Belt—now called "the Ghetto"—and had about 900 families under my responsibility. In view of my experience in New York, and my courses at the New York School of Social

Work, I was considered relatively senior and had a salary of $1,800 per annum, which was quite good for those times. It was certainly enough to maintain myself, to purchase books, to go to the best restaurant I have ever been to—a Romanian Jewish restaurant, called after its owner, Strulevitz, in the area of the first Jewish settlement— once or twice a week, and to contribute a bit to the support of my parents who were having a hard time. It was the best time of my life. My "clients," as they were called in the jargon of social workers of the time, were admirable persons, almost without exception. They were dignified in the face of adversity, courteous without self-abasement. I learned a great deal from my long hours with them; I learned a lot about the history of the Negroes in the South and in Chicago and, above all, I learned about character, moral steadfastness and good humor. It is doubtful if they got as much from me—all I did was report on their unemployment and their needs for clothing, etc. A simple machine would have done what I did but the simple machine would not have learned from them what I learned.

At the University, I attended classes that were given at 8:00 o'clock in the morning or at 8:00 o'clock in the evening. (Many of the graduate students until the Second World War, were employed as teachers in Chicago high schools or in the Park Service or as teachers in the many small colleges in and around Chicago, and could attend classes only before or after their regular working hours.) I think that the only classes in sociology that I took were those of Wirth and Blumer.

I had also the opportunity to hear Frank Knight deliver a profoundly stirring discourse, "The Case for Communism: From the Standpoint of an Ex-Liberal," in a crowded lecture hall (122 Social Science Research Building) under the auspice of the "Community Club." I will not describe the lecture here since I have already written about it in "A Gallery of Academics, Mainly in Chicago."[3] All I wish to say here is that the lecture was one of the most profoundly moving experiences I have ever had. For the first time, I was able to see a thoroughly serious person. It is no wonder that Durkheim used the word "*serieux*" to refer to the "sacred." Knight never allowed the text of the lecture to be published although it was reproduced in "planograph," as a substantial booklet. Knight was dismayed by this unauthorized reproduction. I came by a copy (I think from Maynard Krueger) and then lost it by lending it to Franz Neumann who never returned it. More recently I acquired another from my undergraduate pupil Christopher Gustafson, who reproduced it from Knight's typescript in the archives of the University of Chicago. All these grand events took place in the autumn of 1932.

One evening in the spring of 1933, I attended a lecture on the condition of the unemployed at the Goodman Theater of the Art Institute of Chicago. It was apparently an important event; the lecture was delivered by one of the most esteemed figures of Chicago civic life of the time and many social workers came to hear the speaker whose name I cannot recall; he was dead in earnest. Quite rightly. He was, I think, a sort of socialist. Mrs. Wirth, a clever, very amusing woman was a leading social worker in Chicago. Louis Wirth, who was also very interested in social work, having been a social case worker at the Jewish Social Service Bureau in Chicago in the first half of the 1920s when he was a graduate student working on his dissertation which became *The Ghetto* and thence one of the classics of the Chicago School of Sociology, attended the meeting with her. I too attended. On the way out, Wirth stopped me and told me that he had a sum of money at his disposal to pay for a research assistant for the coming academic year and he wanted to know whether I would be interested. I did not hesitate. He asked me to call on him when I could. I did so shortly thereafter and was told that the research assistantship, which would provide at a salary of $86.11 per month, was for an investigation of "the methodological presuppositions of German sociology." Wirth had a *faiblesse* for discussing "presuppositions." (It later culminated in the methodological appendix of *The American Dilemma*. Myrdal had the same eagerness to discuss "presuppositions.")

Unfortunately for our project, I could never get Wirth to tell me just what he wanted me to look for. There was a certain amount of German literature on the *Voraussetzungslosigkeit der Wissenschaft* and on *Wertfreiheit*. There was a certain amount on the differences between the *Naturwissenschaften* and the *Geisteswissenschaften*. I am far from sure, even now, when I see how a coherent project could be made of it, something worthwhile could have been made of it.

The fact was that there were not very many German sociologists writing theoretical or empirical works, the methodological presuppositions of which could be analyzed. A great deal of German sociological writing was definitional and classificatory. I could not see that there was much value in analyzing the underlying conceptions of the nature of science in general or of sociology in particular of those definitions and classifications. For the most part they were vague definitions and illogical classifications. What end would be served by analyzing them? Looking back at it now, I see that the implicit substantive postulates about the nature of man and the nature of society could have been made out of those works. This might have been worthwhile doing, but I doubt it.

At that time, I did not (I was probably not competent) to take on myself the responsibility of formulating a project. It would have been a preemption of the privilege to which Wirth was entitled officially and by his seniority. I waited in vain for specific instructions, meanwhile reading Rickert's *Naturwisssenschaften und Kulturwissenschaften* and *Die Grenzen der naturwisssenschaftlichen Begriffsbildung*, Weber's *Wissenschaftslehre,* van Below on *Soziologie als Lehrfach*, Spranger's *Über die Vorassetzungslosigkeit der Wissenschaft* in the transactions of the Prussian Akademie der Wissenschaften, Windelband's *Geschichte und Naturwissenschaft* in *Präludien*, etc., etc. Much of what I read was rather poor; it was by authors who knew little of the real work done by natural scientists, humanists and social scientists. I made a considerable number of attempts within the limits of deference and time to bring Wirth to tell me just what he wanted. It became clear to me he could not formulate the project or even respond specifically to my accounts of what I was reading. It is possible that he was so busy with other things that he had no time to elaborate his thoughts and he never asked me to expand my own ideas in response to a half-page statement which he had written for the Social Sciences Research Committee in order to obtain the grant. However, it did not go on this way indefinitely.

When I first visited Wirth in September 1932, he told me, as I have already mentioned, of Mannheim's desire for the translation into English of *Ideologie und Utopie*. Wirth said that he would try to arrange it. My presence and the furthering of the project on "methodological presuppositions" were very favorable to the fulfillment of Mannheim's desire and Wirth's promise. Hence I was set to work on the translation. This was around the end of 1933. By sometime in 1934, the translation of the original book, of an article by Mannheim on *Wissenssoziologie* in the *Handwörterbuch der Soziologie* and of a new introduction, specially written by Mannheim, were ready in draft form. I revised my translation and then Wirth and I sat down to give it a further revision. We did it very painstakingly, weighing Mannheim's vague and suggestive terms over and over again to find an adequate equivalent. We met every morning from about 9:15 until lunch time and then again in the afternoon, when he was not teaching or out of the city. The number of hours we spent together was very impressive—six or seven daily. Of these six to seven hours probably two or two-and a half were spent on the work of revision. The rest of the time was spent by Wirth on unexpected visits from other teachers, with visitors to the university from other universities—in those days Chicago, being the railway "hub" of the country, impromptu academic visitors to The University of Chicago were very frequent. There are not many such visitors now. (Visitors came from almost anywhere, occasionally a student.) Wirth was very hospitable and when visitors wanted assistance, he was usually very eager to help them. He always insisted in having the outer and inner door of his room open so that passers-by in the corridor could see him and he could see them. When I occasionally shut the door, he would get up from his desk and open it so that it stayed open.

Sometimes the visitors just "dropped by for a chat"; at other times they discussed university business. Sometimes they engaged in denunciations of the president of the University, Robert Hutchins. Very little of this business was confidential; only rarely did Wirth ask me to leave and to come back in half an hour.

A frequent visitor was Robert Park who might come in two or three times a day to discuss something that he was reading and which had stimulated him. He always remained standing, usually pacing back and forth in the small room, always alert, good humored, always panting with excitement over what he thought was a new insight or a new discovery. There was never any talk about persons, never any group, nothing about university or departmental affairs. I have said, on another occasion, that Park belonged to that rare category of "seekers" who hunger after truth that always eludes them. I remember nothing specific of what he talked about but I received from these meandering monologues a deeper impression of intellectual seriousness and Park's underlying preoccupation with the collective self-consciousness which he could never articulate. This was a phenomenon that preoccupied Park's attention ever since his doctoral dissertation *Masse und Publikum* more than thirty years previously and for which he never found a formulation satisfying to himself. He was then about seventy years old, very strong and always capable of being interested by something new that was illuminated to him by an old light or by something that he had known before but which he now saw in a new light. Park's intrusions, unknown to the larger world, were the best part of my work on the translation of Mannheim. Wirth did not speak much on these visits. He was very deferential to Park; and Park obviously looked upon Wirth as a fit intellectual confidante.

IX

By the time I met Wirth, the world had ceased to interest him as it had when he wrote his dissertation *The Ghetto*. Looking back at these situations in Wirth's room nearly sixty years ago, I can see that Wirth was not deep enough to be Park's intellectual heir. Wirth did not have Park's capacity for unremitting intellectual obsession.

Naturally, I came to have a fairly clear picture of Wirth as a result of the opportunities. Wirth was obviously a man of outstanding talents; he had a good memory, excellent verbal capacities, at one time— well before I met him—he read widely. He was also a very popular teacher of undergraduates, particularly in the general social science survey for first-year students. A few years ago, I came across a Chicago graduate who told me that Wirth's lectures in "Social Science I" remained in his memory as the best thing of his happy undergraduate career at the University of Chicago. He was not the only one who told me such a story about Wirth as a teacher.

With all his gifts, he did not have the capacity to be alone in a small room, the source of many of man's misfortunes, according to Pascal. He sought the distraction of the presence of other persons. I think that at one time, he was on the way to becoming a wise and reflective person, but for some reason had turned aside. Quite apart from his desire for the company of others, he might have been driven to spending his time serving on committees and delivering lectures from which he might have received honoraria which are derisory by today's standards but which taken together might have come to several thousand dollars annually. Although Mrs. Wirth had a relatively well-paid position as a senior social worker, the Wirths (Louis and Mary) were hard pressed financially throughout the 1930s. They needed his "outside earnings." After Hitler's seizure of power, Wirth brought out of Germany about eight relatives and maintained them until they found their own way. He brought out his father and mother and numerous brothers and sisters—perhaps there were other, more distant, relatives. This was a very demanding obligation. His action was exemplary. He saved his family from extermination; but it laid demands on him that tore him away from intellectual work. There is much more to be said about Louis Wirth, who is now nearly forgotten, except for his association with Mannheim and for the essay "Urbanism as a Way of Life" which his then protégé, Herbert Goldhamer, said that it was mainly his, i.e., Goldhamer's own composition. Of this I can say nothing, except that it is probable that Goldhamer's assertion is true. Goldhamer was a very modest man. The essay has a geometrical mode of argument that was characteristic of Goldhamer and not of Wirth. There were other instances where Wirth became a co-author of a paper without putting his pen to paper for more than his signature.

These observations about Louis Wirth are a digression from my account. I have entered into them because he was an interesting man for whom a slight turn of the wheel of fortune might have led to relatively lasting accomplishments in the academic world. For better or for worse, I owe him a great deal. It was because he appointed me as his research assistant that I entered upon an academic career. He also played an important part some years later in keeping me in the University, after my first year of teaching when the new head of the undergraduate department of social sciences wished to replace me by one of his own protégés.

In later years, there was an increased distance between Wirth and myself; I had never been intimate with him or presumed to be equal to him. I never addressed him by his first name. He did not like my appointment to the London School of Economics, an advancement which, in his eyes, raised the independence of me. He also disapproved of my collaboration with Talcott Parsons of whom he was very critical, perhaps because he—Louis Wirth—had also aspired to be a leading sociological theorist. He did not like my association with the Committee on Social Thought that was more or less a creation of Robert Hutchins. He thought that by joining the Committee I had become a follower of President Hutchins of whom he, together with Frank Knight and Harry Gideonse, was a passionate opponent. He and those two colleagues accused Hutchins of wishing to impose a quasi-Aristotelian or Thomistic bondage on the University; Hutchins and his friends' denunciation of the social sciences as trivial, superficial, ignorant and amoral was very injurious to Wirth's devotion to the social sciences.

I was not a follower of Hutchins, least of all in his Thomistic Phase; but I thought that he was a man who stood for the highest standards in undergraduate education, was a brave proponent of academic freedom and had many other merits as well. In any case, I did not approve of either of the parties to the dispute about the merit of the social sciences or about Hutchins' intentions. I thought each of them overstated the case, imputing base motives and caricaturing the position of the other. Furthermore, Hutchins had left me an entirely free hand in my thorough recasting of the Social Science II that was obligatory for students in their second year. I thought and still think that the disputes centering on Robert Hutchins, of which the polemics of Wirth, Gideonse and Knight against Hutchins were only one, did the University much harm. During the war, I wrote to that effect to a friend who indiscreetly summarized my views to another friend and so the message passed from one person to another to the point were it became, "Edward Shils thinks that Louis is foolish." That is the form in which it came to Wirth. Naturally, he was offended. That was a sad ending to a relationship from which I have benefited and for which I am grateful.

I would add three more observations to this already excessively long digression on Louis Wirth. The first is not essential to this autobiography of my effort to discern, delineate and differentiate the collective self-consciousness. It is that Louis Wirth jettisoned Park's intellectual legacy; he allowed it to disappear from the department of sociology instead of improving and extending it, and making it more exact and rigorous. That was an injury to the understanding of society and to the quality of the department of sociology at the University of Chicago. The second observation bears on his influence on the department of sociology at the University of Chicago. I do not think that he can be blamed for its decline. The fault there lies with the narrowness and irresponsibility of the two seniors, Ogburn and Burgess. Wirth could probably not have done much to offset their negligence.

Finally, returning to my task, I ask what I learned from Wirth that helped me in my intellectual path. I have already said how much I owe him for the opportunity he afforded me for entry into an academic life. Beyond the opportunity to be in contact with Park and Knight and to read a lot of books, some good and some poor, the answer must be: practically nothing. It grieves me that I have to say this.

X

My years as a research assistant and then as an instructor in the College were not well used. I read too many books too randomly, worked on trivial tasks like "Urban Housing" and "Urban Education" for the National Research Planning Board, wrote a number of long and useless articles surveying the literature of sociology from about 1933 to 1935, and other miscellaneous things which kept me very busy. It was all utterly unfocused. It was only in 1938 when I took on the task of reconstituting the second year Social Science Survey—Social Science II which was called "Freedom and Order"— that I began to find my way. I then studied Hobbes, Locke, Bentham, and the two Mills, some legal and constitutional historians. In the more than three years that I worked on that course, i.e., until the entry of the United States into the Second World War, consensus was revealed to me as the proper context of individual liberty and the individual's pursuit of his own "interest."

That was by no means the fault of Louis Wirth. It took me some time to see through Mannheim's sociology of knowledge. I could not quite see that his sociological interpretation of *geistige Gebilde* made *geistige Gebilde* into epiphenomena. Sometimes he treated ideas or knowledge as a part of action. This was his pragmatist tendency, which was more prominent in his revision of our translation than it was in his original version of the book. Sometimes he treated them as functions of social positions, as *standgebunden*; he thought this freed him from the narrowness of Marxism, but it did nothing of the kind. As I have already remarked, I was aware that Mannheim in his more theoretical analysis had no place for the autonomy of intellectual activities. He seemed not to think that there are criteria of validity that the mind is capable of applying in its activities of observation and reasoning. He took for granted that the bias introduced by the desire to believe could be expunged or held in check. Moreover by his emphasis on *Standesgebundenheit* (situational dependence) he left no place for the continuity of intellectual traditions. (He did not adhere to this view in his one major piece of research, namely, his essay "*Das konservative Denken.*") Despite my skepticism about the sociology of knowledge because of its denial of the partial autonomy of the cultural sphere, i.e., the sphere governed by intellectual or cultural tradition, I read Mannheim's *Mensch und Gesellschaft*, when it appeared in 1935, with excited pleasure and proceeded to translate it into English. (Mannheim greatly expanded the translated text, but in doing so, he did not improve it.) He had become convinced that the solution to the problems of modern society lay in planning. When he spoke about the "modern world," he usually had Weimar Germany in mind. Once again, he thought that the crisis of the 1920s and 1930s was an outcome of the mixture of planning and laissez faire. I was skeptical of that and said so in an essay that appeared in the *Journal of Liberal Religion*. Mannheim responded in a very gentlemanly way.

At this time, I also translated a number of Max Weber's essays from *Gesammelte Aufsätze zur wissenschaftslehre*, part of *Wirtschaft und Gesellschaft* and *Wissenschaft als Beruf*. Some of the translations I used as required readings for the second-year undergraduate survey course. Others remained unused and I published them after the war.

I also translated *Der Doppelstaat*. This was an interesting book that I translated from the German manuscript; the author, Ernst Fraenkel, was a German social democratic lawyer who had come to the United States as a refugee. He intimated to Nathan Leites that he would commit suicide if the book could not be published since he counted on it to make his reputation in the English-speaking world. (It had not been published in German). Leites, with characteristic generosity at the expense of others, told me the harrowing tale, which was false, of Fraenkel's impoverishment and desperation.

I translated other things as well, including Simmel's *Grossstadt und das Geistesleben* that I introduced as a required text for the Social Sciences II course.

None of these scattered activities were of any substantial intellectual value for me. Financially they were all unremunerative, although I have regularly received royalties from *The Methodology of the Social Sciences* published by the Free Press; it continues to sell very well after forty years, despite about 160 uncorrected typographical errors in the printed text.

None of the books that I translated has left much of an imprint on my own sociological or moral or political outlook. Max Weber's

writings on *Wertfreiheit* commanded my agreement, and the ignorant disavowal of "value-free science" in recent years has not impressed me in the slightest. What Max Weber had to say about the
rationalization of universities had taken its place in my views about
universities, but little beyond that.

I did get one thing from these translations beyond an improved
understanding of Max Weber's methodological ideas (which do not
interest me very much). In Fraenkel's manuscript I encountered a
reference to Schmalenbach's essay *Die soziologische Kategorie des
Bundes*. But since at about the same time or even a little earlier, I had
purchased the three volumes of *Die Dioskuren*, in the first volume
of which Schmalenbach's essay was originally published, I can
scarcely assert that the translation of Fraenkel's manuscript even had
that beneficial result.

However that may be, Schmalenbach's essay was valuable for
me because it separated the collective self-consciousness of
Gemeinschaft—the spirit of *Gemeinschaft*, the intense solidarity—
from specific primordial conditions to which Tönnies had attached
it. Schmalenbach had distinguished the intense collective self-consciousness of *Gemeinschaft* from the ecological—biological and local—referents. This was very important for me. It fitted in with Park's
analysis of the urban society as a spatial pattern and a moral order.
Park never succeeded in linking the two into a coherent whole.
Tönnies, in contrast, had not separated them.

In the monograph "Values, Motives and Systems of Action" that
Talcott Parsons and I wrote more than a decade later, we did make
both the distinction that Schmalenbach made between orientations
of action and object-properties and the linkage between them quite
explicitly. But we did so very abstractly and very incompletely. We
spoke about ascriptive properties but we did not enter into what were
the properties that were ascribed and the grounds of their ascription.
Nevertheless, having reached that stage opened the way for a better
understanding of collective self-consciousness. We did not reach
that state in that monograph. I think that Professor Parsons never did
reach it; to speak of "common values" was no advance.

XI

There were some years in the 1950s when I read nearly all the
publications in sociology in English, French, and German. Of course,

it would be impossible to do it now with so many sociologists writing in so many more journals. On the whole I learned little from that reading, at least that I can attribute to any particular sources. I read a fair amount of history especially of France and Germany of the seventeenth, eighteenth and nineteenth centuries. But the best thing I did was to read *Wirtschaft und Gesellschaft*, some parts of it over and over.

Except for Frank Knight and Robert Park, I did not find any of the teachers of the university of Chicago interesting. Park was present only for a short time in that decade. Lasswell was certainly very clever and I owed my interest in the study of psychoanalysis to him. He was very friendly to me in a puzzling, kindly, and cautious way. I was for years not at ease with him nor he with me. I saw Knight frequently and appreciated him greatly. I studied Max Weber with him in a seminar in which Milton Friedman, George Stigler, and Herbert Goldhamer were the members. (Michael Saper was also there; Goldhamer and I were the only ones who never missed a session.) I hung on his sagacious words.

I knew most of the members of the Graduate Faculty of the New School of Social Research and the *Institut für Sozialforschung*. I liked some of the members of the former, particularly Hans Speier, disliked at least in principle and to some extent in fact most of the members of the latter.

Early in the 1930s, I became friendly with Alexander von Schelting and Arvid Brodersen who spent the year 1933-1934 at the University of Chicago as Rockefeller Fellows. Von Schelting had just published *Max Weber's Wissenschaftslehre* which after sixty years still remains the best book on the subject. He was of Russian-Dutch extraction who had lived in Heidelberg after 1920 when he became editor of the *Archiv für Sozialwissenschaft*. He was an elegant, vain, rather handsome very Russian looking man, a homosexual who did not flaunt it—pedantic, charming, sometimes tedious, refined in taste, in food and manners—altogether a very exceptional person. Brodersen was a Norwegian, also handsome—like von Schelting tall, handsome, slender. He had written a dissertation under Vierkandt in Berlin. He too was elegant in manners, not pedantic like von Schelting, never tedious. He was a Georginaer and had written a book *Stefan George als Deutscher und Europäer* published by Die Runde, a Georgian publishing firm. These two gentlemen were of a sort I had never met before.

They contrasted strikingly with the cultural philistinism and parochialism of everyone else I knew at Chicago—except for Park and Knight. Lasswell was very conscious of being a Middle Westerner by origin who had by design made himself into what he thought was a person of universal culture. (It is far more complex than I say here. Park and Knight, who were distinctively American, were not weighed down by it because the whole wide world was their object. The others were not preoccupied with Europe or the Orient; they were unaware of them. They were not uncritical patriots; that was not an issue for them. They were just provincial. American provinciality and European centrality were not categories which were pronounced in their minds.) Von Schelting and Brodersen clung to each other as genuine Europeans. Schelting was inclined towards haughtiness but he never said anything disparaging about the United States in my presence; although I do recall his muttering in the winter of 1937-38, when he had to stand in a queue at the cloak room at the South Hall Library at Columbia University at the end of a winter afternoon, "What a country, where a professor has to wait in a line in order to obtain his overshoes!" There was none of that in Brodersen, who as a Norwegian must have felt at home in the Middle West among so many Scandinavians. He was an extremely fastidious person but he was also more open to contact with other human beings; he was an affectionate person so he was more at ease in the United States than von Schelting.

They adopted me as a surrogate European. My smattering of European knowledge must have impressed them. Von Schelting was especially impressed by my knowledge of the contents of the *Archiv*.

Our circle was enlarged by Herbert Goldhamer, who was always rather reticent but also impressive when he spoke. He was a man of good judgment, rather too positivistic intellectually and inwardly a little of a fellow-traveler which he hid from me for many years. There was also Torsten Gördlund, a tall, reddish faced Swede, a protégé of the Myrdals and Eli Hechscher, intimate with W. I. Thomas and Dorothy S. Thomas, who spent several years in Sweden where Mrs. Thomas has been working at the Institute of Social Research in Stockholm on international mobility in Sweden. Gördlund was close to my age, von Schelting was about seventeen years older than I was, Brodersen about ten years older. Gördlund was a warm-hearted roughneck, also tender and sensitive. At the margin were Ottokar Machotka, a sociologist from Brno, and Sylvia Thrupp, also

Rockefeller Fellows. They too came to our seminars but they were marginal to them because they were shy or less intelligent. Fifteen years later, through my friend Thomas Donovan, I helped to save Machotka from imprisonment and perhaps death at the hands of the Communists in 1948, when they seized power in Czechoslovakia. Miss Thrupp I myself rescued from the University of British Columbia in my effort from 1945 to 1946 to appoint able scholars to teach in Social Science II. As in most other cases of my rescues from the provinces, their gratitude was negative and became visible at once!

The seminars were really no great intellectual affair but they brought me very close to von Schelting and Brodersen, and to Gördlund although somewhat less so. My friendship with von Schelting was suspended during the war and was taken up after the war and it ran until his death about fifteen years later. The same with Brodersen, although that lapsed through my neglect in the later 1960s; but I always retained a very affectionate recollection of his delicacy of being and his interest. He was not of the first rank in intellectual power—unlike von Schelting—and when he became a professor of sociology in the Graduate Faculty of the New School of Social Research, he acquired the language and views of contemporary social science which did not fit him at all.

Much as I liked some of them, I did not find any of those Europeans intellectually valuable to me. I suppose that apart from Knight and Park, Talcott Parsons was the only person who moved in the direction in which I began to move very vaguely in the 1930s; of course, he was far ahead of me. I stood in awe of his accomplishment of *The Structure of Social Action*. I was however not so interested in it because it was not about society.

One sociologist whose writings I esteemed was Everett Hughes. He appeared to me the best disciple of Park. He had a broader scope than Wirth, was more concrete than Parsons; he had many very penetrating insights but he had little gift for generalized formulations. His sensibility was deeper than his capacity to formulate it in more general terms. In this respect he was more like Park who, however, had an unceasing drive to obtain a more comprehensive view. Hughes seemed to me to be the most interesting person in the sociology department in the 1930s. (I think he came back to Chicago in 1938). We never hit it off. He was very sensitive to discipleship and he might have thought that I belong to Louis Wirth's circle and must not be lured or welcomed into his own. Of course, I was not in anyone's circle. Maybe that looked to him like conceit or truculence and I made no attempt to dissuade him. However that may be, I received no stimulus from him.

Much of my effort in the last two years of the decade of the 1930s went into the reconstruction of the Second Year Undergraduate Course in Social Science at the University of Chicago. I think that that was a major achievement; but like many such achievements it did not last, largely because the colleagues who were needed to teach it after the war, although full of praise for it in retrospect, were not up to it intellectually. I think that it gave us the best undergraduate general social science course in the world. It was in my efforts in that course that the idea of consensus began to appear but only faintly. A Hogarth Pamphlet, *The Price of Liberty, An Ex-German looks at Britain* by a German refugee economist at Manchester, Adolf Löwe, was of some interest to me in this matter.

At about the same time, I began to develop ideas about social stratification. When a few years earlier I first read books about social stratification—perhaps Sorokin's *Social Mobility* was the first one—I thought that these social scientists were writing about a very different thing from what I had considered to be social stratification. It was perfectly obvious to me that they were writing about something very different from those things connoted to me by the word social stratification. My mind kept going back to Proust's *À la recherche du temps perdus* with its innumerable, extraordinarily subtle references to the sense of superiority and inferiority. I thought that social stratification was about social superiority and inferiority as more precisely about beliefs about superiority and inferiority. This idea was not entirely absent from the works that I read; but the works themselves were about differences in income, wealth and occupation, particularly about occupational distribution and about movement from one occupation to another. I wrote an analysis on the classificatory—"socio-economic"—scheme of Alba Edwards used by the United States Census. It was accepted for publication by *Social Forces*; but I withdrew it after William Ogburn spoke contemptuously of it at a meeting of the Society for Social Research at Chicago. Ogburn might have been right about that particular paper; but he was wrong in principle. He did not see what I was getting at.

I think that my best contribution of that period was hidden in Talcott Parsons' essay on social stratification that I read, ostensibly anonymously, for the *American Journal of Sociology* to which he had submitted it for publication. I wrote a very long report on this manuscript. I think it was about thirty foolscap pages in length, hand-written, which Professor Burgess unthinkingly sent to Professor Parsons. The latter recognized my handwriting and my foolscap sheets. He changed the character of the paper very markedly in accordance with my suggestions so that the paper that appeared in the *American Journal of Sociology* was a rather different paper from the paper as it was originally submitted. In my notes on Professor Parsons' paper, I expounded there my views about statistics as a phenomenon of evaluation of attributes such as wealth, ancestry, power, education, benefits conferred on community, etc. Herbert Goldhamer and I dealt very schematically with this idea in a paper of which only the first part was published in the *American Journal of Sociology* in 1939. It was called "Types of Power and Deference."[4] (This was my last publication in that journal.)

The view that I set forth at that time argued that "ranking" was a phenomenon of belief or opinion and that, like most opinions, it was not only ambiguous, rarely consensual, and often ambivalent as well. I thought that ranking was dependent on "knowledge and evaluation of status relevant properties" (which I later called "referents"); and that that knowledge and the criteria of evaluation were vague, inevitably often incoherent and changing in degree of precision and differentiation in moving from known and seen persons to unknown and unseen persons. In any case, it appeared to me obvious that any realistic analysis of social stratification had to accept the fact that status—or deference—was not to be regarded as unilinearily distributed. It was not like income or wealth. It was not like occupations which also could not be classified unilinearily.

My paper on "Deference," written in the early 1960s, carried this analysis further.[5] This paper had a great potential for changing the entire understanding of social stratification; but it has not succeeded in doing so. I have, however, brought the analysis further only in more recent years in my analysis of collective self-consciousness but this had still to be put into definitive form.

In June 1940, when France and the Low Countries were being overrun by the German armies, I wrote on the invitation of Gunnar Myrdal a study of "Social Stratification in the Negro Community." I have never published this paper and it is unknown to practically all students of the subject. It was based on my own recollections of the Negro community of about seven years earlier and an intensive study of the results of a few major field investigations, autobiographies, etc. It did not postulate to construct a unilinear ranking and it did not assume a consensus.

It is, of course, conceivable that the "status system" of a society could be consensual but only in a vague and loose form and certainly not with respect to fine differences. If the statuses are clustered into larger, more inclusive strata such as middle and lower class, there are bound to be ambiguities at the boundaries even if there is an approximation to consensus. Where there are ambiguities at the boundaries, there is bound to be dissensus. As fine differentiations, they can only be made by persons who are near them or who have much information at a distance.

This was, in my view, a defect of Lloyd Warner's *The Status System of an American Community*. Warner did perceive correctly that "status" was a matter of cognition and evaluation, which the resulting status was a part of opinion and was not an automatic consequence of occupation or income without the intervention of the beliefs or opinions of those who perceived and evaluated the income and wealth. Nevertheless, Warner's study, like other studies of this sort, postulated unilinearity and consensus. It also postulated the similarity of the judgment of the person whose perceptions and evaluations decided the rank of another persons and that other person's self-ranking. There are many important aspects of social stratification to which I have not referred here. I mention it here primarily because it has a place in the meandering road that I was traveling in the direction of the present state of my reflections on collective self-consciousness.

XII

I should also mention in reviewing my intellectual history of the 1930s and the diverse paths that have led me to my present views about collective self-consciousness, my rejection of ideological politics. In the second half of the 1930s, various American observers of developments in Europe said that liberal democracy could not compete successfully with the totalitarian powers, the Soviet Union, Germany, and Italy. Those societies, they asserted, had a fundamental consensus, a faith shared, throughout their societies and fervently experienced. The Western, liberal democracies, they said, were at a disadvantage because they lacked such a consensual faith; they were raddled by conflicts, disagreement about values, etc. I thought this view was wrong.

I recall that Louis Mumford wrote a little book with a title something like *A Faith for Living*. I did not like it. I do not know why fairly serious persons who were not Nazis, Fascists, or Communists could believe such obviously untrue propositions. It was not only an obstinate refusal to consider the easily accessible evidence of conflict and suppression; it was also an utterly wrong understanding of the nature of any society and of ordinary human beings. Only intellectuals could have been so wrong-headed. I was exasperated by the readiness of leading intellectual like Lewis Mumford, Reinhold Niebuhr, and many others to think that only a comprehensive, more or less completely consensual, explicit, systematically coherent, and continuously salient doctrine, compelling in action, could provide sufficient motivation to sustain the devotion and effort required to enable the liberal democratic societies to withstand and triumph over the Nazis and the Communists on the battlefield or in "the struggle for men's minds." It must be remembered that the great figures of sociology had propagated a view of modern society which was not too different from which the writers I have mentioned. From Comte's "critical stage" in the development of society, Durkheim's organic solidarity, and Tönnies' *Gesellschaft*, modern society was portrayed as a condition of hyper-individualism and disintegration. It was a very widespread view.

I had already encountered this view while I still lived in Philadelphia in Tawney's *Religion and the Rise of Capitalism*, where an "overarching faith" was attributed to the Middle Ages in contrast with modern society which was putatively without any internal moral and ties. Tawney did not contrast modern bourgeois society with Fascist Communist or National Socialist Society; he was a loyal Englishman, a patriot, who never said such things in either of the two great wars. The common interpretations of T.S. Eliot's *The Wasteland* were part of this view. I had encountered it later in Elton Mayo's *The Human Problems of an Industrial Civilization* with its intimation that the industrial civilization was doomed because of the dissolution of the solidarity of a *gemeinschaftliche* society. These views did not appeal to me, despite my great admiration, later affection, for Tawney, or my admiration for the urban sociological writings of Simmel and Durkheim. Mayo had read Durkheim and seemed to accept that a society with organic solidarity was really a society without solidarity and was threatened with "disintegration." Mayo believed that a society needs to have something like an "over-arching" faith in order to go on in a decent way without falling into severe internal conflict or complete demoralization. It was my view in the late 1930s that the totalitarian powers gave only a spurious appearance of such a faith; on closer inspection, the apparent consensus was maintained by the suppression of and intimidation of those who held opinions divergent from those of the rulers. Most of my contemporaries, if they thought about the matter at all, would have subscribed to it. I think that Louis Wirth and Karl Mannheim believed it—Wirth simply as a thing to say (as at the beginning of his introduction to *Ideology and Utopia*), and Mannheim because he thought that all liberal democracies were the same as Germany just after the First World War and in the years just before the Nazis became the rulers of Germany. Even Park in his dark moments thought this way about Western society. Knight in the autumn of 1932 was not too far from it.

XIII

The coming of the Second World War made a great difference to me. It caused me to concentrate my mind on Germany. I had over the years acquired a scrappy knowledge of modern German history and my study of Max Weber's writings, especially the political writings, forced me to acquire more knowledge than I otherwise would have had. My acquaintance with many German refugees gave me a certain familiarity with German things.

From 1942, I was in constant contact with Germany through German wireless broadcasts, the German press, and interviews with German prisoners of war. For an extended period one of my major tasks was to write a weekly report on German civilian morale. I was also able to learn much about the internal life of the German army from and about the "home front" interrogations of German prisoners of war.

I had the advantage of a group of remarkable British colleagues, mainly psychiatrists and psychoanalysts in peace-time, many of them connected with Tavistock Institute before they joined His Majesty's Forces. Two who stand out were Lt. Colonel Henry V. Dicks and Lt Colonel A.T.M. Wilson. Dicks was a very thoughtful man who spoke German excellently. Wilson was one of the most brilliant men I have ever met. The movement of attention from macrocosm—the morale of German civilian society—to microcosm—the morale of combat units at the front (and sometimes the reverse movement) was invaluable to me; but it would not have been so valuable without the intellectual company of Dicks and Wilson. Neither had ever studied sociology but they were none the worse for that. They were more psychoanalytic in their outlook than I was; both of them had been professional psychiatrists before the war whereas I had only dabbled in psychoanalysis.

I had read a bit of Freud in Philadelphia in the late 1920s; but I had no opinion about it. Even at that time, I thought that *The Future of an Illusion* was a feeble performance. Even if religious beliefs were untrue, Freud's treatment diminished their grandeur. The book lowered the dignity of human beings. In Chicago I had a little more opportunity or necessity to learn about psychoanalysis. There was, for one thing, Harold Lasswell, for whom I had a distrustful curiosity and even respect. He was so clever and he was so alert to so many important things. It was on the basis of my good standing with Lasswell that I persuaded him to take Nathan Leites as his assistant (unpaid) in 1936.

I had met Leites in New York around Christmas 1935. I used to go eastwards for about a fortnight at the end of the year—one week with my parents, one week in New York where I used to stay at the YMCA for about two dollars a night. During the day I went to bookshops or ate delicious French meals at Bonats (alongside the Post Office) for about thirty-five cents. Leites was ingratiatingly agreeable to me; I am not sure why. It is likely that he expected me to do something for him. I certainly did.

Leites at that time was on a fellowship from some Jewish organization, perhaps a fraternity. He lived in the fraternity house on the campus of Cornell University. He felt very unhappy there; it turned out that he was usually unhappy everywhere. He told me that his scholarship was transferable to any other house of that Jewish fraternity. I knew vaguely of a Jewish fraternity house at 56th and Woodlawn Avenue. I told Leites that he should come to Chicago, where I could try to arrange something for him.

When I returned to Chicago, I went to Lasswell's room (326 Social Science Research Building). I told Lasswell about Leites whose sharp wits and learning impressed me even in our brief conversations. Lasswell agreed at once to my proposal that he appoint Leites to an unpaid research assistantship in the department of political science.

This was a major event in Leites' life. It was also of some significance for me, too. Leites took to psychoanalysis at once with the concentration, rigor, and speech of absorption that were among his main characteristics. At first I was his only acquaintance so I had to bear it as well as I could. I suppose he found me the least unbearable of the persons he met in Chicago because I still remembered a fair amount about second-rate French novels and novelists of the twentieth century and I had also a rather wide ranging although fragmentary view of continental socialism and communism. Leites had been a social democrat and was in fact the Wunderkind of the leading social democratic intellectuals like Salomon, Speier, Alfred Braunthal, Krichheimer. I think that he had published an article jointly with Kirchheimer in the *Archiv für Sozialwissenschaft* (on Carl Schmitt's *Legalität und Legimität*).

Leites had a disposition to read only one or two books on a subject but to read them so exhaustively that nothing was lost. By reading the chief books on a subject, with his extraordinary ability to absorb its content, he could be something close to a master of the subject. He did not simply commit the book to memory; he reconstructed it and systematized it. He became very devoted to psychoanalysis. I suppose that he believed it. He certainly mastered it. In consequence of this, I too read more psychoanalytic literature. I was not so persuaded by it as Leites was. Nevertheless, I became sufficiently familiar with it that I was once invited to present a lecture to the Chicago Psychoanalytic Society.

I ought to tell a little about Leites at this point. He was about 5'10" or 5'11," straight and compact, spare in construction. He walked with a rapid stride. He had a small round head, bald already in his mid-twenties, pink-cheeked, smiled readily, mechanically, simulating congeniality and agreement. He had a good sense for the amusing enormities of his contemporaries, a hypersensitivity to vulgarity, a hatred of the "banal," and an incapacity to resist boredom. Simulations that did not engage him caused him to close his eyes involuntarily; although if his advantage were at stake, his eyes remained open and bright and eagerly assenting to whatever the boring person said. When little was at stake for him, his eyes closed rapidly. I think that he did not really fall asleep because when he opened them, he gave evidence that he had heard what was said.

Leites was remarkable both for his eccentricity and his extraordinary intelligence. He spoke avidly, wrote rapidly—the later in a code, partly Latin, partly German, partly French, partly English. He was exceptionally speedy in forming a conclusion or generalization and he was not uncertain of the validity of what he said. He had a vast memory for what he read—less for what he experienced from other human beings—and his capacity for speedy and precise recall appeared to be equally great. He also had an unyielding capacity for work, for concentrated, rapid and intense intellectual exertion. The only deficiency of his extraordinary intellectual qualities was the utter lack of common sense. Although he thought that the mechanisms of psychoanalytic theory were operative in all other human beings whom he studied, he had perfect confidence in his own ratiocinative capacity. He could not tolerate vagueness or uncertainty or an explanation that was consistent with the poor theories of psychoanalyses.

He was not only unrealistic about a world that he could not release from his attention; he was also one of the unhappiest men I ever knew. He suffered from loneliness; but he could not stand the company of most human beings. It is my impression that in later years he forced himself to appear to enjoy the company of his intellectual inferiors; but I doubt whether he ever did enjoy it.

He was also very acutely unaware of his remoteness, lack of sympathy for other persons, perhaps even of his preoccupation with himself; and he tried to overcome it. He was extremely compulsive and in any moment were there was a lot at stake for him, he became even more so. He knew about this under ordinary circumstances and tried to appear "normal" as if his analyst had ordered him to be "normal," to simulate "spontaneity" and "affection." I think that he could not bring it off. He was perhaps the most intelligent person I have ever met and one of the most learned; but his understanding of the world of human beings came to nothing despite his very large gifts. From observing him, I learned that theory is not as good as common sense in the contemplation of human beings.

Yet, I also benefited from him. For one thing, before I went to Europe in 1942, he helped to maintain a sense of intimacy with European things. He was a passionate Francophile—I was not but I had some intimacy with France through reading novels, autobiographies, literary journals, etc. I had the same condition of being an "honorary Frenchman" as I later had of being an "honorary German" or an "honorary Indian." Some of the first two, I owe to Leites. There was no one else whom I knew in Chicago who carried with him the overtones of French and German intellectuals and political life as much as Leites did. I was already in this state of mind before I met Leites; but there is no doubt that he animated it in me for the fifteen or so years in which I was in good relations with him as anyone could be. There later developed a distance between us because I was critical of the schematic unrealism of his work. He on the other hand thought that I was too eclectic, too content with vagueness and uncertainty. But I benefited from him enormously. One of the things I got from him was an intimacy with psychoanalytic ideas. I could never have read as much of that literature without his presence and later that of Lasswell.

Thus, when I was introduced to Wilson by Karl Mannheim one evening in the winter of 1942-1943, I was sufficiently familiar with psychoanalytic theory to make an impression on Wilson. Wilson thought that because I was said to be a sociologist, I could contribute to the work that he and his colleagues from the pre-war Travistock Institute were doing. Soon thereafter I was introduced by Wilson to his colleagues in the Directorate of Army Biology under Brigadier J.R. Rees. John Rickman and Wilfred Bion were members of the group. They had done original work on officer-selection; they devised the "county-house test." Dicks seemed to do miscellaneous jobs with high level German officers who had been taken as prisoners of war. I admired all of them greatly; they were an extraordinarily intelligent lot of men. I enjoyed their company and learned a lot from them. I do not think that they learned much from me; but they seemed to think that they could. I am much in their debt, and it is right that I should acknowledge them.

After the war, I was a member of the governing body of the Tavistock Institute of Human Relations and a regular participant in its weekly seminars, attended by John Rickman, Wilfrid Bion and others. I saw a good amount of John Bowlby, who was much influenced by Anna Freud. It was, in short, a remarkable group of men, one of the best I have ever encountered. I cannot say that I even adhered strictly to any of the propositions of psychoanalysis, the general theory of which I find much too simple and much too narrow, and the particular clinical explanations I find a complicated thicket of ad hoc and excessively ingenious and ambiguous propositions.

It all began one evening in Karl Mannheim's study. That was the beginning of my explorations of the primary group. My first serious—still very elementary—effort to understand consensus or the integration of society owes a great deal to the cosmic accident that brought me into contact with the splendid intelligences of the Directorate of Army Psychiatry and the Directorate of Army biology. My desire to read and understand Max Weber, my interest in Germany and the accidental encounters of the war (in which Karl Mannheim also played a part since it was he who introduced me to Wilson) laid out the direction that I have been trying to explore and clarify ever since.

I think that it was in connection with the effort, arising out of my collaboration with Wilson and Dicks, to understand the conduct of soldiers in combat that my interest in primary groups, in Cooley's terminology, took form. It had not been in my consciousness before the war. Although I had read much of the literature that bored me, the object did not take form in my mind's eyes. Most of my pre-war interest had been in what later came to be called "political sociology" or political philosophy. My interest in "toleration" was more concerned with the demand for consensus and the willingness to live in a society of only very partial consensus, the demand for uniformity or indifference to uniformity or the principled insistence on the acceptance of divergent opinions. I juxtaposed tolerance against ideology, i.e., against the all-embracing, unified view of the world, conformity in action. I should not over emphasize the coherence of my views. I did not bring together my aversion towards a "faith for living" and my interest in toleration, which was in fact mostly an interest in the historical development of the idea. I did not bring these two notions together, although I should have done so.

My observations and reflections during the war added another object to my intellectual interests. At first, I did not at all see the connections between my denial of the durability of a comprehensive, intense, universally adhered to belief, religious or political, my further assertion that such a belief was unnecessary and damaging to the order in a liberal democratic society, my interest in toleration, and my "discovery" (it was a "discovery" as far as I was concerned) of the influence of the "face-to-face" group in the conduct of individuals and on the coherence and effectiveness of a large corporate body like an army.

XIV

My views about the ways in which individuals are bound to each other in solidarity and mutual support, in conformity with the rules of their collectivity, i.e., with moral consensus, were precipitated during the academic session, 1945-1946, when I was back at the University of Chicago.

It was then that I wrote the paper on the *Wehrmacht*.[6] I began that essay with an effort to put into order the impression I had gained during the war and to interpret the internal solidarity of the German soldiers in the face of the severe reverses they met toward the end of the war. During the war, my colleague Henry Dicks thought it was a consequence of the desire of the German soldiers to demonstrate their manliness. At first I shared this view; later I found it insufficient. That bravery did not require solidarity. This appeared to me to be evident from the reading of the documentation that we had. The *Fronterlebnis* seemed to me to be more than the experience of the gratification of withstanding danger or a by-product of it. *Kameradschaft* was often referred to by German soldiers and by the German authors who wrote about them. That was a different phenomenon from bravery. Some soldiers would have been brave without the support of their comrades, others were sustained in it by their comrades. They were made brave by their solidarity with their comrades. The brave were made braver, the more timorous were encouraged into bravery by their membership in the small group of brave soldiers.

This seemed to me at that time to be an immediate personal relationship, a group constituted by mutual attachment of the members of each other primarily by virtue of their personal qualities.

I contrasted this with the solidarity of an ideological group. In an ideological primary group there is a commitment to the realization of an end prescribed by an ideology or the living-up to a norm prescribed by a demanding and comprehensive doctrine. At this time, I interpreted ideology generally to refer to a set of consistent beliefs of a wide range of reference, requiring strict adherence, which was rigorously obligatory for their believers and which entailed irreconcilable hostility towards all those who opposed them. An ideology is the set of beliefs of a collectivity that may be widely dispersed territorially. It can be participated in by primary groups, the members of which are in each other's presence and who are attached to each other both as persons and as the embodiments of the qualities possessed by virtue of participation in the values which are the object of the ideological beliefs. The more ideological the group, the less the personal element.

My interpretation of the conduct of the German soldiers and their persistent adherence to their oath of loyalty (*der Eid*) appeared to me to indicate that it was not solely the personal ties of comradeship that held the German soldiers to their military task. There was some element of attachment to the whole—to the German army, to Germany or to the German people. The latter was however only one element, indispensable but not preponderant. National Socialist convictions or ideology seemed to play a very small role, if any role at all, in the functioning of the front-line units.

I think now that the dichotomy of personal primary groups and an ideological collectivity in my characterization of the solidarity of the combat units of the *Wehrmacht* was an oversimplification that obscured the fact that the solidarity was formed around an accepted task. Personal attachments were certainly significant; but it was engagement in the common task of fighting and remaining intact.

This was all very well as a confirmation of my skepticism regarding the role of National Socialist ideology—or any other ideology, for that matter—in the daily life of soldiers—or civilians for that matter. It did not however throw any light on the fundamental problems of the bonds that hold primary groups together or which hold societies together.

In one respect, the paper on the *Wehrmacht* was an extension of my pre-war view that no society can be pervaded completely by an ideology, that no ideology is completely shared by all the members of society and that the coherence or order of effectiveness of any society over any period of more than a few weeks or months must be seen as dependent on ties other than ideology. (I did not intend to deny that ideologists do not occasionally gain very powerful positions in society and that they can exercise great power, but not through their success in persuading or coercing all the members of their societies to adhere strictly to their ideologies.)

My rejection of the view that an ideology, that is, a dogmatic belief, explicitly articulate, unqualifiedly salient, coherent, compelling, comprehensive and universal in its reference and consistent was needed for the maintenance of a society. The effort to find an alternative was one side of my argument in the paper about the *Wehrmacht*. The emphasis on comradeship (*Kameradschaft*) was part of that effort. It inclined towards the idea that the coherence of large collectivities constituted by coherent small groups linked to the larger group through intermediate individuals (e.g., sergeants or junior officers). I did not want to dissolve large societies entirely into primary groups. I wanted to present what I thought was a truer picture of modern societies in which there is some attachment to central institutions and central symbolic configurations with relatively little of that attachment being direct, intense, continuously salient, and wholly consensual. I was willing to agree that there is intermittently such an attachment to the center; but I denied that it was utterly compelling, exclusive and continuously and unqualifiedly salient. I wished to reduce it to a state of intermittence and shifting from one part of the society to another.

I have from the beginning had an aversion against interpretations of society when I see it in categories such as complete consensus or complete "atomization," complete *Gemeinschaft* or complete *Gesellschaft*. That was the intention that emerged as I worked on "The Cohesion and Disintegration of the *Wehrmacht*." I wanted to reach a more realistic view of the pattern of coherence of a large society, which would do justice to its pluralism and recognize how, at the same time, the constitution of those smaller collectivities contributed to the maintenance of the whole. The solidarity of the military primary group in an object of the attachment of its members was contributory to the maintenance of the whole, in this case the German army as a fighting force.

In this way, I found myself with a twofold task. The first was the discovery of the character of the tie which holds a relatively large society together sufficiently for it to continue. The other task was to discover the nature of the personal tie.

XV

In the summer of 1947, at the University of Chicago, I pursued concurrently these two divergent paths that had a single destination. I delivered a course of lectures to which a seminar was attached. The course ran over about twenty lectures; the seminar had twenty-four weekly sessions lasting for two hours. The topic was "Consensus and Liberty: The Social and Psychological Conditions of Political Democracy." (The manuscript still exists in Chicago.[7]) There I tried—not very successfully—to develop my ideas about consensus in a large society, such as American, British or French society. I defined consensus as a state of "affinity" or sense of "affinity" of its individual members with each other—nothing more than that, just enough to impose limits on the actions of individuals. I did not define it as agreement about values, or agreement about procedures or about substantive ends; I argued that it was attachment to the society as such and to its members as parts of that society. I think that that was a step in the right direction.

I was still moderately sympathetic with psychoanalytic ideas; but I did not speak of "identification"—a term which I have always rejected because it meant too many things. It did not distinguish among: (a) identification as the individual's designation of himself as a member of a particular group, as a reference to oneself as an American, or as a Frenchmen; (b) identification of the individual with the other— an individual or a collectivity—with stress on the identity or likeness of qualities of the individual and the other individual members of the collectivity; (c) identification by the individual of himself, i.e., discerning his own condition of being a distinctive, individual entity, coterminous and continuous with his body, in other words, the individual self-image. (Harold Lasswell spoke frequently of identification in any and all of these ways; and for that reason so did Nathan Leites without questioning it. I did not find the term satisfactory.) The term identity is still used in these senses about individuals and collectivities; but it does not distinguish between the constant stable factual existence of the individual or the collectivity as seen by an external observer and the self-consciousness of the individual or the consciousness of the individual as a member of the collectivity or simultaneously the collective self-consciousness of all the members of the collectivity. When it is used in the form of "collective identity," it fails to distinguish between collective self-consciousness and the stable continuous existence of the collectivity as seen by external observers. Even if the ambiguities are avoided, a more fundamental ambiguity remains. This is a task with which I still have to cope.

Despite the unresolved difficulty, it still makes sense to assert that this "sense of affinity," this "attachment to the whole," this "feeling of unity" or "perception of oneness" with the other members of one's society or one's group, or what I now call, unsatisfactorily, the collective self-consciousness is not constantly present or salient or equally participated in by all the members of the collectivity. I saw it as an intermittent phenomenon concurrently co-existent with conflict. These variable patterns of collective self-consciousness function to hold the conflicts in check; but it is not certain that they will do so sufficiently to prevent any disorder at all. Collective self-consciousness is usually sufficiently strong to come into operation when conflict threatens to become so severe, so disruptive of order, so disturbing to the rest of society, etc. The rest of the time it could be dormant, although even then effective, in influencing actions before they ever approach the threshold of disorder, i.e., of becoming disruptive of important processes or activities.

XVI

In the autumn of 1947, I followed the other path towards gaining an understanding of the social bond. I gave a course of about eight lectures in the Michelmas term at the London School of Economics, "The Primary Groups in Society." I prepared it very carefully and it was moderately well attended. I covered the literature of sociological research as it was at that time. I did more than justice to *The American Soldier*, finding in it things that were really not there but which have since been attributed to it, and to Roethlisberger and Dickson and the rest of the literature of industrial sociology which was then beginning its brief surge. Cooley was exhumed and exhibited, the literature of rural sociology likewise, and an excellent book by an American, E. Wright Bakke, about the unemployed in Greenwich.

I thought it was quite a good course but Joseph Ben-David many years later expressed disapproval. He probably had unworthy motives for doing so. One outcome of the course was a section or chapter of *The Present State of American Sociology* on "Rediscovery of the Primary Group" which later writers accepted as having really happened. But whether there was such a rediscovery or whether it was I who "rediscovered" what no sociologist worth his salt could have ever ignored may be left unanswered here.

The theme of the lectures was that larger collectivities, armies, villages, factories, political parties are sustained by the strength of the primary groups which they incorporate. I argued that for most of the members of the primary groups, the ties to each other without exception were entirely personal, the exception was a person who participated in the values of the larger collectivity. Attachment to him on the part of most of the members meant they acted in accordance with those values without participating in them. That was an ingenious and excessively schematic view of the matter; but there was probably something in it. I gave the course again in Chicago in the early 1950s and it was the basis for *Love, Belief and Civility*.[8]

XVII

In the summer of 1948, I wrote an essay on "Primary Groups in the American Army" about the American army, based on the data in *The American Soldier.*[9] I came to the same conclusion about the United States Army as I had about the German *Wehrmacht*. I interpreted these data to show that the solidarity of the primary group, i.e., the small unit, was an important feature of military life. (It was one paper in a book edited by Robert Merton and Paul Lazarsfeld in a series, called *Continuity in Social Research*, suggested by me to Jeremiah Kaplan of the Free Press).

I do not think that there was much that was new in that essay; it probably did not go beyond what I had written in the paper on the *Wehrmacht*. It confirmed my view that the extent to which primary groups (I later called them personal primary groups) were formed and maintained, affected the action of soldiers in combat.

This seems very self-evident now; but it was probably not so at that time. There had been too little sociological study of the military until after the Second World War—-the paper on the *Wehrmacht* was a pioneer work at that time—so I cannot say that it represented an advance in sociological thinking before. It was probably very obvious to any professional sergeant but they did not write sociological papers. The American military at its higher levels was insensitive to the "message" for many years as was shown by their "replacement-policy." It was only after about thirty-five years that they conceded that keeping the same units intact to the extent that casualties made it possible was the right thing to do. I was told that the paper on the *Wehrmacht* had something to do with that change in policy; but whether that was in fact the case, I do not know. Whatever it was, that did not solve my problem of the nature of the bond (or the structure of the relationship of coherence or attachment) in small face-to-face groups or in large corporate bodies of whole societies.

XVIII

In the summer of 1949, I wrote an introduction to a new edition of the translation of Georges Sorel's *Réflexions sur la Violence*. Georges Sorel had been a fascinating person for me when I was an undergraduate. I read all of his works, in French and Italian, including his correspondence with Croce. (Much more has been published over the past sixty years). I had wanted to write a book on him. I had a very large set of notes; but I never got around to writing the book or even an essay. Yet he continued to interest me because his intellectual peregrinations gave me a better insight into the wrongness of the distinction between "Left" and "Right" in politics, and into arbitrary association of socialism, rationalism, and "liberated" morality. When Jeremiah Kaplan accepted my suggestion that he reprint Hulme's translation of the *Réflexions* together with a translation of the hitherto untranslated appendices by a pupil in one of my courses in Chicago, Jack Roth, to whom I had proposed that he work on Sorel, I was pleased because it gave me an opportunity to repay a debt incurred in my youth several decades before.

What I wrote in that introduction was very different from what I would have written in 1930. When I re-read the *Réflexions* in 1950 and went over my old notes, I saw things that had never occurred to me previously. I discovered that Sorel's ideal was an exemplification of what I had only recently come to designate as an "ideological primary group." Perhaps the use of the term "primary group" to refer to a collectivity which was not constituted by situations in which the members were in the presence of each other was not justified. On the other side, an ideological collectivity was similar to a personal face-to-face primary group in the sense that that was a "fusion of selves"; the individual was transcended by the collective self-consciousness; individual self-consciousness made way for the preponderance of collective self-consciousness.

An ideological group, by definition, is not a group constituted by personal relations, by the attachment to individuals as persons. It is a group in which the attachments are between individuals who are not viewed, in principle, as persons but as the embodiments of the qualities that are none other than belief in the ideology, possession by the ideology.

For Sorel, the socialist movement was nothing more than a prelude to the *grève* générale—the "general strike"; the "general strike" was everything. The "general strike" which had been much discussed as a technique for the advancement of the working class was for him primarily a state of possession by an exultant belief; it was what I would call a state of ideological possessions. It was a state of complete solidarity. It was not socialism, it was not a means to socialism. It was to be a moment of complete consensus. Sorel did not, as I recall, say anything about how enduring it could be. It was simply an intrinsically valuable state of complete absorption of the individual into the proletarian collective consciousness. That was its value. That is what Sorel meant when he spoke of the general strike as a "myth." The realization of its alleged objective was less important than the elevating experience of solidarity. It was the moment of heroic solidarity of the working class. The heroism was not so much heroic comradeship in the presence of physical danger as it would be in the field of battle, but the exhilarating sense of unity in the class struggle against the bourgeoisie, like the *Kameradschaft* of the *Fronterlebnis*.

There were other aspects of Sorel's ideological disposition with which I did not deal but which were related to his stress on intense solidarity in which the individual is completely transcended. His hatred of *"les artisans de la vie facile,"* of hedonism and individualism is one of these aspects of the ideological character. His rigoristic moralism as manifested in his affirmation of the execution of Socrates (*Le Procès de Socrate*) was one aspect of his praise of the superiority of a more intense collective self-consciousness. His wandering from one ideological sect to another—from Syndicalism as he understood the *bourses de travail* to the *Action française*, of which the *camelots du rois* were an ideological sect or primary group—-and then his ultimate embrace of the Russian revolution, its "heroic period," testify that he was an ideologist of the purest strain. His socialism was only pretext for being ideological. Sorel hated Durkheim for all sorts of reasons; but one of them must have been Durkheim's treatment of mechanical solidarity as inferior to organic solidarity. Sorel regarded individualism as morally degenerate. He had a passionate aversion against civil society.

The aim of establishing an entire society as solidary as a primary group, in which there was a transcendence of individual selves, has been a prelude to tyranny. The ideal of the constitution of a liberal, democratic large society on the lines of the primary group, as was aspired to by Charles Cooley, and the ideal of re-establishing a society in accordance with the pattern of *Gemeinschaft* are untenable. No large society can exist in such a form. Efforts to reconstruct a society under the domination of an ideology are likewise impossible. Yet, even though these efforts to organize society that will operate under an all-pervasive, stringent moral code are bound to fail, they contain in themselves the germ of a fundamental truth. To find and to define the pattern of a civil collective self-consciousness is a task of the highest urgency for statesmen and for serious students of society. To discover the pattern of the moral order of a large-scale liberal democratic society remains a major task.

XIX

From 1945 onward while I was trying to clarify my ideas about consensus and the pattern of integration in primary groups, I was also actively associated with the Federation of Atomic (later American) Scientists. At first I was interested in the international control of the production of nuclear weapons. As the possibility faded, its place on the agenda of the Federation was taken by responding to attacks by politicians and journalists on physicists and chemists for allegedly divulging the secrets of the production of nuclear bombs. At first I began to write about the pattern of a system of international control nuclear weapons. This never got very far after a draft that I wrote in September 1945; then I busied myself writing about the course of the discussions in the United States about international control. I wrote fairly frequently in the *Bulletin of the American Scientists* and a substantial pamphlet on *The Atomic Bomb in World Politics* for the National Peace Council in London. By 1948, it became very clear to me that no scheme for international control was going to be established, primarily, although not entirely, because of the recalcitrance of the Soviet Union.

When the civilian control of atomic energy became enacted into law, the Federation and the *Bulletin* turned their attention to the questions of secrecy in scientific research. I had not thought of secrecy before except when I read Simmel's chapter *Das Geheimnis* in *Soziologie*. But Simmel did not really touch on the problems of secrecy in science. I had to think more about secrecy; I had also to think more about the autonomy of science and the freedom of scientists and about academic freedom in general. I benefited greatly from making the acquaintance and then gaining the friendship of Michael Polanyi, to whom I was introduced by Szilard in 1946 (of this more later).

In the 1930s, I had taken it for granted that the enquiries into "communism" in the universities such as were conducted in certain states by committees of the state legislature were almost always unjustified and useless. There were very few Communists in the universities and except for a very few institutions like the City College of New York, they were too few to cause mischief. In any case, the investigative committees produced evidence that the handful of Communists were a danger to the social order or the national security of the Untied States. I was sort of a liberal in those days, but certainly not a collectivistic liberal and more emphatically not a fellow-traveler. Still, I had friends among the collectivistic liberals. Socialists were rarer. How could one live in any American university in the 1930s and not know one of them. I did have sympathy with one socialist whom I knew personally and who was falsely accused of being communist or otherwise subversive—but this was after the Second World War. I had no sympathy whatsoever with the Communists and fellow-travelers and did not grieve over their discomfiture. But I thought that it was wrong and injurious to public life for the investigative committees to make such clamor about them. I did not like the state of alarm that Senator McCarthy and his base associates no less vulgar or mendacious or persecutory than the Communists themselves were creating in the country.

I wrote with some frequency in the *Bulletin of the Atomic Scientists* of which I was a co-founder with Eugene Rabinowitch and Hyman Goldsmith. I think that I was no less critical of communism than Senator McCarthy and I surely knew more about it. I thought not only that what he was doing was unnecessary; but also that it introduced a pernicious ideological element into American life that was disruptive.

Unlike some of my friends in the Federation, I was in favor of secrecy of scientific research on military matters. But I did not think that the commotion stirred up by Senator McCarthy and Congressmen Dies and Fish did anything to protect secrets from Soviet spies. It was not because I thought that Communists and fellow-travelers were trustworthy persons that I took to writing against McCarthy and his fellow-travelers. I was in favor of surveillance that would keep Communists and their fellow-travelers away from things which should be kept secret. I was favorable towards infiltration by the Federal Bureau of Investigation of Communist organizations. What troubled me was the infringement by McCarthy and his ilk on the rules of civil society; they were a threat to the loose consensus that is needed in a democratic society. I thought that I saw the danger that ideology would triumph over civility, that American society would become polarized between the zealots who, in ignorance and bad faith, supported the Soviet Union, and the anti-Communist zealots like McCarthy, who were less organized and who had no doctrine such as Marxism had but who were equally dogmatic in the intolerance of divergent opinions. I did not wish to see patriotism discredited by association with persecutory nationalism. I did not wish to see collectivistic liberalism driven into alliance with Communist totalitarianism. That is what I saw as a tendency in the United States.

These were the reasons that led me to write *Torment of Secrecy* that I worked on in 1954, while I was also working on *Love, Belief and Civility*.[10] It was of a piece with that work. Underlying the whole thing was my quest for the better apprehension of the patterns of loose consensus as a mode of coherence in a collectivity and as a mode of attachment to a collectivity. *Love, Belief and Civility* was the broader work; it was intended to be a fundamental theoretical work, covering the entire range of collectivities from families and friendships to the churches, societies and states. *The Torment of Secrecy* was intended as a practical work aiming at the clarification and calming of American opinion. It sought to criticize and isolate ideologists and to promote civility. I doubt whether it did either.

The incivility of McCarthy was followed by the incivility of the left which gained a new vitality when part of it became somewhat liberated from the supine, sub-service of the Soviet Union and its agents. The New Left—-born from the suppression by the Soviet Union of the Hungarian rebellion in the autumn of 1956—-was a prelude to antinomianism or nihilism. In the United States, the reduction of Senator McCarthy by a Mormon Senator from Utah freed the cowardly intellectuals of the left who had been frightened out of their wits by the Congressional investigators, crawled out from under their beds where they had hidden. It took them some time to afresh their effrontery. The beginning of the student disturbances in Berkeley nearly a decade later showed them that incivility with impunity was a very feasible proposition. They have never looked back since.

The task that I undertook in *The Torment of Secrecy* has not been resolved. The situation in the United States now is perhaps more serious than it was in 1955. The aggressiveness of the extremists and the weakness of the center which needs civility and which should be its protector have both become aggravated.

Morality has come under the protection of the irreconcilable fundamentalists who have been driven into incivility by the radicalism of the leadership of the Christian churches. The nihilists on the other side, freed from the burden of explaining away the misdeeds of the Soviet Union, hold the liberals to ransom. I am not confident that any progress that I have made in clarifying the pattern of civility, i.e., the collective self-consciousness of a civil liberal democratic society has brought the two main currents of conservatism and liberalism out of their bondage to their extremist partners.

The Torment of Secrecy had its concrete point of departure in the agitation of some American legislators and journalists about the disclosure of knowledge about the construction of atomic bombs that was legally to be kept secret. There was a lot of not very good debate about the issue. Collectivistic liberals, about the only kind of liberals there were in the United States at that time, said that "nature does not have secrets" and that it was vain and wrong for the Untied States Atomic Energy Commission and other interested governmental bodies to try to maintain secrecy *vis-à-vis* the Soviet Union. Some must have said that because they were sympathetic to the Soviet Union and wished to strengthen its position *vis-à-vis* the United States. Others were liberals less devoted to the Soviet Union but they believed that once the official report on the production of the atomic bomb written by Henry Smyth was published, the Soviet Union had sufficient information to proceed and that the retention of scientific and technological secrets bearing on nuclear weapons would not hamper the Soviet Union in its efforts to construct such weapons. Others thought that there were advantages for the United States in retaining a lead even if only for a few years. I was inclined to this position that seemed to me to be the most reasonable one.

I had been desirous from September 1945 of sharing American scientific and technological knowledge in this field with the Soviet Union if an adequate system of international control over the production of weapons could be established. I wrote out my scheme in September 1945 and thereafter I wrote fairly frequently in favor of international control. When however the Soviet Union adamantly refused to consider at all any scheme of international control, I accepted the necessity of secrecy, even though it was no guarantee of enduring security for the United States. (My writings on this subject are to be found in *The Bulletin of the Atomic Scientists* from 1946 to 1949 and in *The Atomic Bomb and World Politics*.) *The Torment of Secrecy* examines the fascination aroused by secrecy and the ways in which the excitement generated by that fascination could be disruptive of the consensus needed for civil order.

As in most of my writings, I saw in the preoccupation with the divulgence of secrets a demand for complete consensus; and, thus, damaging to the partial and limited consensus needed for order in a civil, liberal democratic society.

In my reflection on consensus both before and after *The Torment of Secrecy* I always remembered that it was only a limited consensus that I thought of. Not only is a complete consensus impossible in any society, but it would also be undesirable. It is not desirable for everyone to agree about everything and to place the unity of society above every other value; yet there are times when the value of the society, as it is, must be placed above all other values. Ordinarily that is not desirable; but when the society is in danger, then it must be given precedence and it is then that a far-reaching consensus is desirable. No liberal democracy would be possible with such a consensus.

Pluralism is itself antithetical to a comprehensive continuous consensus about the value of the society and its good order. Pluralism postulates the privacy of autonomous, voluntary institutions. It postulates their freedom from intrusion, regarding the rules that should prevail within the institution regarding who is to be admitted and regarding what goes on within the association. I thought, but only very vaguely, about the privacy of individuals, their friends and their families. (Of course, the participants in these relations are rightly subjected to the obligation of consensus.)

I thought of privacy as the immunity from surveillance by private and governmental bodies and individuals, immunity from undesired communications, immunity from disclosure of information about activities in the private sphere, immunity for the control or seizure of private property, and unwarranted trespass or search or seizure in zones regarded as domestic or private.

I had for many years been concerned about the privacy of individuals and families. I abhorred the intrusions of the popular press and latterly the self- defined "quality" press, into the private relations of individuals of no public importance and even into those of persons of public importance. I have always regarded the intrusiveness of the press into the personal sphere as obnoxious in the extreme. Later I found Justice William Douglas' justification for abortion in *Roe vs. Wade* as an unjustified extension of the right of privacy—as if privacy was a protection from prohibition of criminal actions, like a murder within a family. I did not think that the right of privacy could guarantee against surveillance for any actions. Privacy did not confer immunity against surveillance on warranted suspicion of espionage, the arrangements for subversive or criminal action. But the suspicions had to be warranted.

I must admit that I did not give these matters much thought before the Second World War. The issue came on me from several directions after the war. The need to think about secrecy and publicity in connection with scientific research by indirection made me think about the difference between secrecy and privacy.

It was against this background that I came upon the problems of privacy in a wider intellectual and social context than I had ever considered them before the war. I first attempted to deal with them in *The Torment of Secrecy*. Publicity in science, privacy in personal relationships, autonomy in voluntary associations, the guarantee of private property: all of these were necessary features of a civil, pluralistic liberal democratic society.

In the final chapter of *The Torment of Secrecy*, I discussed these matters in relation to the conditions needed for a pluralistic civil society. In that chapter, I argued for a modicum of consensus between liberals in the American sense (collectivistic liberals as I later called them) and conservatives including genuine individualistic constitutional liberals and genuine tradition-loving hierarchical conservatives, and the refusal by those several groups to support any alliance with the Communists and fellow-travelers on the liberal side or with the proto-totalitarian, populist zealots on the other side.

I was not in favor of the persecution of the extremists; although I did not think that they merited the freedom that the constitution and liberal opinions of the American judiciary granted them and for which the American Civil Liberties Union contended on their behalf. They seemed to me, in their feebleness at that time, not to be a danger to the civil society, of which they were irreconcilable enemies. The Communists were indeed agents for a foreign power and they fell far short of the obligations of citizenship. Because of their subversive intentions or at least their subversive desire, I thought that they should be kept under surveillance. I thought that this was being sufficiently well done by the Federal Bureau of Investigation and that, in any case, the task of surveillance of subversive intentions and espionage was not being done by the various legislative investigative committees. Instead, they created a most disagreeable commotion; they persecuted a small number of more or less innocent persons, they detected no spies, there was no great danger of subversion. Senator McCarthy and his collaborators did not perform any function necessary for the well-being of American society. Instead, they were a danger to civil society because they obtained the publicity which they sought from the press and radio, and early television; and much more important, they alienated further the traditionally alienated intellectuals of the literary world and they alienated the academic intellectuals who had not been alienated as they subsequently became.

Senator McCarthy and his staff, while purporting to protect secrecy (they never had any evidence of breaches of secrecy not already well known to those who were officially responsible for knowing about them), committed many infringements on the privacy of their victims. (I do not include political beliefs as falling within the range of privacy.) Meanwhile the American popular press continued with few inhibitions on the infringements on privacy that they had practiced for many years and even the respectable press began to do the same thing.

Two further developments drew me further into the considerations of privacy. One was the increasing appetite of governments in liberal democratic societies for more information about their citizens coupled with the computerization of government records which made the bringing together of data on particular individuals possible. Social scientists wanted to have these data available to them; they said aggregated data was much less valuable to them. They were right; but their claims raised important issues regarding ethical aspects of social research.

Then, in quite another kind of situation, the relations between immunity from disclosure or publicity and social research were given dramatic expression. A professor of the university of Chicago, as a member of a group studying the jury system, "bugged" the deliberations of a jury in Wichita Kansas, i.e., he placed hidden recording devices in the room where the jury held its deliberations without having obtained any of the juror's permission. There was a resounding uproar (I read of it in the *Times* (London) while I was living in New Delhi). I had some relations with that research project that was conducted under the auspices of the Law School of the University of Chicago. When I returned to the United States, I wrote several papers on the problems of privacy and sociological research.

These papers dealt with problems that I had not seen before. If one regards public knowledge in a civil liberal democratic society as a good thing and a rational and informed opinion as a necessity, there is a justification for social research, quite apart from its merits as scientific knowledge. It contributes sound knowledge to the cognitive consensus. However, if social research is to be limited by the respect for privacy, this is a limit on intellectual freedom; but it is also a reaffirmation of the rightfulness of privacy. It excludes certain sections of society from cognitive consensus. The argument for privacy is an argument for the proposition that there are things that should not be disclosed, that there are things no one has a right to know about. The phenomenon is an extraordinarily complicated one. But the important point is that there are parts of society that should be and are in fact immune from public knowledge and from deliberate efforts to acquire knowledge of those parts. In a way, these entries into the subject of privacy and my arguments for secrecy are arguments that cognitive consensus no less than moral consensus need not be omniscient in its objects nor universal in its adherence. Privacy had an important function in civil society; it is a barrier against universal politicization. At the same time, it must not be a forge for subversion and disorder.

XX

I first established personal contact with Michael Polanyi in the autumn of 1946. I recall telephoning him from a call-box on or just near Kings Road, perhaps in Lincoln Street in Chelsea. I had been given his telephone number or more likely his address by Leo Szilard before I left Chicago in September of that year. I must have written to him when I first returned to London at the end of September so that in a return note he asked me to telephone him. But I do not remember our first meeting. Was it at the Athenaeum? He used to go there often and that is where I met him frequently for lunch. I thought that because I had my introduction to him from Szilard that he must be interested in the international control of atomic energy (a euphemism for the atomic bomb); but when at our first meeting I found that he became deaf whenever I mentioned it to him. He was not interested in discussing the prospects of international control; no, not in the slightest.

I had been interested for more than a decade in academic freedom but my views were rather primitive. I had made a fairly detailed study of academic freedom—-or rather infringements on academic freedom—-in the teaching and in research in the Social Sciences in the United States in a paper first published in the *Annals of the American Academy of Political and Social Sciences* in about 1938 and thereafter I continued my interest. The question of security and secrecy of scientific research having to do with nuclear energy (especially for military purposes) sustained that interest.

I found that Michael Polanyi was not interested in the problem of secrecy. I quickly adjusted myself to this; I ceased to be astonished by it. I accepted the conditions of conversation with him. Aside form his deafness to my efforts to start a discussion with him on these topics, he also did not want to hear anything about Karl Mannheim or Karl Popper. One afternoon when he came to my room at the London School of Economics, just as I returned from the seminar that I gave with Popper, and suggested that we should go to Popper's room and take him out to dinner. He was deaf to that. Thereafter I ceased to mention Popper to him. I got on exceptionally well with him.

It was easy to get on with him. Except for his deafness, he was exceptionally forthcoming and friendly. He obviously took to me at once. He spoke beautifully. He had a slight continental accent—-just slight enough to become aware that English was not his native language. His diction was perfect. His sentences were perfectly formed. His voice was like music; it had a resonant quality. He was a genuinely eloquent speaker in public just as he was in conversation. One heard the echo of delicate bells in his voice.

He was about five feet nine in height. He was perfectly proportioned in body. He was of a dark tincture in complexion and his eyes had a central Asian appearance, like many of the Hungarians. They were beautiful eyes, slightly sad but very active and mobile. He was not always observant of physical things in the world around him; but he was quick to respond to anything said to him, if it interested him. He spoke as if he had reflected on what he said. His speech in conversation was a finished product. That is why it was so painful for me to see and hear him at our last meeting not long before he died. He had lost the capacity for speaking in that beautifully molded way; he would begin a sentence with all of his old beauty of voice and diction but he could only say the first part of a sentence. Words did not come to him and he would forget the first part of the sentence, stopped, put his hand to his face, and try again. But again and again, the first clause was broken off. He was still affectionate, still smiled in a most handsome manner but the power of continuous speech had been lost. Mrs. Polanyi told me that he had outbursts of temper with her, reprimanded her, etc.

His upper teeth protruded very slightly, just enough to make his upper lip extend outward a little but not at all in any disfiguring way. He was always elegant in dress without a trace of dandyism. When so many academic Englishmen were dressing in ragged garments (Tawney was a paragon of raggedness and bagginess), Polanyi's garments always appeared to be extremely well cared for. Like other English academics, he wore a sleeveless pullover. He did not smoke cigarettes or cigars. He might have smoked a pipe; but I do not think that he ever did so in my presence.

As far as I can recall, I think that our first conversations had to do with academic freedom and particularly the freedom of science from government intervention. He was not at all concerned with the civil freedom of academics; he took that for granted.

He was much preoccupied with the efforts of Bernal et al., to promote the "planning" of science. To counter this, he had formed with Dr. John Baker, the Oxford botanist, the Society for the Protection of Freedom in Science that had published about eight pamphlets, several of them written by himself. The most notable was a lucid, and original statement of "The Principles of Academic Freedom." This was an adumbration of the brilliant essay that he published in the first issue of *Minerva* "The Republic of Science." From these pamphlets and from his Riddell Lectures delivered at the University of Durham in 1946 on *Science, Faith and Society*, I learned a very great deal. This small book was the source of much instruction for me.

XXI

Only once in my life have I set out to be a "system-builder." That was when I entered into collaboration with my friend, Professor Talcott

Parsons, who was a system-builder on the scale of the powerful figures of the nineteenth century in philosophy, law, and sociology. Professor Parsons loved systematic thought. He was as deductive as the vague data and the ambiguous categories of sociology permit. He went further than anyone else and I think, more fruitfully, since he had a similar point of departure. Compare his results with, for example, those of Leopold von Wiese whose *System der allgemeinen Soziologie* did not have such a fruitful point of departure.

In the second half of the 1940s, which was the only period in my life when I was officially responsible for teaching sociology in a department of sociology, I believed in the redemptive power of systematic theory. I thought that it was necessary for the guidance and fructification of empirical research of which I have always been a partisan, although sometimes one who is very dismayed by what comes out of it.

My collaboration with Professor Parsons came about in the following way. I had known him from 1936 when he taught one summer in Chicago; it was that summer that he asked me to read the manuscript of his great work, *The Structure of Social Action*. It was a work of remarkable learning and powerful ratiocination. Then there was the episode of the paper on social stratification, already related here. In 1943 he came to London to deliver several lectures at the School of Economics. I arranged a small party for him to meet my friends of the Tavistock Institute.

Later he asked me if I would collaborate with him on a scheme already provided with funds for elaborating the conceptual foundations of sociology. It reminded me of the fiasco of a decade and a half earlier when I was set to work on the methodological presuppositions of German sociology. This time, however, it would be a work of thinking, not analyzing a non-existent or arid body of literature. I accepted his invitation and spent some time in Cambridge (Massachusetts). It was a happy time for me. It was a pleasure to be with a person who so much enjoyed intellectual exertion; he loved to think. That he did not think as precisely as was desirable is not to be held against him. He had more confidence in the susceptibility of the nature of society to the discipline imposed by the mind—a very pardonable fault. He did what he did as well as it could be done. At that time I thought what we were doing was eminently worth doing and probably realizable. Looking back at it after the lapse of about four decades, I think that it was not realizable, certainly not in the four

months in a single stretch in Cambridge and then briefer meetings of
a day or two at a time in Chicago and Cambridge, plus a very considerable amount of correspondence and sending manuscripts back
and forth.

However that may be, we did it. I think that our direction was the
right one. We regarded our task as putting Max Weber—and
Tönnies—in order. It is worth mentioning that we never spoke of
Durkheim or Pareto in the course of our work. We referred to Max
Weber every few days. I kept thinking of Tönnies, too, but only
about the structure of the *gemeinschaftliche* relations, not of the primordial referents. Neither did Talcott Parsons respond to Tönnies'
failure. As already mentioned, I had read Schmalenbach's *Die
soziologische Theorie des Bundes* that separated the relationship from
its referents. (As I recall, Theodor Geiger failed to do this in his
article in the *Archiv für Sozialwissenschaft* in about 1928).

Our collaboration could not have been more agreeably concluded.
We usually met at 9AM in his room in Emerson Hall where we sat at
the corner of a rectangular table. We talked and talked, taking as our
point of departure, the topic of the previous day's discussion. We
talked until we went to lunch but only after we made some notes on
the results of our discussion that morning. Then we went to a lunch
of sandwiches and salad in the seminar room of the department of
social relations (about ten yards from Professor Parsons' room). Then
we went back to discussion, going forward from where we had left
off before lunch. At about four o'clock, we wrote out the main conclusions of our discussions. Sometimes he wrote them, sometimes I
wrote them. After 5:30 we broke off, taking the written results home
to ponder on in the evening. From time to time, we met again in the
evening if something especially interesting seemed to be on the verge
coming into view. There were times when he telephoned at 7:00 AM
to tell me delightedly of some good idea which had occurred to him
since we had parted.

Once a week or once a fortnight, we conducted a seminar for the
professors of the department of social relations. It was like the
Almanach de Gotha of the social scientists of that time. Clyde
Kluckhohn, Henry Murray, Samuel Stouffer, Florence Kluckhohn,
Erich Lindemann, Fred Baler, Robert Sears and Jerome Brunes came
most of the time. I think that George Homans seldom came although
I do remember him shouting with the freedom that comes from be-
ing of Brahminical ancestry. "God damn it, Talcott, shut up! I'm

speaking!" This was not unintelligible. Professor Parsons was an extremely slow speaker, halting between clauses and between sentences. It was not always possible to know when he had finished what he wished to say. On the occasion of one of those pauses at the end of a sentence, George Homans began to speak. When he was just beginning, Professor Parsons recommenced his discourse and George Homans retired from the field. This happened several times in succession. Each time that George Homans began to make his objections or comments (usually the former), Professor Parsons resumed his reflections. After about the fourth such collision, George Homans had had enough. After his outburst, Professor Parsons allowed him to continue.

This sort of thing never happened in our discussions in Professor Parsons' room. Perhaps it was because we sat only about three feet apart, and I always waited until I was sure that he had said what he wished to say. Professor Parsons was already becoming a little deaf and, if he sat ten or fifteen feet away from a speaker, he did not always hear what was said. But he could not have failed to hear what George Homans said on the occasion to which I refer because George Homans had one of the loudest voices I have ever heard. (Once about a dozen years later at dinner in Clare College, I asked an historian whose name I do not recall, whether he had met Homans when he was a visiting professor at Cambridge in about 1955. He said, "George Homans! I never can forget him. He had the loudest voice I have ever heard. One could hear him a hundred yards away.")

I think that *Toward a General Theory of Action* had a distinctive affect on the department of social relations.[11] There were already some strains within the department that had been from the members of the department of sociology, some from anthropology (the social anthropologists), and the social psychologists, clinical psychology and personality psychologists from the psychology department. I recall Clyde Kluckhohn once telling me that his colleagues in anthropology at other universities thought that he had left anthropology because, in addition to becoming a member of the department of social relations, he was also director of the Russian Research Institute. He had also high aspirations as a theorist; but his other obligations were diverting him from the pursuit of those aspirations, while Talcott Parsons was ploughing ahead in a fathomless and uncharted sea of social theory.

I had one clear indication of this one evening at a party at the Kluckhohn's apartment. Mrs. Kluckhohn, who also had aspirations in this direction, said to me with the jocular frankness confined by a little bit of alcohol in a way at which I took no offense, "Ed Shils, you are ruining Talcott. Until your name came along, he was one of us. What are you doing to him?"

These slight strains were, I think, aggravated by a misjudgment on the part of Professor Parsons. When we had completed the main text of *Toward a General Theory of Action*, Professor Parsons wanted the rest of the department to subscribe to it. This was probably the reason.

Professor Parsons had regarded our work as the production of a charter that would provide the theoretical rationale for the department of social relations. In fact, it is possible that it was on that ground that he had persuaded the Carnegie Corporation to provide the financial support for the project. But if that was known to the other members of the department, they did not appreciate to what they were committing themselves.

Since he did not expect them to read all that we had written, we drafted a very condensed version on "The Theory of Action" that was circulated to the members of the seminar. He asked me to visit each of them separately and to deal with their objections and to obtain their suggestions for reformulations and to have them sign the revised paper. They all signed; but I could easily see that it was done more to please Professor Parsons than for any other reason. I sensed then that there was a slight resentment; they thought that in a gentlemanly way, they were being dragooned into doing something on which they had not bargained. When Professor Parsons retired in the middle of the 1960s, the department of social relations was dissolved. The department of sociology was re-established. The anthropologists went back to the department of anthropology. The psychologists went back to the department of psychology and the others became members of the reborn department of sociology.

This saddened Professor Parsons. The department of social relations had been largely his creation. Its dissolution seemed to him to be a repudiation of his aspiration to unify the social sciences. It was probably a hope without a solid foundation. That he believed it was possible testified to his good will, his concern for his university and his discipline of which he was the noblest and best representation of his generation.

I engaged in the work of system-building with enthusiasm but also with reservations. Professor Parsons had even more enthusiasm and no reservations. When it was all over, I began to become aware of the flaws in what we had done, which remains nonetheless a very impressive achievement.

Professor Parsons had a keen imagination about concrete things; he was often very penetrating. I think that he was at his best in the years between *The Structure of Social Action* that remains one of the few really important intellectual achievements of a sociologist and *Toward a General Theory of Action* (and *The Social System* that is a summary of the *General Theory*). He wrote *The Social System* in the summer of 1950 after we had finished our collaborative work; but thanks to the speed of the Free Press and the slowness of the Harvard University Press, *The Social System* appeared about six months before *Toward a General Theory of Action*. In the period between those two works, Professor Parsons wrote about a dozen extremely fine essays on particular subjects on the family, social stratification, Fascism, etc. He was at his best in those works; but after the *General Theory*, his heart was not in such things. His heart was in the "boxes," the "four-fold-tables"—an expository device developed by Samuel Stouffer for teaching elementary statistics but which Professor Parsons adopted as a basis of portraying fundamental features of society. In time he came to think that nature itself was fundamentally a great fourfold box. Once the great structures of boxes had been constructed, Professor Parsons, who in discussing and sometimes writings about concrete things remained as observant and insightful as he had ever been, regarded his insights as really interesting when they could be put into a box, i.e., when they illustrated one of the general categories, processes or hypotheses of the system.

My own view has been different. It might well be possible to construct a coherent logical comprehensive system, with high explanatory power, in which more concrete concepts and hypotheses can be rigorously deduced from my general ones. However, after my experiences at the beginning of the 1950s, I have no temptations in that direction. Neither my tastes nor my capacities lie in that direction. I have no confidence in the illuminative power of a system as differentiated, as ostensibly rigorous, and as vague as Professor Parsons delighted in doing. My interests are no less in fundamental things than were those of Professor Parsons; I have a liking for philosophical anthropology and anthropology of the German sort, e.g., Max

Scheler, Helmut Plessner, P. L. Landsberg, et al. Professor Parsons did not like that at all. Psychoanalysis was as far as he would go in exploring the human nature.

Professor Parsons was inevitably ambiguous in his definitions. He had a very outstanding empathic capacity. Whenever he wrote about relatively concrete situations and when he was not distracted by his categories or boxes, he was outstanding in his analysis of modern societies. Furthermore, although his categories were not easily communicable to others and not more easily apprehended by others, he understood invariably the realities to which they referred. He drew on them when it seemed suitable in his spoken discourse. In his writings, something like the same occurred, although after the completion of *The General Theory*, he wrote less often on concrete things and more often in an abstract, strictly theoretical mode.

I am far from wishing to belittle Professor Parsons' accomplishments and even less his great merit as an embodiment of the highest moral values of intellectual activity. He was, in the latter respect, a paragon of the virtue of an intellectual. And as far as sociological theory, his titanic failures were those of an explorer who undertakes things no one had ever done better.

It might be that what he tried to do in his later years was an impossibility. Perhaps it was only impossible in our present state of knowledge; it might be possible in the future. What has happened in sociology since his death does not encourage confidence in this belief. (I do not see that the data gained by surveys will improve that situation; nor do I think that the recently developed skills in statistical analysis will contribute much either to that substratum of concrete understanding which I am convinced must be a precondition of abstract analysis.) Nor do I think that the adaptation of economic rationalism will bring us nearer to the goal; it combines a spurious precision with a defective common sense. It is far from an improvement.

However that may be, Professor Parsons' way was not a way that I could follow. My aptitude for long sustained, very elaborate abstraction is too weak; perhaps for that reason, my desire to do it was also weak. Whatever the causes, I have not tried to do it, except for that relatively brief period of about three years split equally each side of the middle of the century.

XXII

In the late spring of 1953, I saw a film of the coronation of Queen Elizabeth II. I had been studying W. Robertson Smith's *Lectures on the Early Religion of the Semites* and had been impressed by his statement about Jahweh's membership in Israelite society. The coronation recalled this statement to my mind. I also recalled Durkheim's discussion of totemism as the self-worship of society and Max Weber's observations of intense and attenuated charismatic authority. (Weber did not use those terms but his idea of the *Veralltäglichung* of charismatic authority certainly implied them.) I did not like Durkheim's interpretation because he denied that human beings could believe in the existence of deities outside themselves. I think that because of this unnecessary denial, he failed to appreciate the potentialities of his own standpoint about the sacrality and sacralization of society.

Societies intermittently seek contact with and infusion with the sacred; this is just what the coronation seemed to me to be an occasion for that contact and infusion. I discussed the matter with a friend and former pupil, Michael Young, whom I had helped to found the Institute of Community Studies in Bethnal Green in London and he conducted some interviews with residents of the East End. With these data, information from newspapers and my reading on monarchies, coronations and similar ceremonies, we wrote an essay called "The Meaning of the Coronation."[12]

The coronation appeared to me to be one of those moments of intense charismatic experience, a moment of intense charismatic experience focused on the center, the sacredness of which was being renewed and affirmed. It resembled the state of the working-class in the possession of the charismatic power—what Sorel called the "myth" of the General Strike. (A parallel between sacrality and ideology began to become evident to me.) The brevity of the period of intensity and the restoration to everyday life, that followed soon afterwards, illustrated the general proposition about the intermittence of experience of the sacred and limits of the capacity of most individuals for continuous intensive experience of sacred things. There are moments in the life of societies, moments of crisis, moments of transition ("passages" in van Gennep's sense) in which there is widespread, indeed, common need for contact with the sacred. A large part of the society participates in this renewal of contact from the cosmic center, this reaffirmation of the center of the society. But it cannot endure, but it leaves behind a residue that lives on. A little bit of sacrality will go a long way. Too much of intense charisma results in oppression and intolerance; too little of it—-attenuation to the point of disappearance—-results in disorder and disruption.

I saw the coronation and the popular participation in it as a national communion around the sacrality of kingship. In my interpretation, society was sacralized by having contact with the sacred through ritual of the coronation of the queen. The images on which the national collective self-consciousness is focused are the image of British society, the image of the Queen and the image of the divine. The coronation ceremonial brought British society into contact with the sacred through the bringing of the queen, as the hereditary representative of the British national society, into contact with sacrality. In this manner, through the queen, nationality, civility and divinity are linked. The British people, by virtue of their nativity, their descent and long residence on British territory, were reinforced in their solidarity or their attachment to British society. The coronation ceremony was not just a re-consecration of the throne and the queen; it was a consecration of British national society through the consecration of the queen as the central part of it. By consecration I mean participation in the objectivated symbolic configuration of sacrality.

When "The Meaning of the Coronation" appeared, it aroused the displeasure of social scientists, that is, insofar as they noticed it at all. Professor (later Baroness) Barbara Wootton, at that time a professor of economics in Beford College (University of London) and a person of very outstanding merit, was very distressed by the article and gave expression to her displeasure to my collaborator, Michael Young, who was a friend of long-standing, for associating himself with such a reactionary attitude towards the monarchy. She "cut" him for a long time after that. Professor Wootton was a life-long socialist and traditional rationalist, a thoroughly decent and upright person. To speak of the sacred and to speak of the sacral legitimation of the incumbent of the throne and even to intimate that British society, the British people, participated in the collective self-consciousness focused on the sacralized queen, was more than she could tolerate. Sir Ernest Barker, then professor of political science at Cambridge University and a man of very considerable learning in the history of political philosophy had at least once referred to the monarchy as the symbol of British society; but he had never gone further than that. He sent me a note complaining that I had not acknowledged his priority, but had on the contrary suggested that British social scientists had not gone deeply enough into the significance of the monarchy in British society. There was nothing to his complaint. (Barker had published a collection of papers under the title of *The Tradition of Civility*, of which it was remarked that it contained nothing about either "tradition" or "civility.") A third response was that of the ill-favored Norman Birnbaum, an American from Harvard University, then an assistant lecturer at the London School of Economics. He published a long denunciation of Michael Young and myself for being servants of "the interests." Which "interests" this revolutionary had in mind he did not say; but there was no doubt in his mind that we were iniquitous in our intentions. Later Birnbaum distinguished himself as a friend of humanity by his fervent admiration for the German Democratic Republic.

Some time in the 1970s, on the occasion of the installation of Prince Charles as Prince of Wales, a social scientist of the University of Leiden, Dr. Jay Bluemel, undertook a sample survey of responses to the ceremony. He began, he said, with the intention of demonstrating the wrongness of "The Meaning of the Coronation"; but he was a good enough scholar to say that the result of his survey had confirmed the arguments of "The Meaning of the Coronation."

Since then social scientists and historians have taken to writing about ritual in industrial societies. Naturally, they still think that the acceptance of monarchy is mainly a product of manipulation by the elites; but they have, nonetheless, moved a few steps further. There have been in recent years, about four or five books on rituals and monarchy in advanced societies. Until "The Meaning of the Coronation," this was a subject scarcely ever touched on by sociologists and historians.

The paper was much more superficial than the subject deserves. It did however open up the question of the importance of a sacred center in a large modern society and it threw at least a glimmer of light on the sacral element in civil collective self-consciousness. It did not deal with the primordial element in national collective self-consciousness. That question has only recently appeared on my agenda.

I was trying to delineate that condition when there is sufficient experience of sacrality in society to keep the center acceptable and responsive to them or the peripheries and not so much or for so long that uniformity is demanded. I was beginning to see that the relationship in a primary group of persons in each other's presence was different in quality from the relationship between center and periphery in a large society, i.e., of the relationship of citizens and their government and the relations among the citizens. The solidarity of the "general strike" was patently different from the solidarity of comradeship in a small military unit that was in its turn, different from the relations to the army as a whole or to German society as a whole.

At the time I wrote the paper on the monarchy, I was not as preoccupied with the task of clarifying the meaning of collective self-consciousness as I have been over the past few years. I was however concerned with consensus and, particularly, the loose consensus necessary for a civil society—-which I contrasted with an ideological society. (The paper on "Ideology and Civility" was written about three years later.[13] The book *The Torment of Secrecy* was written between "The Meaning of the Coronation" and "Ideology and Civility.")

XXIII

In the early 1950s, I set to work on this complex of problems in a book that I called *Love, Belief, and Civility*, "love" representing personal relationships, friendships—-in short, personal primary groups; "belief" representing the collectivities formed about doctrines, dogmas, ideologies, including both secular and religious ideologies, religious beliefs about cosmic things; and "civility" being the disposition and outlook appropriate to civil society.[14] ("Civility" was what I had on mind in my lectures on "Consensus and Liberty" in 1947, although I did not call it that.) I intended in this book to analyze the differences between religious communities and civil societies, and particularly to distinguish between ideologies from outlooks. It all seemed fairly clear to me at that time and I thought that I would complete it upon my return from India. The manuscript became rather large (at least 800 pages); but I put it aside in order to go India to work on Indian intellectuals.

When I returned from India, I took it up again but I could not resolve the fundamental problem of delineating the pattern of the transcendence of the individual self in "love" and "civility." Ideologically based solidarity, i.e., the solidarity of persons who see each other as possessing the same intensely experienced ideology and participating in the same "collective self-consciousness (a term I did not use at that time) seemed to me at that time to be more intelligible than the other kinds of solidarity. It has not turned out to be as intelligible as I thought at the time, but the other two kinds of solidarity still seem to me to be more resistant. I am still perplexed by the constitution of solidarity of all and any sorts, whether in the form in which the individual is almost obliterated in a political or religious sect or in the much more attenuated form of the consensus of a civil society.

In the same spring of 1953, I approached the problem in another context. During the war, my colleague Henry Dicks elaborated his ideas about the character structure of what he called "High-F" (Highly Fascist). I respected his views based as they were on his experience as a psychoanalyst as an excellent interviewer (or "interrogator," as they were then called in the armed forces); but I did not share them. Nevertheless, the idea of the "High-F" German soldier made the rounds.

After the war, the New York branch of the Institut für Sozialforschung, the crypto-Marxist group which had been in Frankfurt before the Nazis took charge in Germany, obtained a large grant from the American Jewish Committee to study "the authoritarian personality." They made use, with little public acknowledgement, of the idea of the "High-F" that they located on a scale of "authoritarianism-liberalism." They produced a large book with a large amount of data in which they showed (as one would have expected from Marxists at that time) that Americans were highly disposed towards Fascism. Naturally, according to their theories, capitalism and Fascism had a natural affinity to each other. This thick book was made into the subject of the second volume of the series *Continuities in Social Research*. (The first volume had examined *The American Soldier*). I was asked to contribute my own assessment of the merit of the work. I wrote a paper called "Authoritarianism, 'Right' and 'Left'" (*Studies in the Authoritarian Personality* edited by Richard Christie and Marie Jahoda). I concluded that the authors, favorably disposed to totalitarian ideology but hostile to National Socialist ideology, had so defined liberalism that it comprised fellow-travelers and Communists in the liberal category. I pointed out that certain of the persons classified as liberals were evidently fellow-travelers or Communists and that their characteristics were more like those scored as "High-

F" rather than the liberal with whom they were classified. This caused great consternation in the Frankfurt camarilla and they made efforts to have the paper withdrawn or suppressed. They did not like to have it pointed out that they were sympathetic with Communist totalitarianism; they always avoided any word of criticism of the Soviet Union.

They not only did not like to be criticized on strictly technical and intellectual grounds; they disliked even more being shown to have an apologetic role in relation to communism and fellow-traveling. This is however only by the way. The significant thing is that the Frankfurt authors failed to understand the difference between the ideological and the civil orientations; their criteria of classification of individuals into "liberals" and "fascists" (High-F) or totalitarians was a characteristic defect of those intellectuals who flocked, with more or less acknowledgement, to Marxism.

My study of *The Authoritarian Personality* brought before me once more the differences between the different kinds of consensus, between the ideological and the civil. But it did not disclose to me the structure of the attachment to large societies or the difference between these two kinds of attachment.

In 1991-1992, no claims are made for the ideological view of the world. The Marxist form of the ideological outlook is almost in the same state of abeyance as the National Socialist and Fascist ideological view of the world. But there are always ideologists who even when their ideology is in discredit, yearn for an ideology. It would be too generous towards the human race to believe that we have come to the "end of ideology." When, thirty-seven years ago, I wrote of "The end of ideology?," I placed a mark of interrogation after the phrase. What I meant was that the ideology of Marxism and crypto-Marxism, that particular variant of ideology that had flourished among intellectuals in Western liberal democratic countries showed signs even in 1935 of losing its enthusiastic supporters because the obvious facts of Soviet life did not sustain them. This was before the Soviet Union's interventions in Hungary and in Czechoslovakia, and before the publication of *Gulag Archipelago*. These events certainly did weaken the espousal of the Marxist Leninist ideology but it did not abolish the ideological orientation or the desire for ideological belief or the idea that it is possible to have a society, the solidarity of which is generated by an ideology.

XXIV

The conclusion of *The Torment of Secrecy* was entitled "Towards a Pluralistic Politics." I argued that the pluralism of institutions, parties and beliefs depended on a consensus that limited the range of dispersion of beliefs and the depth or intensity of the experience of divergence, but which still left lots of room for differences in belief. It is not that I think that all beliefs are equally right; but rather that I am convinced that uniformity of belief is impossible of attainment. For this reason it is desirable to allow divergent beliefs—-within limits—-to be freely expressed. There is also some possibility that one can learn something from beliefs divergent from one's own. But there is a plain practical argument; divergences are inevitable and it is injurious to the dignity of the citizenry to suppress views except where they go far beyond what is tolerable for good order in society.

The "pluralistic politics" of which I wrote in *The Torment of Secrecy* was in fact the politics of a civil society. The coherence of a civil society is a far cry from the intense, urgently demanding solidarity of a small military unit in combat; but I saw that they are both members of the same family of collectivities, just as an ideological, political or religious sect is a member of that family. They all have to do with the "fusion of selves" as Cooley called it. From the paper on the *Wehrmacht* written in 1946, to the paper on "Primordial, Personal, Sacred and Civil Ties," written ten years later, I think that I made a little progress towards the clarification of the distinction among these different kinds of the "fusion of selves."[15] Nevertheless, in the paper written in 1956, I do not think that I penetrated deeply enough. Its achievement as I see it now lay in the specification of some of the properties with reference to which solidary collectivities are formed.

Seen from my present standpoint nearly forty years later, the discernment of the primordial as one of these referents now seems like knocking on an open door. It did not seem to me at that time. Talcott Parsons and I had missed the significance of primordiality in *Toward a General Theory of Action*. The term "ascription" (the opposite of "achievement") told nothing about the "object-properties" on the basis of which ascriptions were made and solidary collectivities formed. It seems odd to say, but I think that we were too "individualistic" at the beginning of the 1950s. Although I had regarded the "pattern-variables" as an analytical separation of the elements of the composition of *Gemeinschaft*, we did not ask why "ties of blood" and originating in the same locality were regarded as significant, and why human beings should be classified and regarded as being one with oneself or being "other." This is a question that still requires an answer.

Primordiality became visible to me one day as I was reading Max Weber on kinship on a bus along Oxford Road in Manchester on my way to a seminar at the University. This must have been during the winter of 1952-1953. Like M. Jourdain, I discovered what had long been so obvious to me without my having a clue to why it was so significant. I had already appreciated Schmalenbach's distinction between *Gemeinschaft* and *Bund*, both of which were seen as collectivities of intense solidarity: the former being a solidarity of persons connected by common blood and common locality; while the *Bund* was a collectivity of intense solidarity of persons of common beliefs, desires or ideals. Tönnies had not made that separation between the primordial referents of *Gemeinschaft* and the type of solidarity that arose from it. I had drawn on Scbmalenbach in my analysis of the *Wehrmacht*; but I had not gone deeply enough into the nature of the role of personal attachment in the solidarity of the combat groups.

In September of 1953, I wrote a short paper on "Ideological and Personal Primary Groups," unpublished and lost, in Brown's Hotel London, after a summer spent in Florence studying Robertson Smith's *Lectures on the Early Religion of the Semites*. (The paper was to have been presented on my behalf to the American Psychological Society by a member of the department of psychology at The University of Chicago; I had given a seminar with him at the University in about 1952 in order to try to elucidate some of the obscure ideas of Wilfrid Bion).

In that paper, I was able to bring together Schmalenbach's and Robertson Smith's ideas about solidarity based on beliefs about sacred things. I described intensely solidary religious and political groups as marked by the state of belief by the members that they were infused by a common religious spirit (or ideological idea)—as being in a state of "possession," in which the members believe themselves to form a single whole because that spirit or idea has entered into them.

My aim in that paper was to distinguish between personal primary groups (the sort that Cooley had in mind when he spoke of "primary groups") and what I called "ideological primary groups," e.g., revolutionary sects, religious sects. These were characterized by common attachment to the group, i.e., to the other members by the awareness of the possession by these other members of exclusive, compelling and highly intense beliefs about the cosmos and society.

I had been working on such groups intermittently since the autumn of 1941 in the Belmont Avenue area of Chicago where I interviewed members of the Deutsch-Amerikanische Berufsgemeinschaft—a cover name for a group of German-American Nazis. I brought this together with my knowledge of Stalinist Communists, Trotskyites and other Marxist sectarians. Some of this appeared with the essay on "Authoritarianism, 'Left' and 'Right'" which I wrote in the Spring of that year.

From about 1953 onward, I offered seminars on the sociology of religion. Max Weber, Ernst Troeltsch, and Rudolf Otto were my points of departure. Two Scandinavian books were especially of value, *Agape and Eros* by Anders Nygren and *The Idea of God* by Nathanael Soderblom. (Naturally, Durkheim, too, was brought in; but I did not make much of him.) The charismatic phenomenon was the center of the course; the nature of religious communities.

The nature of the "we" seemed more easily comprehensible when I attempted to describe the state of communion that is basic to a religious community. The idea of communion appeared to be very extensible.

In my seminars I began to detach charisma from the charismatic person. It became something like a holy spirit. I will try to summarize the results of these seminars very schematically.

Let me begin by saying that the "he" whom I perceive has a charismatic quality, if I look upon the charismatic quality in him as a consequence of professed belief, baptism, conversion, etc.; then, I might perceive that "he" has the "same" charismatic quality as I have. We are therefore both possessed by the same charismatic spirit (or quality). We form, therefore, a charismatic collectivity by virtue of the fact that we are both possessed by the same spirit. We are "one" by virtue of the fact that that "one" spirit has entered into both of us. This conception of a spirit is a conception of something outside ourselves to which we can open into ourselves by our own initiative.

The spirit is an objective thing, existing outside ourselves and not dependent on our recognition for its existence. We became aware of it. We ourselves have in varying degrees the capacity to recognize it; but we do not have the capacity to create it. And this capacity to recognize it is not equally shared in any society. Some individuals have it to a greater extent than others.

XXV

In October 1955, I wrote what purported to be an account of the discussions of a meeting of the Congress for Cultural Freedom in Milan. A report had been commissioned from Dwight Macdonald; but what he wrote was so characteristic flippant and light-headed that Irving Kristol, then the editor of *Encounter*, begged me to save him from embarrassment by writing a more serious account of the conference. In the issue following the one in which my essay appeared, the essay by Macdonald was published with an introductory note by Kristol saying that it was an "alternative view," such was the straightforwardness of a great editor.

Like Samuel Johnson in his reports of the debates in the House of Common, I made it up. I did so by picking out a few bits from the various papers and discussions and shaping them into more explicit form that expressed the potentiality of the discussion rather than what was actually said. The discussions were, as a matter of fact, rather heterogeneous; but they were scattered in the large pile of papers in few states that I could reasonably present. In the report, I made it clear (unlike Clifford Geertz's contribution to the confused discussion of ideology a few years later) that I regarded an ideology as a set of propositions normative and cognitive which are purported to be rigorously logically related to each other in a distinctive system, explaining the whole of society or the whole of the world and history, from which strict directions for the action of its adherents are contained—"the unity of theory and practice"—and which drew a very sharp dividing line between friend and foe. (I had first adumbrated this distinction between ideology and outlook in my paper on Communist and socialist movements that I presented to Robert Park's seminar at Chicago in about 1934.) I asserted in "The End of Ideology?" that it was impossible for an ideology to pervade in an exclusive, enduring and comprehensive way any whole society and even smaller collectivities. I said that it was impossible to rule a society in strict conformity with an ideology for any extended period and over the entire range of the society's activities.

I had thought this ever since the late 1930s. In 1955, although it was before Khrushchev's report of 22 February 1956 (at the Twenty-Third Party Congress), I saw that there was beginning to appear signs that the beliefs in the validity of the Marxist ideology were beginning to fade, because it was being found that Marxism was untrue, that the Soviet Union did not correspond with the account given by the Marxist ideology of the nature of a socialist society, etc. I also said that the ideological element in society could never die away completely because the ideological disposition would always be present in a fairly strong way in some human beings and that the responsiveness to it on the part of others was likewise a deep and permanent part of the potentialities of very substantial minorities of the population in any society. I implied fairly clearly that under normal circumstances of society, ideological receptiveness of the mass of the population in any society would be at a low level of intensity. I thought that we were coming into a period in which the substance of Marxism that had been the regnant ideology among many Western intellectuals since the 1930s was being shown to be false. Since ideologies do have an intellectual content, the intellectual content of the Marxist-Leninist ideology was being refuted daily by the actions of the Soviet Union and its satellite Communist parties. But quite apart from the evacuation of its intellectual pretenses, the ideological impulse was not sustainable indefinitely and without diminution.

This brief paper was not very original. I had been thinking along those lines for nearly twenty years. Furthermore, even the originality of the title was not so novel. Raymond Aron had already used it as the title of the concluding chapter of *L'Opium des intellectuels*. The chapter was called *Fin de l'age ideologique*? Raymond Aron must have sent the book to me in Chicago while I was in India since I did not read it until my return to the University in the autumn of 1956. We had both placed a question mark at the end of our titles that were practically identical.

In 1959, Daniel Bell took this title for a miscellany of his essays but he removed the question mark, which was ill-advised. He was taken rudely to task by the vociferous radicals in American academic life. The radicals were enraged that anyone would dare to hint that they were, contrary to their confident expectation, doomed to defeat and discredit. Bell retracted some of the assertions that the radicals had come to the end of their tether. For some years his naive prediction of the enduring "end of ideology" provided a gleeful opportunity for radicals to crow over the discomfiture of their adversaries. Several anthologies reproducing the various writings on the "end of ideology" appeared, trying to save the radicals' face. Nevertheless, I never retracted; and I have turned out to be right. The Marxist ideology has indeed come to an end; although, with characteristic unrealism, some American and British academics are trying to salvage what they can of it.

XXVI

At the conference in Milan, I presented the paper "Tradition and Liberty: Interdependence and Autonomy."[16] I had long been skeptical of individualistic rationalism that asserts that every human being is, under just conditions, a self-contained, intellectually and morally self-sufficient entity, fully capable of self-regulation, of making the best decisions regarding his own interests. But for all this to occur, he must live in a regime of freedom. This view, although in some respects admirable because it contrasted its ideal with a state of tyranny in which no one except the tyrant is self-sufficient, seemed to me to be very superficial and narrow-minded.

Traditions are seen or have been seen by individualistic rationalism as tyrannical, almost as tyrannical as individual tyrants, made worse in some respects because by diffusing tyranny throughout the society which accepts the traditions rather than permitting the tyrant to be precisely located and rebelled against. Human reason, emancipated from superstition has no need of tradition.

These two views about the self-sufficiency of the individual and the seriousness of tradition have not often been put down in written form but they are nonetheless widely believed by genuine liberals and collectivistic liberals. Even a thinker as powerful as Professor Friedrich Hayek came close to this belief in his essay "Individualism True and False," delivered in Dublin in 1945. I remember trying in about 1946 to lead him into an admission of the importance of tradition. He had in that lecture criticized Descartes' "false individualism"; but my effort to win him to an affirmation of tradition left him cold. Perhaps I argued poorly; perhaps he was not listening to what I said. In any case, Professor Hayek did change his mind so that when he came to deliver the Hobhouse Memorial in 1978 he spoke of tradition in an appreciative way, as the wisdom of the human race.

Frank Knight was one of the three serious persons among my elders who had a good word for tradition; but even he was quite ambivalent about it. Park frequently spoke about traditions but he had no view as to whether they were good or bad. They were for him as they were for William Graham Sumner, simply inevitable and that was it. Michael Polanyi was the other. He went further and stressed the importance of tradition in the growth of scientific knowledge; but he too could not be drawn, at least by me, into any conversations about tradition in general. Karl Popper was the third person and he was also the most forthright and trenchant in his argument for a rational theory of tradition. But he, like Polanyi (and Heisenberg), spoke about tradition in science and that confined the scope of his observation about tradition to science, where the working and benefits of tradition are clearer than they are in morals and politics.

It was the last with which I was concerned in "Tradition and Liberty." I argued that although freedom was the freedom to depart from widely held traditions, freedom could not exist without traditions that set limits and fields of action for freedom. I said moreover that the freedom-sustaining and freedom-limiting traditions must exist at least in the sphere of the sacred. In other words, certain political traditions had to be regarded as sacred and not subject to changes in accordance with fluctuations in taste and changes in the definition of interests.

There was no response to these arguments except some objections from Daniel Bell. Professor Bell thought that my interest in consensus had already been somewhat improper, if not scandalous. I suppose that he was an individualistic rationalist at that time. My interest in the sacred and tradition seemed to him to go beyond the boundaries of intellectual propriety. I never asked him what he had in mind and he never referred to it in our conversations. I have noticed, however, that not long ago, he delivered a lecture on the "Rediscovery of the Sacred." I wonder whether he recalls his strictures of a third of a century ago about the enormity of speaking about the sacred.

This, however, is a trivial aside. More important was the fact that I was giving temporal depth to consensus. Tradition is consensus through time. It makes the past state and the present state of a society into a single society. The boundaries of a society reach different distances into the past in accordance to the duration of the effectiveness of a tradition. Some traditions are new, others are older. The parts of the society maintained by the latter traditions are the older parts.

Tradition begins to make fresh sense when looked at in a form of collective self-consciousness. Just as collective self-consciousness constitutions a society in the present, a tradition incorporated into collective self-consciousness makes the society not just factually identical or continuous with the past. It makes it part of a single entity, changing in character and population, but retaining throughout the time the characteristic set of self-reproducing institutions and the collective self-consciousness in which the dead are included in the collective self-consciousness of the living but in which the living are not included in the collective self-consciousness of the dead (who no longer possess or participate in the collective self-consciousness.)

Between 1956 and 1958, I wrote three papers that put forward the same theme. (1) "Ideology and Civility" published in the *Sewanee Review*; (2) "Primordial, Personal, Civil and Sacred Ties," which I delivered on the occasion of the tenth anniversary of the British Sociological Association in London. (It was later published in the *British Journal of Sociology*); and (3) "The Concentration and Dispersion of Charisma" presented at the American Sociological Association in Washington and published in *World Politics*.[17]

In all of these papers, I was trying to delineate what were the properties of the ideological view of the world and of ideological collectivities. In the first paper, "Ideology and Civility," I did not make any distinction between religious institutions and earthly institutions, i.e., institutions with earthly objectives. There are however very important differences, above all, as given in the definition of their objectives.

In my teaching of the sociology of religion that I offered a number of times in the 1950s, I tried to deal with the same problem with special regard to churches and sects, i.e., the problem of the properties of religious collectivities. This entailed an examination of the attenuation of the charismatic in churches in comparison with the intensity of the charismatic in sects. It is interesting that although religious sects are fairly similar in the great world religions, the churches or similar large-territorial religious bodies differ markedly in their corporate form. It is necessary not only to examine the historical conditions under which these different types of religious bodies originated, but more important, for my purposes, to find out how the corporate form is related to the kind of redemption offered by its scale and the techniques and arrangements for obtaining it.

It is also necessary to analyze the relations between earthly institutions and religious institutions; particular attention will have to be paid to the connection between the various kinds of earthly political, economic and social order in relation to the kind of religious territorial and parochial organization of the religions in particular societies and, not least, the conditions of conflict and peace (including indifference) between the institutions of the earthly and the transcendental spheres of society. Within societies and in the various world religions, there are varying degrees of civility and ideology.

Again, I think that it is very important to work out the various patterns of the collective self-consciousness for each of these variations. Particular attention will have to be paid to the way religious collective self-consciousness coexists with collective self-consciousness of collectivities with earthly objectives.

This brings me up to 1957-1958, when in "The Concentration and Dispersion of Charisma" I carried my ideas further on the stratification of the distribution of charisma, the inequality of charismatic quality, and the susceptibility and possession of it by those who believe themselves to possess it. The charismatic person, i.e., the one who believes that he is possessed by or of charisma, believes that other persons are susceptible to the charismatic quality or that they are impervious to it or that they can acquire it in varying degrees of intensity.

The dispersion of charisma is a process in which charismatic potentiality in the periphery is aroused through contact with a more intensely charismatic person or institution. It is a wider sharing of attachment to—-participation in—-a sacred entity, represented in the individuals to whom it has been dispersed. Each of the individuals is, in consequence of dispersal, endowed with (or has had attributed to him) some of the essential quality of the sacred. A collectivity is formed by the simultaneous and similar relationship with the sacred external to the collectivity but also entering into it.

I had long been interested in the Protestant sectarian idea that every human being contains a spark of divinity, which has to be nurtured by self-discipline and study of sacred books and by the contemplation of the divine. This pointed in the direction of the proposition that the voice of the people is the voice of God. A society in which this was believed was bound to have a strong tendency to be a democratic society. It stood in contrast with societies in which the ruler was thought to be the intermediary between divinity and society, or in which a ruling family was hereditarily charismatic or in which charisma is usually a matter of attribution rather than being the inherent quality of an individual as certain common readings of Max Weber made it out to be.

The idea of the dispersion, concentration, alternation and intensity of charismatic quality was already made clear in Max Weber's discussion of the routinization of charisma that is in fact nothing else than the infusion of charisma of a relative low intensity into an institution. Still, the new formulation made these implications explicit. The idea first occurred to me in the course of my study of the new states of Asia and Africa in the second half of the 1950s. These studies had grown out of my interest in Indian intellectuals and then in the intellectuals of other societies of the world that had recently become sovereign. It struck me that the rulers, while very uneasy about their tasks, were excessively confident about the superiority of their capacities to those of which the holders of certain offices were charismatic *ex officio*. This was the first time that I perceived that these rulers had no confidence in the capacities of their citizenry. They seemed to think that their power as such legitimated them, qualifying them to disregard and suppress critics and to seek support from the mass of the population only through acclamation. It occurred to me that they regarded the lower classes of their societies as lacking the fundamental qualification for a voice regarding governmental policies. This contrasted with liberal-democratic societies where there was a modicum of fundamental respect, although far from complete, for the mass of the population. I interpreted this as belief of leading politicians and higher civil servants in the poor countries of Asia and Africa that they alone were the possessors of charismatic qualities, while the rest of their society was utterly lacking in those qualities and hence not worthy of the esteem which is a prerequisite of a liberal democratic order. The contrast between the new states of Asia and Africa and the liberal-democratic societies of the West was the difference between the concentration and dispersion in the distribution of charismatic qualities and susceptibilities and the intensity and attenuation in the experience of the charismatic.

So implicit in these ideas was the notion that charisma is an attributed phenomenon and is attributable to strata, collectivities and institutions that, on looking back at, I am surprised that about six years elapsed between the publication of "The Concentration and Dispersion of Charisma" and "Charisma, Order and Status" (1964).[18] The latter is the more fundamental paper; but I should have seen its main theme earlier.

I might permit myself a biographical detail to contribute to an explanation of this long lapse in taking an intellectual step that should have been taken earlier. From 1960 to 1977, I taught every term of the year. For several years, I taught two terms in Chicago and two terms in Cambridge. From about 1965 onwards, I taught three quarters a year in Chicago, and two in Cambridge which meant that I taught more than all year—-at least two courses per term for eleven months in the year.

In 1960-61, I began to edit *Minerva: A Review of Science, Learning and Politics*, a quarterly that I edited with great severity. This meant rewriting nearly all the articles which I published, adding my own ideas and material to them, corresponding with the authors in great detail and remonstrating with them with schoolmasterly zeal. I should add that I practically never rejected a paper without a detailed explanation to the author. Sometimes a paper would go through three or even on rare occasions four revisions before being accepted for publication. In those days, I also read all the galleys and pageproofs. (I had the assistance of excellent young women through most of these years, never more than one at a time but in all but two cases, of high intellectual and moral quality as well as cheerful and patient. I must express my gratitude to them without naming them.)

In addition to this, I was also a chairman of the Committee for the Comparative Studies of New States at The University of Chicago. I also taught three summer schools each a month long, in India, one in Agra, one in Delhi and one in Bangalore. That was also a demand on my time and energy, since I and my two assistants lived in the same hotel with the students who were young and middle-aged, teachers of sociology, political science and anthropology from India, Pakistan, Singapore (with a few from other South Asian countries). In another year, I spent about three weeks in Delhi for the National Education Commission in the course of which I wrote the three chapters of the report dealing with universities. In all these activities, I became acquainted with a splendid group, mainly of men but with a few women among them. Some of them have become eminent scholars like my friend Professor André Beteille of the Delhi School of Economics.

On top of all this, I was much taken up with the affairs of *Encounter* and the Congress for Cultural Freedom and in the crises having to do with the disclosure about the support of the Congress by the Central Intelligence Agency. I was very taken up indeed.

In the month of September of 1967, I had to send a long telegram, as many as two-hundred words in length, every few days to the other members of the board of trustees of *Encounter*—-Sir William Hayler, Andrew Schonfeld, and Arthur Schlesinger—-to resist their efforts to dismiss the editor and to dismantle the magazine. I was successful in the end, but it took time.

I tell all of these details (which put together now impress even me) to explain why it took me six years to move from "The Concentration and Dispersion of Charisma" to "Charisma, Order and Status." Of course, I was not intellectually idle during these rather busy years. I did write several papers on deference and social stratification. I wrote the paper on "The Idea of Mass Society" that I regard as one of my most interesting papers and moderately original, too, in its turning of the tables on the vulgar critics of the vulgar culture of "mass society," i.e., Horkheimer, Macdonald, et al.; but I did not write what I did to refute those characters. I wrote it because it was true and had to be written if the world was to be understood.

I tell all these petty details solely to account for my failure to proceed more speedily from one stage to another in the development of my ideas about "sacred" or "charismatic ties" and for my failure to return to the idea of "conscience collective" which I had first encountered thirty years before in my immature study of Durkheim for Professor Cailliet's seminar at the University of Pennsylvania.

XXVII

I think that after about 1958, I ceased to add to the manuscript *Love, Belief and Civility*. It was not a deliberate decision to do so. I still had a lot to do on it. I have especially to continue to work on what has been my central problem, namely, the different kinds of bonds that I enumerated in the paper written in 1956 "Primordial, Personal, Sacred and Civil Ties." One of the defects of the large manuscript was its insufficient treatment of primordial ties and their relation to sacrality. Practically everything that I have written in the past thirty-five years has grown out of problems that are in the course of my work on this book. I think that in writing papers intended to clarify certain points encountered in the writing of this book, especially those having to do with the major section on belief, I became so preoccupied by those undertakings that I ceased to concern myself with the book as a whole.

Thus, although I put the manuscript aside, I did not put its problems aside. They have remained with me ever since then. Most, if not all, of the papers that I have written since then deal with the main problems of *Love, Belief and Civility*.

The last thing I did on the book was to re-write a section of the first part into a separate paper (now not to be found) on "The Nature of the Personal Relationship" which I originally intended to send to the *Journal of Phenomenology and Phenomenological Research*. I think this was a pretty good paper; but I could not penetrate more precisely into what I called the transcendence of the self and the fusion with other individual selves into a "we"; I did not attempt to publish it.

I also went back to the meager sources of our awareness of primary groups, mostly Charles Cooley and W. I. Thomas. What they, particularly Cooley, offered was very good; but it was also very slight. Thomas, who should have known better, foolishly thought that the influence of primary groups should be replaced by scientific knowledge. Although the term primary group no longer has the resonance that it one had, it is still at the center of thought about society. Its centrality has not, however, led to a deeper penetration into the character of the relationship. The rock on which *Love, Belief and Civility* was founded is still there. Moliére seemed to have derogated the knowledge of prose that M. Jourdain had been speaking all along. But the nature of prose in contrast with verse is worth understanding. Everyone refers innumerable times in the course of a week to "we" or "us" or "ourselves"; even more often to "I" or "me" or to "you"; and he or she knows what is being referred to. My task, however, is to find out what "we" really is.

XXVIII

At this point I diverge from the history of my efforts to cope with the coherence of primary groups, the consensus of the larger society, with the place of the sacred in the cohesion of society and with collective self-consciousness—-wishing to go back some years to the beginning of my earliest intellectual interest which is also the oldest of my present interests. That is my interest in intellectuals. It will show something of the continuity and exfiliation of my intellectual interests and its increasingly evident connections with my other interests.

When I was in high school, I read a lot of literature—-especially English and some American—-but I knew nothing about writers. In about my senior year, H.L. Mencken came into my field of vision. He was a great discovery for me; I became a Menckenian critic of American society of which I knew only what I had studied in school histories and what I had seen in my family and its friends and in my wanderings in Philadelphia. I was in sympathy with American society as I saw it. I did not know anything about any other society except what I heard from my parents and their friends (mainly my father's colleagues) and our relatives who spoke about the "old country"—-meaning for my parents Russia and for their friends Germany, Belgium and Ireland. Like the ethnic groups which I saw in the various districts of Philadelphia on my Sunday walks, all those countries in their own ways seemed to be interesting and of value; but they did not seem to me to be better than the Untied States, which had the merit that there were no pogroms against Jews, that no one starved there as they had in Ireland in 1840—-still spoken about by Tim Collins, although he must have been born about thirty years after the famine. All of these persons spoke without bitterness of the "old country" and with much appreciation of the United States. The newspapers of Philadelphia were all uncritically patriotic and so was the *New York Times*, the Sunday edition of which I used to purchase. I had not yet begun to read the *Nation* or the *New Republic* and since this was in about 1926 or 1927, they did not yet reach the point of execration of the United States which they attained in the 1930s.

Mencken was as strange to me as a man from Mars. I had not ever read anything like him. Witty hyperbole, hilarious mockery, a certain good-natured benevolence—as bawdy as one dared to become in these days. And immensely disrespectful. I had known nothing of the Bible Belt, of Comstock and Sumner. I had never heard of wiener schnitzel and rostbraten. I knew about beer, and I remember the saloons with swinging doors between into which I had once peered; although I cannot be sure whether my conception of them came from what I think I remember as something which I saw or whether it is a precipitate of Mencken's happy description of "the workingman's university."

I am not sure which of Mencken's books I read first. It must have been the *Prejudices* of which there were about three or four volumes at that time. I read them in the Camden Public Library. Why in Camden, I cannot say; but after having covered so much of Philadelphia, I used sometimes to cross the Delaware River on the ferry and wander about there. It must have been the summer of 1926. I took to Mencken as if I had been born to him. Hitherto I had always been respectful towards authority. It had not occurred to me that one could mock it, criticize it, denounce it. I learned all that from Mencken. Of course, it was all very good-natured; it read as if Mencken rollicked with laughter as he wrote some of these essays. I also read a little while after, the first edition of *The American Language*. That certainly was no stimulus to hatred of one's own society.

It was written with warm appreciation of the roughnecks and greenhorns who produced so many vivid variants in the English language and with respect for the "schoolmarms" whom Mencken mocked; I read it in that spirit. The criticisms of the "booboisie" were as denunciatory as anything I had read in a book up to that time. By the end of the decade and the early years of the next decade, the Great Depression had settled on the United States, the Communist Party came out of its ethnic obscurity and its bohemian holes and corners. I was becoming familiar with French literature of the nineteenth century. I had learned something about the political and moral attitudes of Shelley and Byron and the early Wordsworth. I was beginning to learn something of the intellectual life of contemporary France. (I think that, in my first year in university, I took out a subscription for the *Les Nouvelles Litteraires*). In brief, I entered into the intellectual world since the French Revolution.

In about 1930, I wrote a few paragraphs for my own clarification asking why literary men hated their own country. I was thinking mainly of Flaubert, Baudelaire, the surrealists, Henri Barbusse, and even the coyly unworldly Anatole France whose books were the first I read in French and of the great Russian writers from Pushkin to the revolution of October 1917. By the 1930s, these attitudes were in full flood. I need not recite any of the details of the stampede towards radicalism of American literary men and women. By the end of the 1930s, these anti-bourgeois, anti-capitalistic attitudes had

become almost a condition of life among non-academic intellectuals. But even in the late 1930s, they had not advanced much into the
universities. At the University of Pennsylvania, there were a few
socialists among the teachers most notably Maynard Krueger and
Andrew Biemiller and not many more students. I would guess from
what I was told by Sidney Sufrin that there were about ten members
of the League for Industrial Democracy of which Krueger was the
patron. They certainly were rare enough at The University of Chicago. There were very few fellow-travelers among the teachers at
the university; Frederick Schumann was the only real victim of the
totalitarian temptation. Louis Wirth, I learned after his death, had
been a Communist Party member as a student and was in danger of
deportation to Germany just after the First World War, but for the
intervention of Albion Small. He was surely not a Communist or
even a fellow-traveler when I knew him. Ernest Burgess, who was a
benign and simple person, became a proponent of "social planning"
as were Wirth and Charles Miriam. But that was, after all, the agenda
of honest supporters of President Roosevelt's "New Deal."

I recall that I prepared and delivered a paper in Park's course on
"Collective Behavior" in 1934, on the Socialist and Communist move-
ments. I studied the *New Leader*, the *Daily Worker*, the *Masses* and
the *New Masses* and the manifestos and programs of Communist and
Social-Democratic Parties in Europe. I read Arthur Rosenberg's
Geschichte des Bolschewismus; I had already read Sombart's
Sozialismus und Soziale Bewegung in its sixth edition and I re-read
much of Sombart's tenth edition of that work: *Protestantischer
Sozialismus* which I had first read as an undergraduate. (I had ordered a copy from W.H. Allen on Woodlawn Avenue in about 1930;
I still purchase books from his son, George, being the oldest and
longest customer of that extraordinary richly stocked shop, now on
Walnut Street. George is now about seventy-five and he recently
reminded me that he, too, is a graduate of Central High School—
about twenty graduating classes after my own).

This paper made a very favorable impression on Park, who wanted
me to continue to work on the subject; and he arranged with Harold
Lasswell whom he liked and who liked him, to offer me a research
assistantship to go on with my study on the subject. I was reluctant
to desert Louis Wirth, who had taken me away from my service at
the County Bureau of Public Welfare and brought me into an academic pathway. I was grateful to Wirth for that, although my useful-

ness to him was near fulfillment since the translation of *Ideologie und Utopie* was well on the way to completion.

There is little point to speculate about what would have happened if I had accepted Park's and Lasswell's proposal. It probably would not in the long run have made any significant difference. I might have become a more respectable academic with a Ph.D.; but since I have done pretty well without, it might not have made much difference.

This, however, is a digression. Its significance is that in becoming familiar with revolutionary socialist and Communist movements in Europe and then small counterparts in the United States, I had an ample field for understanding the hostility of intellectuals towards their own societies from the other end of the telescope. I continued through the 1930s to read *belles lettres*. This was one of my attractions for Leites, apart from his belief that I was an influential person. I for my part also benefited from Leites' attachment to Paris, his reading through the files of the *Nouvelle Révue française* and his fascination by France as a whole. I also kept in touch with the political stir among British literary intellectuals. I enjoyed all of this. The upshot of it was that I acquired a rather substantial knowledge of the attitudes of intellectuals of all sorts in the main European countries and the United States towards their own societies from the eighteenth century down to the present.

I must not dwell on this. Much has been written by others on the leftism of American intellectuals. I have written about it myself; the first volume of my *Selected Papers* is very largely about that subject.[19] My interest in it grew to the point where I thought I was ready to write and teach about it.

In the frightfully cold winter of 1946-1947, on the invitation of Michael Polanyi, I spoke about Tolstoy, Oscar Wilde, Dostoevski, Turgenev, Gide, Flaubert, Anatole France, Thomas Mann, Silone, Koestler, and lesser literary figures. I went to Manchester to speak before the Manchester Literary and Philosophical Society on this subject. I met with complete incomprehension and even the courteous but complete disavowal by my host and chairman, Michael Polanyi, who could not understand what I was talking about. (Within a few years, the intellectuals' rebellion of moral indignation, of excessive claims and exaggerated hopes, became a major theme of Michael Polanyi's view of the world. After this experience, wherever he disagreed with me, which was rather frequently, I used to say, "Don't be too strong in your disagreement, Michael. In two years, you will say exactly what I am saying having forgotten that you first heard it from me.")

In the summer quarter of 1948, at the University of Chicago, I conducted a seminar on the social and political relations of intellectuals. That same summer, I wrote a manuscript of several hundred pages on the subject. One part dealt with the social and political relations of intellectuals in societies without sovereignty; I was thinking of intellectuals in colonial societies. I was also thinking of intellectuals in countries that never lost their sovereignty like Russia, China, Japan, and even of the United States *vis-à-vis* Europe in the nineteenth century. This was the beginning of my thought about centers and peripheries.

This latter aspect of the subject of intellectuals in relation to their own society came especially prominently into my mind because the intellectuals in those societies were hostile towards the rulers of their own society and had also become critical of the traditional culture of their societies, although they sometimes espoused and praised it in an exaggerated way.

I thought that I should deepen and make more detailed and intimate my understanding of this subject. I was already fairly familiar with the facts of the intellectuals and their societies in Western countries. I had no first-hand contact with intellectuals in colonial or recently colonial countries and I knew little of their intellectual works or the works about them. A moderate amount had already been written about Western intellectuals; and, although I did not think so well of that literature, it would have required a long and large first-hand investigation to add something which was both new and sound. In contrast with this situation, a first-hand investigation on a group of intellectuals in an important country, about whom little had been written and who were numerous and interesting enough to justify study seemed to be very worth doing. I had at first thought of going to the West Indies where I had some connections but on reconsideration in the light of the first criterion, I decided that India had first claim on my attention.

Accordingly, I began to prepare myself to begin a study on Indian intellectuals in relation to the ruling authority of their own society and the traditional culture of the mass of that society. This was why I spent a large part of 1955 and 1956, in India, observing and interviewing Indian intellectuals, and for about a dozen years I spent about one month each year in India.

I had come to the choice of India as a result of a long and growing interest, dating back to my reading of Kipling's *Soldiers Three* and *Kim*, when I was in secondary school, and my interest in Mahatma Gandhi's civil disobedience movement of the early nineteen thirties. Anyone who grew up in Philadelphia, when I was a boy, could not avoid being interested in Great Britain. The Main Line of Philadelphia was a scene of a deliberate and studied anglophilia. This was very noticeable in the bookshops. We were of course taught English literature at all levels of our education and particularly in Central High School, where we were given a very superior education in literature as well as in all other subjects. Except for Washington Irving, Longfellow, Poe, Whittier, and William Cullen Bryant, we heard nothing of American literature in elementary school. In secondary school, we read William Dean Howells and Mark Twain—-nothing of Melville or James. On the other side, we received a thorough grounding in English literature from the seventeenth to the early twentieth century. It was impossible for a schoolboy in this situation to be unaware of the British Empire. It was against this background that my interest in India developed.

My years in London during the Second World War and at the London School of Economics after the war brought me into contact with Indians. Then the fact that Max Weber had written about India also inclined me in that direction. Furthermore, having decided to study intellectuals in a colonial or recently colonial country, India was far and away the best candidate. It had many intellectuals, many universities, a great indigenous intellectual tradition, a deep contact with modern European intellectual traditions, and it was, internationally, a more important country than Trinidad or Jamaica.

My problem was the relation of intellectuals—-in both directions and in attitudes and action—-to existing governmental authority and to the indigenous traditional society. Given the belief of modern governments that they must draw on the highly educated to serve them as advisors and experts, my main concern was whether long periods of opposition before and since independence had impaired their capacity for government. (I drew this idea from Max Weber's criticism of Bismarck for his breaking the spirit and the governing capacity of the German National Liberals.)

I came to feel a great affection for many of the Indian intellectuals whom I met. I mention M. A .D. Gorwala, a Parsee, a former senior member of the Indian Civil Service, a man of the high rectitude, bravery and devotion to the common good—-somber, alert, modest, who at his own expense published a weekly journal called *Opinion* most of which was written by him. He was a master of English style. Then there was Mr. Nirad Chaudhuri, who is now ninety-five years of age and as much a master of his capacious and tenacious memory as he was almost four decades ago. Prodigious in his knowledge, fresh in his thought, mischievous in his wit and also a master of English style. Sudhindranath Datta, also a Bengali, belonging to a newer generation, not much younger than Mr. Chaudhuri but as a Calcuttan of a culture as familiar with the latest development in European thought and literature as any high brow in Paris or London. They were very diverse.

Mr. Gorwala was broad-faced, with an eagle's nose, broad shouldered and powerful in body, authoritative in tone but also very hospitable, more than a little gloomy in mood and so scrupulous that each night he reviewed his day's activities to make clear to himself where had gone astray and where he could make mends the following day, a faithful reader of the *Meditations* of Marcus Aurelius. Mr. Chaudhuri about five feet two in height, about a hundred pounds in weight, a small round beard, smiling ideas, never dispirited, always indomitable, a rapid reader in French and English, a connoisseur of wine who seldom drank, a connoisseur of food with a good studious wife who was a marvelous cook, with a placidity of appearance and temperament which stood in contrast with Mr. Chaudhuri's incessant talk and wit and a curb on his impetuous actions. Sudhuri Datta, a handsome a man as I have ever seen, graceful and elegant in his conversation with an air of one who has seen an interesting world become boring. There were so many others, old D.M. Bose, once a great physicist, now very fat, smiling, enjoying music. C.V. Raman, haughty and sharp in his disparagement of the Indian scientists whom he had hoped to encourage by his winning the Nobel Prize that he gained by research which he did early in the morning before going to his regular work at the accounts department of the Government of Bengal.

There were many others in Bombay, Delhi, Madras and other towns where intellectuals were gathered together, no less interesting, no less distinguished by their moral bearing and their charming manners and friendliness to me. I have not done them justice. The time I spent with them in India was wonderful.

As it worked out, among the things that impressed me about the Indian intellectuals I studied, was not their admirable character and their intelligence nor was it their critical attitude towards the government of India, although that was certainly very noticeable; it was only in a few cases vehement. Nor was it their at-homeness in India. It was their preoccupation with Great Britain. They thought that real intellectual activity was not in their own country; it was in the West, in Western Europe and, above all, in Great Britain. I was put in mind of the "Westerners" among the Russian intellectuals in the nineteenth century, of teachers in American universities in the last part of the nineteenth century and the early part of the twentieth century in their admiration for German academic achievements of that time and for Oxford and Cambridge. The line of Chekhov, "What is the news from Moscow?" often came to my mind.

When I came to try to put together my observations and reflections on Indian intellectuals, I formulated them in the framework of "metropolis" and "province." I developed these in a seminar in the winter of 1957 on "Indian Intellectual Life" and then in an essay which I contributed to a volume in honor of a fine Indian economist, the late Professor D.R. Gadgil of the University of Poona, and director of the Gokhale Institute of Economic and Social Research. The essay was called "Metropolis and Province in Intellectual Life." This was also one of the major themes of the short monograph that I wrote in 1958 and 1959, *The Intellectual between Tradition and Modernity: The Indian Situation.*[20]

In the autumn of 1958, I wrote a paper for the annual meeting of the American Association for the Advancement of Science; it was entitled, "The Macrosociological Problem: Center and Periphery." A little later, I wrote another essay with more or less the same title for *The Logic of Personal Knowledge*, a volume to honor Michael Polanyi on his seventieth birthday. These were the first occasions in which I put forward the idea of center and periphery before a somewhat larger audience. I had already adumbrated the idea in my paper "The Concentration and Dispersion of Charisma."

At that time there was no recognition of the idea of center and periphery among social scientists, although Charles Galpin and later Robert Park in their ecological studies, Galpin in his *The Anatomy of a Rural Community* and Park and his pupil, R.D. McKenzie, in their studies of the circulation of the metropolitan press in the hinterland were close to it. Much later I saw an explicit reference to center and periphery in one of T.S. Eliot's slender volumes—either in *The Idea of a Christian Society* or *After Strange Gods*. I had not noticed it the first time I read it early in the 1940s.

My work on Indian intellectuals and what I wrote on center and periphery brought a bit closer to each other my interest in the relations of intellectuals to authority (political and intellectual), and my interest is the ties among individuals and of individuals with large collectivities with whole societies. The idea of a center was a statement about the link. Attachment to a center is attachment to its collectivity; rejection of a center is rejection of its collectivity. It is through their attachment to the center of their society that individuals are attached to their society.

The center can be an individual; it can be a group of persons; it can be an institution; it can be a set of objectivated symbolic configurations. In many cases, the group or the individual or the institution is regarded as the embodiment of the objectified symbolic configurations. These three centers are frequently not harmonious with each other. There is practically never one single center, the object of a complete consensus. There are competing centers. There are conflicts within centers and the peripheries are by no means always in agreement about the centers to which they attend. Rejection of a center almost always entails attachment to an alternative center.

As a by-product, an important one, of my work on Indian intellectuals, I began to see Western intellectuals in a new light.

Thus, the phenomenon of the "alienation" of intellectuals in their own societies was a negative variant of the family of phenomena of which the attachment of soldiers to their primary groups, the attachment of religious zealots to their sect and their deity, the attachment of conspiratorial revolutionaries to their cell, their party and their doctrine or ideal, and the civility of the citizen in his attachment to his own society were also variant instances. Consensus about a person, about a society and about an ideal, susceptible of variations, intensity to attenuation, from concentration of attention to dispersion among several competing or complementary centers offered a new pattern of greater complexity than I had hitherto conceived of the relations of individuals and strata to centers and peripheries. But the constitution of the relationships of individuals to collectivities still remained an unsolved problem.

Looking back at the development of my ideas about consensus or as I now call it, collective self-consciousness (a more exact and more evocative, although more awkward, usage), I am struck by my failure to see clearly the connection between my point of departure in the effort to understand consensus and primary groups, solidarity and my more recent writings about charismatic qualities and their distribution and center and periphery. All these things were much more closely related to each other than I saw at first. In retrospect, however, they appear to be very consistent with each other. The later ideas were not only consistent with the earlier ones but they were also advances on them.

My efforts in the middle of the 1950s, in addition to the work on Indian intellectuals and tradition, were directed to primordiality which fell into the category of "object properties," as we called them in *Toward a General Theory of Action*. I thought that we left human beings rather rootless in *The General Theory*. Although Professor Parsons had written excellently about the family and kinship in *The General Theory*, it can be found only under the pattern variables: of ascription-achievement; diffuse-specific objects; collectivity-individual and particularistic-universalism. All of this is certainly true; but it says nothing about the significance of the biological tie or the significance of place or heritage. This seemed to me to be a short coming. In systematizing *Gemeinschaft und Gesellschaft*, we had left out something important.

In the paper on "Primordial, Personal, Sacred and Civil Ties," written in 1956, my interest there was to clarify my ideas on those features of an individual or classes of individuals which caused another individual in the same or different category to regard him or them inside or outside of his own collectivity. I concluded that what we called "ascribed" qualities needed to be differentiated so that there would be a place for "primordial" qualities because they refer to certain physiological relationships and relationships to place. These are ascriptive qualities; but the term ascription does not evoke them. A member of a particular university or college or a particular club might have status ascribed to him merely on the basis of his membership in that association. What I wanted to do was to point out that these were tendencies in human beings to give special significance to physiological filiation and to telluric location on the surface of the earth. The most elementary features of human beings are the facts of their biological relations and their places of birth or long residence. (Why primordial properties are significant is another very important but separate problem).

In my rough classification of qualities—primordial; personal, i.e., affective dispositions of the acting subject and the affective dispositions perceived in other persons; sacred, i.e., qualities possessed by virtue of relationship to a particular deity; and civil, i.e., qualities of membership in the same territorial community or being subject to the same earthly authority exercised over a bounded territory— I was interested in the way in which these qualities when perceived in others as similar to those possessed by himself precipitate a collectivity of which the acting, perceiving subject sees both himself and the other person or persons possessing that same feature, quality or object property as members.

After I published the paper on "Primordial, Personal, Scared and Civil Ties," Professor Parsons asked me, rather gently, whether I was thereby rejecting the "pattern variables." I told him that I was trying rather to deepen them. We did not discuss the matter further, but I was right. The rough classification of object-properties that I made did not, by any means, repudiate the "pattern variables." (It is incidentally an awful term that I agreed to accept since Professor Parsons had devised it some time earlier and was very attached to it. I was not going to make an issue of a foible of a good friend whom I respected so much.) I think that the object properties carried the idea of the pattern variable much more deeply. They are harmonious in the ancestry; they both arose from our effort to systematize the basis of *Gemeinschaft und Gesellschaft* and the first chapter of *Wirtschaft und Gesellschaft*.

I think that we took the existence and the formation of collectivities for granted. The pattern variables could up to a point be used to characterize them but we neglected their constitution. The idea of common values can be fitted into the idea of collective self-consciousness but we did not do it. The idea of common values did not lead us to collective self-consciousness. But this belongs to a later stage.

XXIX

In the winter of 1961, I wrote the essay called, "The Theory of Mass Society" which I have mentioned earlier.[21] It was published in *Diogenes* on the invitation of Roger Caillois, a remarkably gifted self-educated sociologist whom I have always admired but whom, alas, I did not come to know well. In that essay, I asserted that one of the most prominent and characteristic features of modern society was the diminution of the distance between centers and peripheries. I was quite specific and concrete in my reference: I meant an increased deference and solicitude on the part of the incumbents of the centers towards those at the peripheries, greater attributiveness at the center to the desires and demands of the peripheries, more objects of attention in common between centers and peripheries, greater visibility of each to the other, etc.

A closely related analysis of social stratification in terms of center and periphery was a paper that I wrote for a *Festschrift* for Professor Darjab Prasad P. Mukherji of the University of Aligarh and one of the leading Bengali intellectuals of the twentieth century, a man of wide culture and much elegance and personal charm; although I regret to say, a "leftist" in which respect he was no different from most Bengali intellectuals educated in the twenties and thirties who did not have his talents or his sweet disposition. (This paper was entitled, "The Stratification System of Mass Society."[22]) In this paper I analyzed the movement towards equality and particularly the diminished deference granted to properties like descent, ethnicity, occupation, wealth and authority in modern liberal democratic societies. I did not assert that the distribution of these properties did not affect the distribution of deference, but only that they were less weighty in affecting the distribution of deference. I suggested that the attribution of deference was more narrow or less generalized; it was not so much given to a whole person or stratum.

The stratification of deference or status (I used these terms interchangeably) was in modern liberal democracies—-disparagingly called "mass societies"—-less widely dispersed, and it was becoming less salient and less generalized and also less pervasively clarified into strata. Of course, stratification of deference or status has not disappeared and probably will never disappear but it has certainly changed some of the most gravely inegalitarian features. (The essay "Deference" first appeared in *Social Stratification*, edited by John Jackson of Trinity College, Dublin, and then in a somewhat revised form in a *Festschrift* for Harold Lasswell, *Personality, Power and Politics*, edited by Arnold Rogow of New York University.[23])

These three papers, "The Theory of Mass Society," The Stratification System of Mass Society" and "Deference," overlap with each other in their essential themes. The main theme is the closer approximation of the various strata to each other as a constitutive feature of modern societies, i.e., the reduction of the distance between center and periphery. More fundamental is the increased participation of individuals from all strata in the collective self-consciousness of the national society, the center of which is the objectivated symbolic configuration of the national territory, embodied in the institutional centers and in other individuals who are thought to possess the crucial property of territorial nationality. One might venture to hypothesize that the growth of the national collective self-consciousness (nationality, *tout court*) has grown as the stratification or status or deference has receded in the ways indicated. Of course, they coexist together and nationality remains compatible with a quite unequal distribution of deference.

These three papers seem to me now to have a pertinence that I had not perceived previously. The closer approximation of center and periphery may be reformulated as the increased, more salient, more appreciative taking into consciousness of the existence, dignity and even consciousness of the other strata, higher and lower. The approximation of center and periphery is a more comprehensive or more widely extended sense of oneness, with the other sectors of society, of the center with the periphery, of the periphery with the center. The referents or criteria that distinguish them from each other, i.e., those referents which they do not have in common, have receded; the referent or criterion which makes them more equal to members of the same collectivity have become more salient or more significant. They have come more than ever before to form "a single society." It is not just that the participants feel it more acutely and recurrently; they do in fact form more a single society in the sense that there is more attachment to it, more participation in the collective self-consciousness of the society, more interaction among its parts by internal migration, intermarriage, greater focus of attention throughout the society on the same objects, etc.

The coming closer to each other of center and periphery was a more differentiated and I think a more illuminating way of speaking of an increase in consensus. The coming closer to each other of center and periphery is a phenomenon of attachment to a common image of the society and an attachment of the strata or zones, i.e., of individual members of each of the strata or zones, to each other through the shared participation in the image of the society. The image itself is a complex configuration. (I will not go into that right here). The phenomena that I delineated in later years, are really precisions, differentiations, subsumptions and cuttings-across the categories of things I had dealt with twenty-five and thirty years ago.

Max Weber would probably have had no tolerance for any notion like collective self-consciousness; I think that his desire to be a "methodological individualist" would have forbidden it. Yet, the way in which he dealt with the variants of the possession of charismatic qualities, e.g., charisma of office (*Amtscharisma*), hereditary charisma (*Erbscharisma*) and clan or lineage charisma (*Sippencharisma*), opened the way to an analysis that cannot make sense of those phenomena without collective self-consciousness.

When in my paper on "Charisma, Order and Status," written in 1964, I asserted that charisma was an attributed rather than an inherent quality, I was, in fact, opening the way to view charismatic qualities as referents of membership in a collectivity.[24] When charismatic qualities were conceived as being the property of rare individuals, it could not become a referent for the formation of a collectivity unless the members of that collectivity already possess sensitivity to the charismatic qualities of others and receptivity to the diffusion of charismatic quality from other ostensibly charismatically endowed persons. This means that to receive a charismatic influence, i.e., to come under the influence of charismatic authority, the person to be influenced already has a charismatic sensitivity or a charismatic potentiality. Of course, this is a matter of the perception of the self and the perception of others.

Until affected by a charismatic leader, the other human beings in the society were, as I think Weber saw it, entirely without charismatic qualities. But to be receptive they had to have a sensitivity to charismatic qualities in others; some persons are charismatically insensitive or "unmusical." It is perhaps a truism; but without it, the capacity to respond to a genuinely charismatic person, as Weber would have said, seems to me to be impossible.

In the paper that I wrote in 1964 for the centenary of Weber's birth, I made explicit what was only implicit and ad hoc in Weber's writings, namely, the idea of the "charismatic institution." This was a development that was really an explicit statement of what was implicit of the notion of the dispersal of charisma. I did not bring those two expressions of the same idea together at the time but they were in fact variants of the same idea of society as a collectivity that is charismatic to its members. The notion of "attenuation" that I promulgated has also been of rather considerable importance; it is a counterpendant to intermittent intensity. This could be applied to all sorts of settings and attachments; but it is especially pertinent in dealing with the structure of civil liberal-democratic society that I was writing about since the first half of the 1950s (*The Torment of Secrecy*).

I did not at the time see the connections, which were all there, waiting to be drawn into the study of the constitution of society.

XXX

A consequence of my work in India and my teaching and writing about it was contact with persons who were studying about Africa. The most important consequence was my closer association with Audrey Richards, who had befriended me at The London School of Economics before I knew anything about India or Africa.

Audrey Richards was already a famous social anthropologist when I met her. She was probably about fifty at the time. She had a humorously regal bearing. There could be no doubt about her treating all of her colleagues as equals, although some of them at The London School of Economics were already quite famous like Rex Tawney, Lionel Robbins, Fritz Hayek, Harold Laski and Alexander Can-Saunders, the director, some were not yet famous, and some, although interesting, talented and even beloved, never became famous; but Audrey Richards treated them all alike. She was respectful and affectionately sardonic, sometimes in a lovingly motherly way, slightly teasing. She took me immediately into her circle, almost at once; I also became very close to Popper but he was, or at least thought himself to be more an outsider than I was.

Audrey Richards spent part of her girlhood in India where her father was a law-member of the Viceroy's Council. He left India to become professor of international law at Oxford and a fellow of All Souls College. Audrey therefore spent the rest of her girlhood in Oxford. Her father did not approve of his daughters (he had four of them, all of whom became distinguished in various ways); he approved only of sons of whom he had none. Still, Audrey Richards could not be allowed to remain ignorant, so she was sent to Newnham College where she followed the pre-medical course. This was during the First World War when women were not allowed to sit for degrees although they could take the examinations that, for young men, led to them. After finishing at Newnham, something had to be done with her. Either because her family did not approve of her becoming a physician or because she lost interest, she did not continue her medical studies. There was then a caesura during which she served as Gilbert Murray's "secretary" consisting mainly of long walks with him. She then went with her sister, who later became an eminent social worker to work on the relief in Germany of persons who had become ill and impoverished during the war and in the disorders that followed. When she returned, she was once more set upon by her family and relatives who wished to have her settled in life. First she was sent to a secretarial school to learn shorthand and typing; then it was decided that she should become a teacher. For that, however, she would need a qualification. Apparently a qualification was thought to be any diploma or degree. Here, her friend May Wallas, a contemporary at Newnham came to the rescue.

May Wallas' father was Graham Wallas, at that time professor of political science at the London School of Economics. Wallas was a very good and kind man, but a bit schematic. When his daughter arranged for him to meet Andrey Richards, he was prepared for her. He turned to his card file where he kept a list of dissertation topics and found one that for no obvious reason he thought was just the right thing for Audrey Richards. It was "The Noble Savage in Literature and Science." He even had two supervisors chosen. One was Kingsley Martin, later editor of the *New Statesman and Nation*; but at that time a lecturer or assistant lecturer in political science and responsible for teaching about French political philosophy of the eighteenth century. Martin was not a great scholar and apparently had no great interest in supervising Audrey Richards. Later he became known as a lecher; but it is clear that he did not permit that to arouse any interest in the bright young woman student whose intelligence and character forbade him to try his fortunes on her. She left him somewhat depressed. As she walked along a corridor from the refectory in which the desultory interview had been granted her by Kingsley Martin, a tall slender bespectacled gentleman approached, guessed her name, told her that he was looking for her and shepherded her into his room. Then he held forth to her about the wonders of social anthropology, treated her as if she were already his pupil and commanded her to become a member of his seminar. That was Bronislaw Malinowski, still only a lecturer in social anthropology, but already ready for the further ascent of his meteoric career as one of the greatest of social anthropologists of the twentieth century. That was Audrey Richards' beginning of her splendid career as an anthropologist.

She worked in Africa, wrote several important books on food and nutrition in what was then Northern Rhodesia, taught in South Africa and then worked for the colonial offices during the war. When I came to the London School of Economics in 1946, she, too, had recently been appointed as Reader. Although she was a new member of the teaching staff, she had been intimately familiar with the School since she was one of the band of very outstanding anthropologists whom Malinowski, a great teacher and scintillating personality, had turned out in the two decades before 1945. Nadel, Fortes, Schapera, Firth, Evans-Pritchard, all the leading lights of British anthropology had been under Malinowski's protective and engaging wing. Hence when she came to teach at the School for the first time in 1946, she was perfectly at home. She was determined to make me equally at home there. I should add that the shabby rundown School was as comfortable as an old glove; but she made it more comfortable.

That was time when Clyde Kluckhohn, Margaret Mead, and Ruth Benedict were "doing personality and culture." I already had some connections with psychoanalysis through my association during the war and then with the Travistock Institute after the war. I was interested in it, a little skeptical, open to persuasion. I think Audrey Richards was the same in her attitude towards this new attractive field in which there seemed to be a hidden trap. She suggested that we conduct a seminar together. I gladly agreed. I think we did it for several years. In that time, I learned a lot of social anthropology from her and from the speakers we invited to the seminar.

She went out to East Africa to found the East African Institute of Social and economic Research; I left the School. I only saw her once in the period before I came to Cambridge. She sent me offprints occasionally and I remembered her with admiration and affection.

At about that time another link was formed between us. This was Lloyd Fallers. Lloyd Fallers had been a much liked and respected pupil of mine in Chicago just after the war. When Audrey Richards was at Northwestern University in the summer of 1948, she discovered him on a visit to the University of Chicago. She took him with her to the London School of Economics and then she took him to

Kampala; later her colleague and then successor at the East African Institute of Social and Economic Research which she had founded in Kampala in 1950 (or 1951). Fallers was a first-class man, excellent intellectually and as decent and honorable a human being as one could find. When he returned to Chicago to finish his dissertation and then when in 1959 he became professor at The University of Chicago, together with David Apter, we established the Committee for the Comparative Study of New States. Audrey Richards came and spent a quarter with us. But by this time, I had already gone to Cambridge.

At Cambridge, a little after my arrival, an Afro-Asian Studies Centre was founded with Kenneth Bernaill, an economist interested in economic development as director. After about a year, it was dissolved and replaced by an African Studies Centre and shortly thereafter by a South Asian Studies Centre under the directorship of Benjamin Farmer, a geographer and a very gentle and sensible person. I was elected very shortly thereafter to the Committee of Management of these two centres. I was the only person astride both of them.

When I arrived in Cambridge, at the beginning of the 1960s, Audrey Richards was already there. She had resigned from her directorship at the East African Institute, installed Lloyd Fallers there in her place and taken up a fellowship at Newnham, her old College. Shortly after her return, she was pressed by Ruth Cohen to accept the responsibilities of deputy or assistant principal of the College.

We had a happy reunion. She was more kindly than ever, regal without the airs of a *grande dame*, always one for a joke or an amusing anecdote, often about friends, always told with affection.

Beginning in 1961, Audrey Richards, who had become director of the African Studies Centre, and I began to conduct weekly seminars running over two terms at the African Studies Centre in Cambridge. We did this every academic year through the 1960s. Most of the papers presented dealt with Africa. I also lectured on the New States of Africa and Asia at Cambridge through a good part of the 1960s and well into the 1970s.

In addition to the two terms each year, for about six or seven years, I also conducted every Friday afternoon a seminar in the department of anthropology at University College London. It was a general seminar, but most of the participants were anthropologists who had worked in Africa and most of the papers presented at the seminar were on Africa. I never became an expert on Africa although

I became fairly familiar with the literature on the subject in books and periodicals. I had already known a fair amount of the literature of British social anthropology on Africa and for the purpose of my teaching at Chicago and Cambridge during the period I became moderately familiar with the contemporary politics of a number of West and East African states.

I wrote only a few things on Africa. One I began in the mid-1970s as a monograph on African intellectuals. It was intended to parallel my work on Indian intellectuals; it still exists in draft. I did not bring it to the point where I thought it fit for publication; it would have required more time than I could spare for the task; and when I ceased teaching about Africa in about 1977, I fell behind in mastering the increasingly voluminous literature by Africans and on Africa. I stopped my research on African intellectuals because I found inept their efforts to be authentic or original. I stopped teaching about Africa because the amount of literature in newspapers and periodicals was too great and because despite numerous changes in personnel, the events and outcome of political changes were too uniform to hold my interest. Not having ever been a master of the literature on Africa as I had become on India, I gave up African society as a subject of study. I have continued, however, to follow African universities, although there too I find conditions too uniform.

I also wrote a short essay on "The West African Intellectual Community" which was mainly a proposal for the establishment of an Association of West African Universities. This was objurgated because it did not cover all of African universities. More than a decade later, exactly such an Association of West African Universities was formed. Yet, much of my African studies were not completely a waste of time. They did leave an imprint on my general sociological views, particularly in my efforts to gain an understanding of the constitution of society. This may be seen in my essay on "The Integration of Society," found in *Center and Periphery* and in Weiner, Myron (ed.), *Modernization: The Dynamics of Growth*, the Voice of American Forum Lectures, 1966.

From my fairly superficial study about Africa that included about six visits and listening to many seminar papers by persons who had lived or done field work there, I learned more than I had known previously about the tension between primordial attachments of lineage and locality and civility, about the weakness of a center divided from the periphery (or peripheries) by primordial differences, and about the fascination of and repugnance towards alien centers. I observed in Africa the disaster for a society of the absence of a consensus, binding together the different sectors of society. The main African traditions are parochial primordial traditions. These ideas were not generated *ab ovo* by any study of Africa; they were already present but seeing, reading and thinking about Africa brought them forward in my mind. They were fortified by the observation of the vicissitudes of African society.

XXXI

My editing of *Minerva* began in 1961. *Minerva* deals with universities, higher educational policy, the history of universities, science policy, the history and administration of scientific institutions and related subjects. I have read all and probably re-written once and in many instances several times, the majority of the articles that run from 5,000 to 12,000 words. For some years I also translated or summarized reports and documents from German and French. This has taken up about one month of each year. During the years of the "student disturbances" in the latter part of the 1960s, I also wrote a "Chronicle" which in 1968 was seven hundred handwritten foolscap pages in length. This has been done alongside my teaching, research and writing.

The editorial work on *Minerva* has been close to my main intellectual interests. It might have been more fruitful, if only I had known how to take advantage of it. One thing that I have succeeded in doing partly through my influence on my late friend and former pupil, Joseph Ben-David, who, with Robert Merton, was one of the two serious sociologists about scientific activities and scientific institutions, was to have Joseph Ben-David, under my insistent criticism, develop the categories of center and periphery in the analysis of the history of universities and in the growth of scientific knowledge.

Movements of Knowledge (about which more later) has certainly benefited from my work as editor of *Minerva*. In a sense, I have been at work in the sociology of knowledge despite my disapproval of the ideas on the subject contained in *Ideology and Utopia* and in the "strong programme of the sociology of science" by the group mainly at the University of Edinburgh. One of the consequences of my efforts to improve my authors and myself has been the recognition that science is not "an institution."

Scientists participate in institutions. Scientists, in conducting scientific research, in engaging in scientific discussions, in teaching a science, are performing scientific activities. These activities are not science; they are activities that acquire or create scientific knowledge. Science, that is, scientific knowledge, is a body of propositions—a body of objectivated symbolic configurations. I had been thinking along these lines ever since I read Hans Freyer's *Soziologie als Wirklichkeitswissenschaft* in about 1934. The growth of new propositions from earlier propositions testifies to the existence of intellectual or cognitive traditions. If cognitive tradition exists, it means that the knowledge of a knower at any one time is, in part, drawn from previously existing knowledge. Mannheim allowed no such place for tradition in his sociology of knowledge. The previously existing knowledge is a constellation of objectivated symbolic configurations. It has an existence to which those who live long after its discovery are able to draw upon.

To admit that knowledge—cognitive propositions—had an existence independent of the persons who put it forward seems to have appeared to Mannheim to have been a regression to the idealism that he thought he had overcome. That was something which Mannheim's sociology quite particularly did not allow for. He could not agree to the autonomy of knowledge. My own views were moving further and further apart from Mannheim's. At that time, I had not reached the position that I now espouse. Nevertheless, I was firmly devoted to *Wertfreiheit* as a logical possibility and as a rule and standard to be observed by academics in their teaching and especially in their research. The idea of the autonomy of objectivated symbolic configurations (as I began to call the constituents of the cognitive sphere) was greatly aided by the appearance of Karl Popper's "Epistemology without a Knowing subject." (This essay was reprinted in *Objective Knowledge*.)

Durkheim's *Les Règles de la mèthode sociologique* about the objectivity of the social fact, its *sui generis* character, came back to my mind. But I applied it to scientific knowledge and to knowledge in general. I did not disagree with Durkheim about the objectivity of the social; but I thought that if one were to study academic intellectuals who were committed to the discovery and the transmission of the truth, then one would also have to recognize that. What he meant, however, was that for any particular individual the "social fact" was objective. The sphere of objectivated symbolic configurations was objective for everyone in the sense that it is not a phenomenon of physical existence or of a psychological state of mind. Of course, it would never have come into existence without the exertion of human minds and it could not grow without the exertion of human minds, many of them, each adding and modifying what the other has created.

My clarification about the nature of scientific knowledge and my intention to formulate more exactly my views of the autonomy of knowledge owes a lot to Hans Freyer on the objective mind, to Michael Polanyi, and to Mannheim himself.[25]

I also owe a lot to the contributors to *Minerva*, especially some of those whose work I rejected, and also to those whose work I rewrote from top to bottom. Of course, I would not consider for a moment those who regarded scientific knowledge as a mode of conducting social conflicts, of exploiting the poor, of taking advantage of ethnic minorities and of suppressing women. They were beyond the pale; fortunately, they have kept their distance from me and from *Minerva*. Nevertheless, I abhorred the ease with which academic social scientists allowed themselves to be bullied by agitators into the unresisting renunciation of their previous declarations of loyalty to the ideal of objectivity and of "respect for facts."

Academics—-not just sociologists—-rationalistic, unsentimental, even scientistic scholars, practically never demurred when they were charged in the second-half of the 1960s by ignorant students and younger colleagues with attempting to shore up the capitalistic system by their scientific and scholarly research. I speak here primarily about the generation of scholars who were already mature (or who were old enough to be mature) in the 1960s and 1970s. Regarding the generation after them, the situation has become much worse. I am convinced of the necessity of affirming the autonomy of knowledge. Whatever the uses to which it can be put, whatever its involvement in chains of practical action, whatever the motives of those who have sought it, the propositions of scientific or scholarly knowledge are true or false on the grounds of evidence gained from the methodical self-critical observation of the phenomena to which they refer.

My editorship of *Minerva* was in a way a continuation of the work I had done for *The Bulletin of the Atomic scientists*. In the 1940s and 1950s, I had only to come to the defense of scientific activity and scientists from ignorant rough political demagogues who had no responsibility for the integrity of science and scholarship. Since then, when I have been compelled to insist on the autonomy of scientific knowledge, I have had to argue for it against university teachers, persons who have gained the doctorate from distinguished universities, and decent young graduates who presumably are preparing themselves for a life of scholarship.

In expounding the argument for the autonomy of scientific knowledge, I did my duty as a citizen. But it was also a step forward in my own intellectual activities. The development of my ideas about the objectivity and autonomy of scientific knowledge has served me in a most helpful way in developing my ideas of collective self-consciousness. Of this more later.

XXXII

In 1973, I was invited by the University of Kent at Canterbury to deliver the T.S. Eliot lectures. I was of course left free to choose the subject of the lectures. Previous lecturers had nearly all been men of letters and they had lectured on literary subjects. I could have chosen to lecture on the subject which I had been working intermittently since the beginning of the 1930s, namely, intellectuals and their relations to their own societies and on which I had already published a fair amount. Instead, I chose to devote the four lectures of the series to tradition.

I had always thought (albeit vaguely) that this subject had not been treated with sufficient understanding by sociologists. Max Weber, who made traditional legitimation into one of the three main categories in his analysis of authority, did not satisfy me. After an excessively narrow definition, he had gone into an impressive analysis of feudal and patrimonial types of authority, while traditionality outside the sphere of the exercise of authority was practically entirely disregarded. Even in the exercise of authority, Weber's conception of tradition was too narrow. He did not deal with the function of tradition as a norm, the appropriateness of which is self-evident to those who are subject to it. Weber did, it is true, refer to "stereotyping," by which he meant the reproduction of the pattern of action, that pattern of past performance, being accepted as the norm for the prospective action. Weber sometimes asserted that stereotyping is a consequence of the fear of magical powers that will be offended by innovations. There were also suggestions in his writings that stereotyping is the same as a mechanical or reflexive habit.

Both of these views, although they probably apply to certain situations, are inadequate as a conception of tradition. In his remarks on the routinization of charismatic authority, the role of traditionality is treated very scantily.

One would have thought that Tönnies, who wrote so understandingly well about *Gemeinschaft* and *die Sitte*, would have given a fuller treatment than he did. Even Alfred Vierkandt's *Die Stetigkeit im Kulturwandel* gave me little help. Durkheim and his protégés likewise. In the United States, the works of Thomas, Park and Sumner that might have been thought to be full of understanding of tradition were rather bare. Every nationality and every major religious community, past or present, offers evidence for it. Literary historians and critics have always invoked it; but except for T.S. Eliot, they never seem to have thought about what they were doing. I know those are strong statements. Nevertheless, the unthinkingness with which the word tradition was used troubled me.

In contrast with this, T.S. Eliot's essay of 1924, "Tradition and Individual Talent," although full of enigmatic remarks, offered a glimpse into the function of tradition in literature and in general which needed to be and could be carried further. Michael Polanyi's *Science, Faith and Society* gave me some insight into the place of tradition in scientific research. Karl Popper's "Towards a Rational Theory of Tradition" is one of the best things written on tradition; and it was courageous as well to have presented it before an audience of rationalists and progressivists. (It was published in the *Rationalist Year Book*.)

Tradition had been on my mind for some time. The world seemed too deeply covered by it. It was pervasive even in a society where many foolishly considered change as a good in itself and for tradition as something only to be abolished. Without tradition there would be only random flux, unless human beings were rational enough, without anything to start with except their own physiological organism, to work out a set of contracts to respect each other's property and physical integrity. Obviously that never happens. Yet, social scientists often write as if society is traditionless or should be so (William Ogburn was the great exemplar for that foolishness.)

Both as a point of departure which sets the conditions of intentions to change and as a set of patterns which (in) themselves by the sheer fact of their existence requires that more attention be given to tradition. There is more to tradition than that.

The strong attachment to things that have come down from the past or which are thought to have done so, the belief that the past was a better time than the present, the desire for knowledge of the past and the belief that occurrence in the past legitimates present action are omnipresent evidence that, whatever social scientists and rational sages might say, human beings are not always eager to escape from the past. They want to have it near them. Frivolous scholars like Professors Hobsbawm and Ranger might think that tradition is an invention of the ruling and exploiting classes to hold the lower classes in subjugation; but they have never asked themselves why the ruling classes decided to "invent" tradition. Did those classes change the past by accident or as a device of exploitation? It never occurred to the two distinguished professors of London and Oxford universities to ask themselves whether the "inventors" of tradition had any ground for thinking that the "invention of the past" was a good idea that might render the exploitative dominion more secure. But even though the inventors of the "invention of the past" are fools does not exempt serious persons from trying to understand the phenomenon of the manifold relations of the present to the past. That is what I tried to do in *Tradition*.[26]

Tradition is one of the most pervasive phenomena in the world. The word is constantly adduced by sociologists, anthropologists and historians to identify a mode of action or thought or to explain actions; but no one went into it. I decided that I had to do it.

In the spring of 1955, while I was in Bombay, I had, as mentioned previously, written a paper called "Tradition and Liberty: Antinomy and Interdependence" in which I argued that political freedom was not a creation *ab ovo*. It required the support of a tradition of liberty and traditions of attachment to society that sustained and delimited liberty. Before my departure from Chicago, after I had sent off *The Torment of Secrecy* to the publisher, I wrote an essay of about fifty-five pages stating my views on the matter. From that I made an outline of about the same length.

After my return to Chicago in 1956, I conducted a seminar on tradition on the basis of that detailed outline or syllabus. It went reasonably well, at least, well enough for me to give a similar seminar in the spring of 1958 at which a number of very good papers were presented. I learned a lot from them. From the detailed syllabus, I then produced a manuscript of about 200 pages in the late

1950s. That was the basis of a long paper, "Tradition" that was published in *Comparative Studies in Society and History* in about 1958. I delivered the Eliot lectures in Canterbury in the early 1970s. These were based on a manuscript of about 150 pages from which I gave the four lectures. Then began a long period of rewriting. It must have gone on for about five years since I was still working on it nearly full-time at Leiden and then at Leuven, about seven years later. I finished it in Leuven in the flat that I had been given in the old chapel of the Beguinhof.

I did a great deal of work on it. I studied the history of art and the history of Western classical scholarship as well as the history of the tradition of learning in Islam and China. I acquired a great deal of knowledge that I found difficult to assimilate at the time. I had to jettison most of it because I could not master it in a satisfying form. The things that appeared essential kept eluding me. Usages that had appeared simple and straightforward caused me much perplexity. It seems to me now that I would have less difficulty than I had then. One point stands out, and that is the importance of the past, not just in the genetic sense of "causing" what happens subsequently, nor as a restriction of the range of choice of alternatives by offering a few dominant alternatives to thought and action. I did not grasp the significance of the way in which the image of the past makes the present state of a society, and how the past and present state are united in the collective self-consciousness, so that, although the temporal sequence is abolished, the present and the past of the society are experienced as parts of the same thing. The collective self is constituted not just by contemporaries but by predecessors as well.

I did not see the way in which collective self-consciousness performs the function of making the past—-a past without reference to time—-an equally constitutive part of the same thing as now exists. The society of the past and the society of the present come through the collective self-consciousness to constitute a single society. In this phenomenon, tradition is not what is handed down to the present, nor is it simply the awareness of past as a product of what is remembered and orally transmitted or left in documents or constructed from documents. It is the perception of the past as part of the present moment. For example, the Battle of Gettysburg is part of the present even though I was born half a century after it. Similarly, the Jews of the European Middle Ages and of Hellenistic and Roman antiquity are present to me. Tradition in this sense makes a single nationality out of events widely separated in time.

I am not sure that my work *Tradition* advanced me in my effort to clarify my ideas of the structure of the large society. It did however open the way for me to apprehend better the temporal constitution of society by treating tradition as a consensus of earlier generations and later generations.

A paper of that period, delivered at a meeting of the American Sociological Society, on the temporal unity of society and the indeterminateness of its temporary boundaries opened up the question as to whether we should not regard tradition as the consensus between generations. This meant that the collective self-consciousness of a society had some of the following connections with the past. One, the currently held image of the collectivity, i.e., that held by its living members, is formed from images of the past and present of the society. The image does not refer only to the society in its present state; it refers to its past states as well. Two, the acting subject in his relations with others in his collectivity orients himself towards past as well as present members of his collectivity. National heroes of the past are seen primarily as bearers of the referent of nationality, or it might be of any other collectivity. The subject forms a collective self with them, with the qualifications that in the case of relations with the dead, it is a unilateral relationship.

Collective self-consciousness is not only a participation in a self that embraces anonymous and known members of the society of the present. It entails participation in a self that embraces members of the society, known and anonymous in the past.

The members of a collectivity see their fellow members not just with respect to what they are at the moment but also with respect to what they have been in the past. Indeed one could say that the definition of what the other individual is at present is arrived at by knowing what he has been in the past. That individual bears in himself properties representing or symbolizing quite remote pasts. This observation applies to objectivated symbolic configurations as well as it does to collectivities. (The achievements of the past are contained, for example, in contemporary scientific propositions. The recognition of one scientist by another entails the recognition not only of the past achievements of the particular individual scientist but also of his participation in the tradition of science, i.e., his possession, although unspoken, of the achievements of scientists of the past, as the postulates of his work in the present or recent past.)

When I delivered the lectures and then for some years thereafter when I was revising, over and over again, the manuscript from which the lectures were delivered, I had not yet reached the point where I undertook to elaborate the idea of collective self-consciousness. This was another instance in which the potentialities of an idea were later drawn out when they moved towards convergence with some other ideas of mine.

Consensus was such an instance; it was vague and undifferentiated at first; bit by bit other ideas appeared without at first a clear connection with consensus. Later their place in relation to consensus became more differentiated—-although still not enough! The same was true of tradition when I first worked on it; it was what the living generation drew into its present image of the past and acted in accord with what was offered by it.

My ideas about the constitution of society were at first entirely limited to the more or less simultaneous or concurrent collocations of the patterns of a territorially bounded collectivity. The work on tradition implicated this by an "unfolding" in the past patterns of the territorially bounded collectivity (the boundaries of which were not identical through time).

That is the way it was when I first worked on tradition: I was not explicitly trying to develop my views on collective self-consciousness. But I vaguely grasped the notion of the temporal depth of collectivities entailing the past referents of collective self-consciousness. When I developed further the idea of collective self-consciousness, that potentiality in the idea of tradition come out relatively clearly. That is, as clearly as my ideas ever came out.

XXXIII

Not very long after that, I was invited to deliver the H.M. Jones lectures at the University of Belfast. H.M. Jones had been the principal of the Belfast College Institute. He left a substantial sum to the Queen's University on his death. This was many years earlier, but the University did not get around to inaugurating the lectureship in his memory until about 1975. At that time, my friend, Sir Eric Ashby, was then chancellor of the University and another eminent scientist, Sir Arthur Vick, who had been director of the Atomic Energy Establishment at Harwell, was vice-chancellor. I decided that I should choose a subject that would conform with the interest of my two patrons on the growth of scientific knowledge and on science policy. I called the lectures, "The Distribution of Knowledge." The lectures were about the growth and spread of knowledge, particularly scientific knowledge with and between societies.

I took as my point of departure the ideal aspired to by Condorcet that foresaw the future progress of mankind as lying in the universal possession of knowledge. This entailed a comprehensive cognitive consensus in all adults, in principle, of the entire human race. This is an ideal that has been largely pronounced in the societies that made the greatest progress towards some of its preconditions, namely, universality of school attendance and universality of literacy. It still exists in fragmentary form in those societies: the ideas of universal higher education, lifelong education, recurrent education, etc., and the potentialities of the "Internet" that will make all existing knowledge available to everyone on the computer screen. Similarly, there are the recurrent accusations against the development of science into specialization and similar criticisms of specialization in higher education and the sporadic efforts to broaden at least undergraduate syllabi, then to the usually ignorant praise of multi- or interdisciplinary studies and research. These are all later day survivals, in a debased idiom, of the ideal of a society and even ultimately of the whole human race guided by reason and sound knowledge, sharing a common culture, and, hence, unified and beyond the horrors of war and persecution.

It was and is not the intention of *The Movements of Knowledge* to join the pogrom against the Enlightenment.[27] It was a noble age. Its ideals have been abused by emancipationists who have carried part of its ideal out to its logical consequences. More conservative thinkers have more reasonably criticized the ideal for its unrealism and its self-destructive regard for the manifold ways in which even its partial realization has depended on many elements that are, in fact, alien to rationalism.

It was to a much greater extent the intention of *Movements of Knowledge* to arrive at an understanding of how collectivities that are formed around the collective possession of bodies of knowledge are constituted, how they expand and contract, and what are the limits of their expansion. It is not entirely out of the question that there will come a time when the human race as a whole shares a common collective self-consciousness formed around the image of a single body of knowledge in which all human beings, except infants, participate. It might not be out of the question over a very long time, providing that the human race changes in a very far-reaching way its intellectual powers and interests. I do not foresee any such far-reaching changes. I do not foresee, although it is said already to have happened, that primordial sensibilities will evaporate, that intelligence and creativity will be released from their present restraints and that talents will become equally distributed. None of this will happen in the foreseeable future. It is therefore interesting to examine the scale and potentialities no less than the limitations of the formation and expansion of collective self-consciousnesses.

I then began to prepare the ideas of *Movements of Knowledge* for publication. As I continued on the task, the manuscript changed in size, form and content. In order to deal properly with scientific knowledge, it became necessary to distinguish it from humanistic knowledge, from religious or transcendental knowledge, from wisdom, from technological knowledge, from self-knowledge, and from knowledge of society. Each of these kinds of knowledge required a large part of the manuscript for itself. In each part, the particular kind of knowledge was described, distinguished from the others. The central part of the work is about the characteristic modes and conditions of growth of each particular kind of knowledge, its extension or link with other kinds of knowledge, the expansion within societies, and then the expansion between societies and civilizations. Under expansion, I include the movement of knowledge into practical action; I do not confine myself to the application of scientific knowledge to technology. The work as it stands is focused primarily on the phenomena of growth and expansion; but it also deals with the institutional and cultural setting in which this growth and expansion occur. By cultural here I mean the setting of other kinds of knowledge, different from the kind in question. Much historical matter, the history of education, the history of universities and technical colleges, the history of numerous disciplines, scientific and humanistic knowledge and the institutions in which it is cultivated and transmitted, the history of religious beliefs, religious communities and religious institutions, etc., have been adduced and brought into relationship with growth and expansion.

There were large introductory sections on the objectivation of knowledge, on the topography and sharing of knowledge, and on the principles of the classification of types of knowledge. There were also sections on the growth, extension, expansion and recession of knowledge. The manuscript grew larger. It was rewritten several times, some parts many times. The parts on the movements of religious knowledge and of scientific knowledge came closest to being satisfactory. The section on humanistic knowledge was not too primitive. The section on the movement of technological knowledge needs much more work; but there is a rather good literature available on this and it would be not too difficult to bring that to a satisfactory state.

I should point out here that in *The Movements of Knowledge*, I have attempted to deal with knowledge in India, China (Japan and Korea only slightly) and Islam as well as with knowledge in classical antiquity and the modern age.

Thus, what began from my interest in the expansion of modern Western literary and scientific knowledge into India from Great Britain, the extension of educational opportunity in Europe and North America in the nineteenth and twentieth centuries and the growth and expansion of scientific knowledge in modern Europe and the United States and in the relations of scientific knowledge and technology grew into a very comprehensive architectonically systematic work. It laid encyclopaedic obligations on me. Nevertheless, I would have gone ahead steadily through a few more revisions and then completion (to the extent that any such work can ever be completed). There was however an obstacle. The obstacle arose from my efforts to deal with the knowledge of society which in most cases is the knower's own society. I asked myself what is the distinctive character of knowledge of one's own society—-its present condition and its past? A problem exists with regard to the knowledge of societies other than one's own.

It was easy enough to write about the disciplines or proto-disciplines that dealt with the physical world, with living organisms, with the transformation of material objects. It was less easy to write about a society's knowledge of itself particularly when it is a question of its application.

I was not concerned with "social science" as a science (which it is not), although most social science is knowledge of the social scientists' own society. I was interested in envisaging knowledge of one's own society as a form of collective self-knowledge.

About twenty-five years earlier I had written an essay entitled "The Calling of Sociology" which I published as an epilogue to a large collection of sections of various works contributing to the theory of Society.[28] In this essay I said that sociology (or social science) was the "self-knowledge of society." That phrase seemed to me to mean something; but I was not clear what that meaning was. It came back to me when I came to revise the section that I called unsatisfactorily "civil knowledge" that dealt with unwritten as well as written and published knowledge of one's own society. I repeatedly asked myself whether a society could know itself. Individuals within a society might know their society; many individuals might know their society. But in what sense could it be said that a society knows itself?

The term seemed less challenging and more straightforward when interpreted to refer to a plurality of the individual members of a society knowing their own society. Then it occurred to me that if many individuals in a society know their own society, it is not at all likely that each of them could have acquired his knowledge separately without any connection to what the others knew. There were certain images in circulation in that society which various individuals "latched on to," i.e., in which, in my later language, they participated. The knowledge of one's own society was in Durkheim's language a collective representation.

Thus, after a fairly unbroken absence of a half-century, Durkheim re-entered my intellectual life. (Of course, I had re-read the *Les formes élémentairs de la vie religieuse* fairly often). It happened almost by accident. The accident was the following. Usually at the last meeting of my seminars, I ask the students what they would like to have a seminar about in the following term. I can follow this procedure because many of my students come regularly to my seminars, some as for many as four or five years in succession. On one such occasion in the early 1980s, a few of the students said they would like to have a seminar on Durkheim. I responded as I always do by agreeing to carry out as well as I could their request. I thought it was a good idea because I wanted also to take up once more the writings of Marcel Mauss, Maurice Halbwachs and Marcel Granet because I wanted to trace the further course of Durkheim's ideas after they had left his mind and had been taken into the minds of his disciples who were men of great learning, great intelligence and great imagination in their own right.

In the course of this, I had to examine Durkheim's concept of "representations collective." As far as he was concerned, they were the simultaneously held beliefs of individuals in the same society. He said nothing about the interindividual interdependence of those beliefs. If this was so, then "collective representations" were nothing more than statistically frequent beliefs. There was no interindividual pattern of structure. But Durkheim was too intelligent to think this when the whole bias of his thought was against such individual intellectual autonomy. Nevertheless, the definition of "collective representations" leaves them simply as a plurality of "individual representations."

I was not interested in saving Durkheim's reputation. I am not like the Marxists who used to say—contrarily to what was evident to anyone free of political passion—"But that is not what Marx meant." I read the great authors for the improvement of knowledge. I read them so that I might be led by them to discover something I did not know before and which they did not know either.

Thus, I concluded that there was something more to the knowledge of society which a plurality (a large number or a small number) of individuals knew about their society; it is something different in its interindividual structure than substantively the same propositions known by a plurality of individuals whose knowledge is interdependent with the knowledge possessed by other individuals. It corresponds to the objectivated symbolic configuration in which a multiplicity of individuals participate.

So it was that collective self-consciousness came to take up such a large place on my agenda. I do not think that this development means that the knowledge which individuals acquire about their own societies is wrong or not to be considered as possibly valid. That is not what I mean at all. Truth as well as error can be a collective possession. The fact that the beliefs of others are taken into account or are accepted as the postulates of one's own beliefs does not mean that the beliefs of the others or of the knowing individual are wrong. They might be based on detached and disciplined observation.

I did not however confine my conception of civil (or institutional) knowledge to the knowledge gained by persons who deliberately set out to observe like Tocqueville and Beaumont or LePlay or Charles Booth or Seebohm Rowntree. I had in mind also the kind of knowledge which ordinary persons who acquire knowledge in the course of the pursuit of their daily round or out of their curiosity, random or focused. They know their own society, too, through their experience of it, by hearsay received from persons who have experienced what they themselves have not experienced and what they have imagined from their experience and from hearsay and reading.

In fact, this pattern of knowledge is not greatly different from the pattern of knowledge of deliberate observers; they too depend to a great extent on hearsay about events and actions that they have not witnessed. Their knowledge of their own societies too is affected by what others know or think they know about that society. This knowledge is reinforced or modified by the knowledge that they have of the knowledge possessed by others.

This much can be said now: knowledge of one's own society is collective self-knowledge (or, collective self-consciousness, as I call it in other contexts.) I say nothing at this point about the significance of this collective self-knowledge in the constitution of society. That however was my aim, even at the time of writing *Movements of Knowledge*. I had to deal with this problem in the third major part of this work that dealt with conversion of knowledge into practice.

As a result of this diversion, the manuscript of *Movements of Knowledge* ceased to move. A few bits of the manuscript have been published: "The Cognitive Expansion from Centre to Periphery," in *Say Not the Struggle*, a collection of papers in honor of A.D. Gorwala, a very distinguished Indian civil servant and publicist, who, as I have mentioned, was a friend of mine; "The Expansion of Ordered European Knowledge" in *Europe und ihre Folgen* edited by Kryzstof Michalski; "The Universal Validity of Science" in *Zeugen des Wissens*, edited by Heinz Maier-Leibnitz and "Tradition, Centre and Periphery: Reflections on the Life of S. Ramanujan," which I recently published in *Minerva*. I have also published numerous essays on the history of universities and the history of the social sciences, which were adaptations of various sections of *Movements of Knowledge* or which will be adapted for incorporation into that work.

At around this time, I began to have in my seminars a rather large number of Korean and Chinese students, the latter coming from the mainland as well as from Taiwan and Hong Kong. They wanted to know about Max Weber. They came in large numbers to my seminar on "Max Weber in Chinese Society." When at the last session of that seminar, they were asked what they wanted me to deal with, many of them said that they wanted a seminar on civil society and Max Weber.

XXXIV

The formation of cognitive communities or collectivities within and between societies and between civilizations is the underlying theme of *The Movements of Knowledge*. Everything in it is intended to contribute to illumination of that theme. I could not have made myself ready to undertake to deal with this theme without this digression of several years when I struggled with collective self-consciousness.

I know that the notion of a collective *self* and of a collective self-consciousness will meet with indifference, or denigration—-like that which was directed to Durkheim three quarters of a century ago. I think however that I am in a better position intellectually to rebuff these criticisms. It is true that my views are even further from the traditional individualistic position than Durkheim's; but I have the advantage of having been in a position to give more detailed attention to methodological individualism than Durkheim did. (Durkheim did not make clear to himself the difference between the collective consciousness and the collective self-consciousness. I attribute great importance to the "self" in this matter.)

The collective self-consciousness resides, more or less, simultaneously, in the minds of a plurality of individuals who form a collectivity by virtue of their participation in that collective self-consciousness. This is not a tautology. They could possibly form a joint stock company or some other association based on contracts among their individual members; but they could not form a collectivity without participation in that collective self-consciousness. "Participation" is a crucial term. It postulates the externality or objectivity of the collective self-consciousness to all of the members of the collectivity. They become members by participation in the collective self-consciousness. The collective self is a part of them as much as their individual self.

The prototype of this phenomenon is the scientific community which is constituted by the orientation of its members towards an objective body of scientific knowledge that is distinct from any relationship of human beings, and by the perception of the other human beings who are oriented as participants in that realm of objectivated symbolic configurations, or in Popper's terminology, "World 3." Each acting subject is seen as a participant by his name as author in a scientific paper or book, or as a scientist in a laboratory, or as a persons described by others as a scientist.

There is a triangular pattern: (1) the acting subject; (2) the objective body of scientific knowledge; (3) the other acting individual subjects, who also participate in the body of scientific knowledge, are seen by each acting subjects to do so. Thereby, through this mutual awareness of the "others'" participation in it, they form the scientific community. (This applies to sub-communities no less than to the "scientific community" as a whole.)

A religious community has the same pattern. The religious collectivity and its collective self-consciousness are also triangular in form. At the apex is the body of knowledge (the image of the deity, the image of he church, etc); at one angle is the subject perceiving his co-subject, in the other angle as participants in the body of religious knowledge. (The participant is visible when he is worshipping in the same church or is describing himself as an adherent of the doctrines of that church.)

The believers in scientific propositions or in the theological proposition about the deity have a relatively clear body of objectivated propositions in which to participate, i.e., to know and accept. Their act of participation is generally open to the observation of their fellow members of the scientific or religious community.

The triangular pattern of the collective self-consciousness is less clear in other types of collective self-consciousness since the image towards which participation occurs is less clearly discernible, there being no precisely promulgated body of knowledge or doctrine. The counterpart of the body of knowledge or religious doctrine is the image of the society, friendship circle, nationality, ethnic group, locality (i.e., local science), occupational category, social class, political party. The acting subject, as such already viewing himself as a member of a particular collectivity and a participant in the image of that collectivity, perceives the other person as a possessor of the qualities that give evidence of his participation in that image.

There is a problem in the assimilation to the triangular pattern of the collective self-consciousness of the scientific or religious community to other kinds of collectivities like nation or lineage or class. In the case of scientific or religious collectivities, the image of the scientific or religious collectivity contains a reference to an entity outside itself, namely, the body of scientific knowledge or the existence of the deity. In the case of the collectivity without an intellectual or doctrinal (a scientific or a divine) referent, the referent on the basis of which the collectivity is constituted is some property like territoriality. The result of the perception of the other individual includes, or excludes, that individual into or from the collectivity, which is represented in the image, which in its turn contains a reference to the property in question.

XXXV

That is how I came to work on civil society. There was another factor in this focusing of my interest on civil society. This was the increasing attention to civil society among the critics of Eastern Europe and China of their totalitarian regimes. Once more, there was a coincidence of external events and a certain point in my own intellectual evolution that led me to work on a particular topic.

I originally called the knowledge of one's own society "civil knowledge." That gave it a bias that will have to be corrected in the coming years when I have taken *The Movements of Knowledge* in hand once more. All societies, civil or uncivil, have knowledge of themselves. It might not be truthful knowledge and it does not necessarily make the society civil.

The idea of a civil society had been in my mind for a long time. I have already referred to my discussion about "pluralistic politics" in *The Torment of Secrecy*, to interest in consensus and its necessity for a free pluralistic society: the years when I was occupied with "mass society," and with ideology in contrast with civility, the dangers of ideology for a pluralistic society, and privacy. My struggle with "civil knowledge" backed me into dealing directly with "civil society."

I began with a long essay on "What is Civil Society?" which I wrote for presentation at the biennial discussion at the Castelgandolfo in July 1989. I followed this with an essay on "Good Manners in Personal Relationship and Civility in the Larger Society" and another on "The Virtue of Civil Society" which I delivered as a lecture at the Athenaeum in London.[29] This led to a paper that I wrote for my Chinese and Korean students "Civility and Civil Society in Chinese Classical Philosophy" that dealt only with Confucius and which is therefore incomplete. (I have still to deal with Mencius, Han Fei Tzu, and Lord Shang among others). The paper was presented at the meeting of the European-American Association for Chinese Studies in Montreal in 1992. I have also written a paper on "Civil, Pluralistic Liberal Democracy: Tocqueville and Max Weber" and "Religious Pluralism in Liberal Democratic Society" (published in *Christians and Jews in a Pluralistic Society* edited by myself and Ernst W. Böckenförde, a member of the German Constitutional Court and professor of public law at the University of Freiburg). This term (autumn 1992) I have been conducting a two-quarter seminar on "The Idea of Civil Society: Hegel, Tocqueville and Weber" to be continued in the spring of 1993.

My views are simple. A civil society is one in which society is superior to the state. It is a society in which there is a large, specifically civil sphere. By this I mean that the economy is one formed around the market of private business enterprises with free movement of labor and free choice of occupations. It is one in which there are numerous private or voluntary associations to perform services for their members and to provide for the welfare of the poor and those who cannot look after themselves. It is one in which private voluntary associations are free to make representations to the state (or government) and to conduct autonomous private institutions like universities, research institutions. A civil society is one in which citizens are assured of freedom of association in voluntary associations and in political parties. It is a society in which the civil sector is politically organized into a plurality of political parties which engage in competition with each other for the suffrage of a universal adult electorate for the operation of representative institutions, most notably the legislative assembly and in which the judiciary is autonomous *vis-à-vis* the legislature and the executive branch of government. There is a free formation of public opinion that means freedom of the organs of opinion including the press, radio and television. It is a society of autonomous religious institutions and communities and a separation *de facto* of church and state.

The civil society is a pluralistic society, since in all large societies membership in which is constituted by residence in the legally circumscribed territory for a certain minimum period, if not by birth, there is inevitably a heterogeneity of ideals and interests which may be freely pursued.

Now a pluralistic society is a civil society when the autonomy of institutions and the freedom of individuals are kept from damaging centrifugality by the sufficient prevalence of civility of the population. The necessity for civility does not require that it be a continuously salient disposition on the part of all of the population. It must be present and effective at those points where conflicts of ideals and interests of the different sections of the population would otherwise permit the outbreak of violence and other types of disruption of the functioning of the social order.

What is civility? It is nothing other than the moderation of the pursuit of interests and ideals which otherwise would diminish the common good. Civility is therefore a concern of the common good.

XXXVI

The fact of "we" and the state of "we-ness" is absolutely fundamental. But what do they mean? The "fusion of selves" is an attractive phrase; but I have not been able to overcome its obscurity and to reduce it to intelligible terms. What I have substituted for it: "collective self-consciousness" might not be any better, but at least to me it seems to resolve the difficulty of treating the "fusion of selves" as a transindividual phenomenon. In my present view, I have made it entirely into a state of mind of individuals in a collectivity in which each individual perceives himself as part of a larger entity, of being in that respect not himself. There are immense difficulties remaining in this.

The perception of being "part of," or "one with" is a perception by the individual's mind. It has a different content from the perception by the individual of himself as an individual. The individual is the mouthpiece of the individual himself when he says "I" or "me" or "my"; he is the mouthpiece of the collective self-consciousness when he says "we" or "us" or "our." The voice are the sounds generated within the physical body of a physically separated individual. But the voice can be set into mobility by that part of the individual which is his own self of that part of the individual which is part of the collective self. When, for example, I raise my voice in protest against the appointment of a professor, it is because the collective part of me takes offense on behalf of the department, discipline, university in which I participate. It is that part of my physical organism which is set into action by the response of that part which participates in the collectivity. But the latter operates through the former. When the individual says "we" or "us" or "ourselves," he is not thinking arithmetically. He is thinking of a single entity and his speaking for a single entity that is not himself. In that sense, he has transcended himself as a separate individual; it is what he becomes when he has transcended his individual self that concerns me.

All these reflections are however reports on later developments in my thought on these matters. I am not confident that they represent a solution; but they at least contain some expression of my dissatisfaction with the metaphysical language of other writers on this subject. The question remains of whether it is possible to escape metaphors in speaking of such phenomena. Maybe all I have done is to substitute a metaphor actually operative in the minds of individuals for a metaphor used by observers to describe a phenomenon that they observe.

I think that the task still remains. It is perfectly all right to claim to adhere to the principle of "methodological individualism," although the claim should not be overstated. The important thing to remember however is that human beings in their own image of the world and in their own action are not methodological individualists. These human beings believe that collectivities are real. They are right in this; they believe that collective selves are real, and they are right in this, too. For myself as an observer, I must learn to do justice to this fact.

What has been said here does not disregard the fact that collectivities are sometimes formed and memberships in them retained by rational considerations of the probability of advantageous consequences for each participating actor. Sometimes the rational calculations of prospective individual advantage support and are supported by the propositions and ties mentioned above; sometimes they are in contradiction to them. I would only say that the "theory of rational choice," asserting that rational calculations of prospective benefits for the calculating person is the only ground on which collectivities are formed and memberships maintained, is extremely unrealistic.

Norms regulating the conduct of the participants towards each other and towards the collectivity as a whole are generated from the experience of participation in the collective self-consciousness. They are norms requiring solicitude towards other members of the same collectivity and of concern for the well-being of the collectivity as a whole. The norms call forth an "other-regarding" activity and attitudes. The substance of ethics could be regarded as the generalization of norms that are precipitated by membership in collectivities, participation in collective self-consciousness.

This does not mean that ethical judgments do not undergo refinement by rational reflection so that they become universally valid. The refinements however are refinements of the fundamental fact of obligation to the community and its members and responsibility for the well-being of its members. The fundamental fact of "oughtness" emerges automatically from the fact of the emergence of a collectivity. Within a collectivity, obligation prevails; towards the outside, there is no obligation. This is very crude but there is some truth in it. (This was observed any years ago by William Graham Sumner in his distinction between "in-group" and "out-group").

The norms arising from participation in a collectivistic self-consciousness are, in their most elementary form, parochial and relativistic. Reflective reason raises them above parochiality and relativism so that they become generalized as valid in relation to all human beings. The very concept of a human being has a primordial component, although it might be overcome or set aside by the perception of civil and sacred properties. These enlarge the size of the collectivity and reduce the parochiality and relativity of the norms generated by the primordial collective self-consciousness.

We come up against some difficult problems here. It would be well to consider them, although a definite resolution is not necessary in order to solve the problems of the triangular structure of the collective self-consciousness. Still they are interesting. First, why do human beings establish collectivities with others whom they perceive to possess certain qualities that they themselves possess? Second, why does the formation of a collectivity entail norms of obligations to other members and to the collectivity itself? Third, why does the perception of primordial, civil or sacred qualities in other persons have a compelling effect on the conduct of the perceiving subject?

The same questions can be raised about personal qualities; but I will omit to deal with them here because different patterns seem to me, at present, to be characteristic of a personal collectivity formed by lovers, spouses, and friends. It might be noted in passing that psychoanalytic theory derives the propensity towards primordial, sacred and civil ties from personal, or more specifically, sexual ties.

XXXVII

From my early concerns with solidarity in primary groups or small collectivities in primary groups and consensus in large collectivities and whole societies, in the 1930s and 1940s, the constitution of collectivities has been my fundamental interest. Growing out of that interest, have been my efforts to delineate the "spirit" of the collectivity, i.e., the beliefs and images around which it has formed and to discover the nature of the attachment of its individual members to it and to each other. I wish to understand the capacities for and the limitation to the expansion of the various kinds of knowledge, the capacities for and the limits on the scale and depth of the various communities formed by different kinds of knowledge.

On the surface *Movements of Knowledge* might appear to be far away from the constitution of collectivities, perhaps even far away from the substance of *Tradition* and no less far away from the study of literary and academic intellectuals and so on. As I recurrently have emphasized in this retrospective view of my intellectual peregrinations, the same fundamental theme has repeatedly (almost I might say, invariably) emerged from the relatively wide range of more concrete, specific and differentiated objects of my attention at each moment. I should therefore say that the ultimate interest in *Movements of Knowledge* is the objectivity of knowledge: the discussion of the cosmos of knowledge, the growth and extension of knowledge and the application of knowledge tributary to the expansion of knowledge, i.e., the formation of communities of knowledge, across primordial boundaries, across the boundaries of class, across the boundaries of large societies, across ethnic and national boundaries, across linguistic boundaries, across the boundaries of long separate and tenacious traditions.

The subsidiary aim of *Movements of Knowledge* is the discovery of the various kinds of knowledge and by the various methods and institutions of propagation through which the expansions have occurred.

Individual self-knowledge is precluded from expansion; it ceases to be self-knowledge if its substance passes into the possession of another individual. Primordial, transcendental, and primordial social knowledge is more capable of expansion than self-knowledge. The religious and the scientific communities are the best instances of the largest expansions of knowledge.

All these various communities formed around different kinds of knowledge are in relations of mutual reinforcement and of obstruction or conflict. With the community formed around each kind of knowledge, there are numerous sub-communities. These, too, are in relation of mutual reinforcement, obstruction and conflict.

XXXVIII

My friend James Coleman's ideas about the working of society—I mean the ideas of his powerfully received book *The Foundations of Social Theory*—-are imaginative and ingenious, but far-fetched and unrealistic; they strain to force all human actions into the procrustean crib of the theory of rational choice. (In conversation he is, of course, far more sensible).

I am probably the only social scientist (!) who asserts that there is a concern for the common good simultaneously experienced in many individuals, in some, even many politicians, and in many ordinary persons, local civic leaders, etc.

I do not argue that these persons think only of the common good. I do not argue that the collective self-consciousness of the society predominates in all their actions or that it has a high position of precedence in the outlook and conduct of the large majority. I argue that it exists to some extent in most large societies and not least in the United States, even at present when my belief that this is so among my own fellow-countrymen is put under tense strain. Most social scientists attribute all action to self-enhancement, self-protection, the exploration and deception of others—"strategies" is the common and revealing word. Yet, I insist that this is not the case, and I am staking the final vindications of my intellectual history or rather assessment of my life-long wrestling and skirmishing with the world on behalf of the truth about itself.

It is anomalous, to say the least. Am I Pollyanna who wished to see only the good and who makes it up if he does not see it? It does not trouble me that the vastly prevailing current of thought, such as it is, of my contemporaries, and of the great ancestors of the analysis of modern society differs from my own views. It is the facts themselves that are more troubling. I do not pay any attention to what my contemporaries say. They are of inferior clay and their disagreement only bores me rather than troubles me. Nor am I put out that my views are in disagreement with the views of Tönnies, Max Weber, and Durkheim. For one thing, the contemporaries who are so far astray from the truth are not as negative in their description of contemporary Western society makes out; after all, most of them believe that if the right persons were in power or if the right institutions are established, the common good would be realized. They seem to think that they—-perhaps they only—-seek the common good; and they often think that there are others in their respective societies who seek it or who are amenable to being persuaded that they should seek it. They think that there is a common good, however perverse their conception of it. They apparently think of something more than their own advantage. But I should not attempt to find confirmation of my own views in the inconsistency of my wrong-headed contemporaries. They do not think; they merely repeat errors that they have acquired from others. They are the victims of a cognitively erroneous collective self-consciousness.

Nor am I troubled that my views diverge from those of the great ancestors, even though I have learned much from them. When I attempt to correct them, it is not because I think that they are totally wrong. My own analysis in many respects, takes its point of departure from their discoveries. My troubles are of a different sort.

I often raise the question with myself whether I am not constructing a figment of my own imagination in my desire to vindicate the society into which I have been born and to which I am so attached, despite its so numerous fallings away from what I think is the right path and the right order of society.

Let me say that I try to take into account these fallings away and not to blind myself to them. I am convinced that despite the numerous instances, profusely reported, of the failures of human beings and of my fellow citizens of the Western liberal democracies, that there is such a fact as civility, and that there is much civility in our society, silent though it often is. Even when silent, it is not wholly without effect. I am convinced that there is a widespread sensitivity to the primordial, however much it is denied and however many instances are reported of a repudiation of primordiality. I think that I am not simply imagining without seeing any corresponding reality, that there is an awe before sacred things. Primordiality, civility, respect for the sacred, a widespread although often submerged civility—-all of these exist.

I think that the truthful element in my analysis lies in the fact that I do not refuse to acknowledge that there are many instances of "rational choice." Nor do I fail to acknowledge the large, very visible, much trumpeted deviation from primordiality, civility, respect for the sacred in contemporary society.

The one postulate of my analysis is that there is such a phenomenon as normality and a widespread adherence to a belief in normality that must constantly reassert itself in any society including our own. I insist that the belief in normality is a fundamental property of any society. This implies that the belief in the validity of normality is a property of the human mind and that it is not a matter of "custom" or "socialization" or "habit" or an unthinking acceptance of a tradition that has no foundation in the real facts of life.

Yet it cannot be denied that many persons do behave contrarily to the rules of normality and they have many vociferous defenders. It is the defenders of abnormality that I must confront. Most of them are relatively recent converts to the defense of abnormality. They deny that there is any such thing as normality and, hence, that there is no such thing as abnormality either. Yet, they come to the defense of abnormality and do so by denying the legitimacy of any assertion that there is a natural law of normality. Why do they do it?

It is not easy to give a definitive answer. I would say first of all that normality is a burden. Any rule is a burden, even for persons who are not themselves inclined toward behaving abnormally. It is a strain because it sometimes entails the repression of natural impulses. But it is also a strain because it is declared by authority; it is intertwined with the functioning of existing liberal democratic society which has encouraged criticism of authority. It allows actions hostile to authority to be performed with impunity. Impunity of recalcitrant acts and words is an encouragement to such acts and words.

There is a hatred among the educated—-among intellectuals—-against their own society. The grounds for this hatred, the motives that sustain it, need not be gone into here. (It is certainly desirable to analyze the phenomenology or the constitution of such hostility.) There is a collective self-consciousness that sustains it; a collective self-consciousness which is inimical to the prevailing collective self-consciousness and which probably is also a potentiality within the prevailing collective self-consciousness.

The existence and validity of normality is denied because it is associated with the exercise of authority. That is what the detractors of normality are really aiming at. Only a few years ago, abnormality was not high on the list of things to be defended by denying normality. The abnormal—homosexuals, unmarried mothers—are late arrivals. They have to replace the poor and the homeless and the Negroes who although still high are not as high as they were. The chief protégés among the Negroes are the juvenile delinquents, looters, rioters, etc. The rest have been put aside.

The discredit of socialism and of the Soviet Union has shifted the list of protégés of the domestic enemies of the existing liberal democratic society. I do not think that the protective abnormality and the derogation of normality are primary objects of the campaign against normality and for abnormality.

XXXIX

I have repeatedly been cast down in self-doubt. Sometimes the idea of collective self-consciousness dissolves. It is not that it yields before the reigning ideas about "identity" that are simply nothing except acknowledgement that individuals call themselves "Germans" or "Frenchmen" or that they live within the bounded territories ruled by separate governments. I cannot accept that. I cannot accept that individuals are not members of collectivities, the outer reaches of which they cannot see. I reject the assertion that these collectivities that cannot be seen are myths, illusions, errors. The collectivities are real in the sense if addressed or invoked or touched, they can go into action. No one can deny that the obedience of the Serbian soldiers against Bosnians or Croats or Slovenians is not simply obedience to an authority with whom a contract has been signed or because they expect to benefit from the booty or because they wish to kill someone, anyone. It is impossible for me to accept that these soldiers act as they do only because commands have been given to them; that they are conscripts, neither willing or unwilling but that they simply do what they are told, and that this is true of their officers, as well and their officers' officers, etc., up to the sovereign, the head of government or state. It is impossible for me to accept that the head of a government simply wishes to exercise power for the sheer pleasure for himself. Does he not exercise that power as a member of, for example, the Serbian collectivity? When he orders his troops to attack Sarajevo, does not that *Serbian* fact of his of his military instrument count for anything?

There is something there. Is that something that I am calling the collective self-consciousness? There is no doubt that individuals think of themselves as members of collectivities and that thinking that makes some difference in their actions. They act as members of collectivities, the collectivities act as collectivities.

Now, what is it that constitutes the individual as a member of a collectivity? I have been saying now for some time that it is the individuals perceiving the other person as possessing the same property, the same property that he himself possesses. I have also been saying that this property has an "objective" existence outside the individuals who are members of that collectivity. I will go further and say that membership in that same collectivity is constituted by participation in that objectivated symbolic configuration. He participates in the *idea* of the collectivity. There would be no collectivity without the idea of that collectivity and even of collectivities in general. My task is to make more concrete and exact what is meant by the idea of the collectivity.

I am now confronting the following problem on which all stands or falls. First, to describe more precisely the "World-3": the image or idea of the collectivity (in religious collectivities, the image of the collectivity and the presence in it of the sacred; in civil collectivities, the image of the political society with its territorial (and sacred) referents; in primordial collectivities, the image of the collectivity and its primordial (blood and local) referents; in aesthetic and intellectual collectivities, the image of the collectivity and its aesthetic or intellectual referents.) Second, to describe the attachment to the other person(s), seen or known, unseen or unknown. Third, to describe *normative obligations* arising from participation (in the image) and from the perception of the other person with reference to his possession of the referents given in the image.

The crux of the matter is whether there is an inter-individual reality of the contents of simultaneously existing individual minds. It would be a "World-3" phenomenon, a kind of consensus, although not necessarily an agreement of the coexistent patterns of minds.

It makes little sense to think of a society of concurrently existing individuals forming a differentiated structure of interacting individuals. Such an image is a distortion because at any one moment all the individuals are not "fully deployed." Now there is one action taking place, now another. The society is a thing realizing itself in time—not just living in consensus with the past, but in linked series of varieties of structures—-daily morning-structure and daily afternoon-structure, weekly structures, monthly, seasonal, annual structures, each a cycle, many or all of the cycles moving within larger cycles, the cycles of individual life times and of generational cycles going with these recurrent cycles. Not all of the cycles are recurrent; all have some uniqueness in them. Yet despite all this movement one is permitted to speak of a society having a characteristic structure over an extended period.

The same kaleidoscopic pattern of minds is likewise possible. It is permissible to speak of prevailing opinion or of collective self- consciousness. To do so may be a distortion, but not more a distortion than any generalization. Taken all together, these cycles are the society as a reality. It is a question as to whether it is intellectually useful to think of this cyclically differentiated coexistent plurality of states of collective self-consciousness, even if it is beyond the powers of any individual mind to describe it.

My view that it must be recognized and taken into account because it is each individual acting subject's awareness or image of that coexistent plurality of states of collective self-consciousness that gives its power to public opinion. Public opinion is indeed nothing but that coexistent plurality of the collective self-consciousness (in many anonymous individual minds), amalgamated into such images as "the public," "the people," "society," "one," "they." It is one of the necessary components of the normative force of the collective self-consciousness. It must be remembered that "the other" in the formation of collective self-consciousness is not invariably a present, known or seen individual. It is the anonymous "mass" of the "society," "the public," "the people," "our people," etc., with whom the image of the society is shared; thus, the image of the simultaneous coexistent, anonymous plurality of individual minds (consciousnesses): collective self-consciousness.

What makes the past society and the existing society into society is their sharing a common "culture," i.e., the common collective self-consciousness that turns out to be a plurality of simultaneous and successive collective self-consciousness.

XL

In this backward glance over the course of such notions and intellectual impulses as I have received and developed over these six decades, I am cognizant of the fact that I can not cite any of my contemporaries and can cite only three elders who have left an imprint on me. These elders are Frank Knight, Robert Park and Michael Polanyi. I have dealt with these men previously. There have been coevals (more or less) with whom I have been very sympathetic, whose ideas I thought were very congenial to my own. These are Michael Oakeshott and, on at least two points—-on tradition and "World-3"—-Karl Popper. Raymond Aron was another; but he did not write on the subjects that were closest to my main interest (except on ideology where I agreed with him on nearly everything). He thought with a penetrating instinct; although had he not tarried to expiate on his observations of general or theoretical import, he would, I am confident, have concluded as much as I have concluded. His was a more decisive mind than mine; he did not ruminate; he came to conclusions swiftly on whatever he put his mind to.

None of my sociological coevals have given me any sustenance. I had much affection and appreciation for Talcott Parsons and, as in the case of Aron, we were almost always in agreement in our analyses; but his way of thinking was rather different from mine; and perhaps in his last fifteen years, after we finished our joint work, he went off in his procedural direction for which I had much less sympathy than I had for his more concrete insights. Robert Merton is a person of high intellectual integrity and devoted to the best standards of intellectual life. I appreciate the orderliness of his mind, the meticulousness of his scholarship, and the dignified gentlemanliness of his bearing; but he ordinarily does not deal with the same order of phenomena that I do. He has read a great deal and he has understood what he has read; but I do not think that his mind runs in fundamental directions in the way in which I have conceived of them. He has deliberately excluded himself from the fundamentals; he declared about forty years ago his determination to confine himself to "theories of the middle range" and he has adhered faithfully to that promise. I think that he had the imaginative power to reach more deeply than he had; but he has too great a sense of obligation to be explicit and precise. He would not be content with the standard of vagueness that I am willing to accept, not as anything definitive but as a step forward from where I was before. François Bourricaud was close to my own way of thinking. He, of course, knew a lot that I did not know, namely about Latin America. And in his last years and in his contribution to the *Dictionnaire critique de la sociologie* (edited with Raymond Boudon), I found him entirely congenial. Gary Runciman, I would class with Robert Merton rather than with François Bourricaud. He has a demand for clarity that I think neither his own insight nor the nature of the subject matter can satisfy; he is a man of the very first intelligence, but he makes the social world simpler than it is.

XLI

All that I have written seems to be very far apart from current sociological discussions in Western countries. The fact is that I do not see any affinity between my ideas and the ideas of any of my contemporaries who are making the running in sociology. Professor Louis Coser, in a review of one of my publications, began by saying that he had always "marched to a different drummer." I had never known that he marched at all, and I do not think that I marched to any drummer at all.

One thing that I would say to my partial credit is that I have never marched with anyone. It would have been better had Professor Coser said that he had always run with a different mob and that I did not run with any mob at all.

Although I have been teaching in universities in the United States and Europe, I have only twice been exclusively a member of a department of sociology, once at the London School of Economics and another time, very briefly, at the Catholic University of Leuven. In Cambridge, there was no department of sociology; in University College London, I was in the department of social anthropology. In Chicago I have been only marginally a member of the department of sociology. When Morris Janowitz was either chairman or a leading figure of the department, I took some part in its affairs, mostly at the behest of Morris Janowitz. I had no sense of intellectual or personal affinity with the members of the department, although I enjoyed the friendly amiability of Leo Goodman and later of James Coleman. I do not think that I ever engaged in serious intellectual discussion with any of the members of the department, not even with Janowitz, who was my protégé. I had got him started in his teaching at Chicago and I supported him in his progress through the university; but I thought that he had no intellectual center of gravity that I could detect. He was lively and vigorous, but his mind was distorted by jealousy and rivalry and he had nothing fine in his make up, moral or intellectual. He loved The University of Chicago and the department of sociology; he was a patriot, and he loved the United States Army, and that was a lot. It is a great pity that he lacked intellectual depth and, if I may say so, honesty. He added untruthfulness to rivalrousness and cruelty. That made him into a fairly useless interlocutor.

I could have talked with Edward Banfield; but he left The University of Chicago at the end of the 1950s. We did teach together on at least one occasion; and I found that his honesty and tough-mindedness made him a good person not only in general, but also in intellectual discussions. One could speak freely to him and what he returned was given with the intention of serving the truth, as John Rickman said once about our Saturday morning seminars at the Tavistock Institute in the second half of the 1940s.

In his old age, Frank Knight was cantankerous and very repetitive, although of undiminished acuity and seriousness. But even in his best times, when I gained from him more than I ever did from anyone else, I gained what I did by listening to him, catching fragments, cherishing them and meditating on them. Of course, being twenty-five years younger than he was, and lacking self-confidence, I could not engage in dialogue with him. With Robert Park, I could occasionally ask him a question; but for the most, I did best by being silent and listening to him as he meandered about intellectually. It is to him and to Frank Knight that I owe the stimulation that set me on the course described in this account. Neither of them could have foreseen where I was bound and I do not think that they would have accepted it with applause; but I do think that overcoming the barriers of words that were unknown to them, that they would have thought that I was a kindred spirit. I hope that that would be so.

My best discussions were with Joseph Ben-David because he was obstinate; and although polite, he did not aim to please by confirmation. I think that most of the persuasion usually ran from me to him rather the other way round. But he was not afraid to say what he thought, although he always did so very deferentially and courteously. Alas, in his last years he was ill much of the time and I could not impose on him with my ideas. He would have been an excellent anvil *cum* hammer for testing my ideas.

The other person with whom I have close intellectual affinity is Shmuel Eisenstadt, powerful and learned. He has been close to me for nearly half a century. He is perhaps one of the very few sociologists of eminence who has used some of my ideas in his work and he has done so in ways so fruitful that much of what external encouragement I had received has come from him. Yet in discussion, especially in recent years, he has sometimes seemed too ready to agree to what I say; but frequently he would say, "but the important question is under what condition." Sometimes I suspect a certain impatience that deference and affection will not permit him to articulate. I would add that he is not a worshipper at the altar of conceptual precision and clarity, and that is where I most need instruction.

Finally there is my young protégé Steven Grosby, who is the most forthright student, intelligent, intellectually curious and learned I have had since the two gentlemen mentioned immediately above. He puts some hard questions to me, but perhaps not as hard as would benefit them since we are so much in agreement.

All in all, I am fortunate to have had Ben-David and Eisenstadt at the beginning of my voyage and Grosby as I approach the end. But of those who are further afield, I gain nothing from them. How could I? They are for the most part crypto-Marxists or disappointed left-over Marxists. I refer particularly to Habermas. How could one engage in a discussion with a man who has hidden his convictions and who had done so for so long that he is unaware of doing so. He is a man who silently admired the Soviet Union, the real lineaments of which he sensed but would not acknowledge and all the while kept the affair entirely silent: an enemy of civil society and a utopian harmonist. How could one discuss with a man whose arguments are a facade for worse convictions. Of Giddens, I will say no more than that he is a very productive trifler who, having lost his Marxist faith, is a lost soul, always trying to turn something up, running after every fashion hoping to catch up with it. Of Habermas it could at least be said that he is very artful, so that political polemics appear to be incidental to serious heightened analysis; in fact, it is the other way around but his artfulness masks this. Of poor Giddens that cannot be said. Bourdieu is nothing except an accomplishment of diligence and publicity.

XLII

It is obvious that my intellectual career has not been a straight one. Although I have taught in many universities sometimes as a regular member of the staff and sometimes simply as a visiting professor, I have only twice been absent from The University of Chicago for more than a year. Except for these two absences, I have taught at the University of Chicago every year since 1938. For most of those years, I have taught three quarters every year; although since 1970, I have taught two quarters a year. It would appear that despite my travels (I have crossed the Atlantic Ocean about 400 times) I have been paradoxically sedentary!

My particular intellectual interests have been, at least externally, more heterogeneous than my career as a university teacher. Political sectarians, armies, social stratification, Roman history, Judaism in the Hellenistic age, revolutionary movements, intellectuals in all countries, Chinese political philosophy, universities—-the list is much longer, the variety much greater. But perhaps like my academic career, I have really been hovering about the same place. What appears to be the basic unity of my diverse intellectual interests and discoveries—-or re-discoveries—-could be an accident or it could be the results of a late effort to salvage the scraps of a random movement of intention. Neither of these interpretations is correct.

There is a genuine confluence, unity and continuity in my thought. The numerous, particular things I have studied were partly thrown into my field of attention by events outside my fundamental direction. The accident of the great depression, my becoming a social worker, my having to become familiar with many Negro families, my meeting Louis Wirth, my translation of Mannheim's books and my friendship with him, the Second World War and my closer contacts with German affairs, my contacts with Indians in London and the formation of the new states of Asia and Africa, the atomic bomb and my contacts with the physicists and chemists on the Metallurgical Project, the activities of Senator McCarthy, my long connections with India, and all the rest of the list, were not part of any plan. How could the great depression or the establishment of a distinguished university in a rough industrial city, the Second World War and the emancipation of the colonial societies of Asia and Africa have been foreseen in a plan? They all created situations upon which I had the opportunity to study and reflect. In each of these numerous and very diverse situations I saw things very different from what I saw in each of the others. The propositions or hypotheses or categories that took form in my mind were very diverse and far-flung. What I wrote about privacy was very different from what I wrote about armies, and these again were different from what I wrote on Indian intellectuals or about political demagogy or immigration or about French Jews. I have written on many subjects and I have on the whole not repeated myself. Yet, there is a signature on everything I have written after my trivial first writings as Louis Wirth's assistant (e.g., "urban education," "urban housing," "the literature of sociology"). I have really been chipping away on the same rock. The rock is a single problem.

What is that problem? It is the problem of all of classical sociological and political theory, namely, the nature and conditions of
consensus or of social solidarity, or loyalty. (Professor Parsons called
it "the problem of order," which is a broader phenomenon than consensus.) That was the problem that Tönnies, Max Weber, and
Durkheim touched upon, circumvented, or tried and failed to solve.
I have tried to do what they failed to do by working towards and
then concentrating on constituents of collective self-consciousness
that were touched on or neglected or passed over entirely or errone-
ously amalgamated with other things. I have done it by bringing
forward elements like primordiality, sacrality, centrality, peripherality,
the objectivity and autonomy of symbolic configurations, individual
self-transcendence and traditionality. I have done so apparently not
caring for the "systematic location" of the phenomena. I am well
aware that I took up each of the particular phenomena of the moment because it interested me as something significant itself. But I
also saw that my view of it was in affinity with my views on a number of other phenomena about which I had written. I did not try to
make my views on all these different subjects fit together into a single
scheme. I think that my friend Talcott Parsons did this incessantly;
all scraps of information had to be made to fit into the scheme. I
never tried to do this. I think that this case of Professor Parsons'
mind is what accounts for the impression of awkwardness, of observations being cast into boxes into which they did not fit.

Despite that, I became aware some years ago that there was a
thematic unity, a continuity and development, in the numerous dis-
crete problems about which I had written or wished to write.

I have accepted, as given, the fundamental elements of the Hob-
besian view, i.e., egoism, the capacity for reasoning, the niggardliness
of nature, conflict and coercion, and the fear of death. Every paper
or book I have written accepts those postulates. The question is:
How do collectivities cohere internally and maintain themselves under
internal strain and external demands and threats?

The things that preoccupy some of the more ambitious writers on
society in recent years, power, class, competition and conflict, and
the exercise of power and class conflict, inequality and revolution—
all these favorite topics of Marxists and neo-Marxists and crypto-
Marxists and persons who want to be Marxists although they no
longer believe in it—-are real things; but they are secondary or derivative from those with which I have been preoccupied. The same

may be said about "modernization" or the near nonsense into which that process has been reduced by conversion into "modernity," and then by wanton minds, into "post-modernity."

None of these things make sense. They cannot be adequately described and their causes cannot be understood without reference to primordiality, sacrality, centrality and peripherality, traditionality and the objectivity of the symbolic sphere.

These are the features of human society that have emerged before my mind in the course of long intellectual wanderings. I think that they were all there in implication, but hidden, from the very beginning. Until I wrote the foregoing pages, I have never scrutinized my various intellectual products to see how they were connected with each other. I was too busy to do this, too busy with writing other papers, working on books, reading on the subjects of the papers or the books, teaching and so on.

Nevertheless, when I began a few years ago to write about collective self-consciousness, I began to see that I had not been taking up one topic, finishing it, taking up another, repeating, then taking up and finishing it many times. I saw that the same theme as constantly reemerging, reemerging in a more complex form and making the preceding themes re-appear in contexts that extended them and brought them into relationship with each other.

I would be pleased with this outcome, the testimony of a steady intellectual character were I not so daunted by the need to continue with the task. Walt Whitman said, "Allons, the road is before us!"

Notes

1. *Movements of Knowledge* is the unfinished manuscript written by Shils during the last fifteen years of his life. It is discussed at length in the later sections of the *Autobiography*. Today, it is to be found in Shils' papers in The Regenstein Library of The University of Chicago.
2. For Shils' understanding of consensus, see "Consensus" in Edward Shils, *Center and Periphery—Essays in Macrosociology* (Chicago: The University of Chicago Press, 1975).
3. Reprinted in Edward Shils, *Portraits*, ed., Joseph Epstein (Chicago: University of Chicago Press, 1997).
4. Reprinted with the title "Power and Status" in *Center and Periphery*.
5. Reprinted in *Center and Periphery*.
6. "Cohesion and Disintegration in the Wehrmacht in World War II," reprinted in *Center and Periphery*.
7. Today in Shils' papers in the special collections department of The Regenstein Library.

8.   See below for Shils' discussion of this unpublished manuscript written by him.
9.   Reprinted in *Center and Periphery.*
10. *The Torment of Secrecy* is available in print, having been reissued by the publisher Ivan R. Dee in 1996, with a new introduction by Daniel P. Moynihan.
11. *Toward a General Theory of Action* was republished in 2001 by Transaction Publishers.
12. Reprinted in *Center and Periphery.*
13. Reprinted in Edward Shils, *The Intellectuals and the Powers* (Chicago: The University of Chicago Press, 1972) and Steven Grosby, ed., *The Virtue of Civility* (Indianapolis, IN: Liberty Press, 1997).
14. This over 800-page long manuscript is in Shils' papers in The Regenstein Library. Despite revising the manuscript many times, Shils never finished it. However, his ideas for his seminal papers during the 1950s and 1960s have their origin in this manuscript.
15. Reprinted in *Center and Periphery.*
16. Reprinted in *The Virtue of Civility.*
17. Reprinted in *Center and Periphery.*
18. The latter essay is reprinted in *Center and Periphery.*
19. *The Intellectuals and the Powers* (Chicago: The University of Chicago Press, 1972).
20. *The Intellectual Between Tradition and Modernity: The Indian Situation, Comparative Studies in Society and History,* Supplement I (The Hague: Mouton & Co, 1961).
21. Reprinted in *Center and Periphery.*
22. Reprinted in *Center and Periphery.*
23. Reprinted in *Center and Periphery.*
24. Reprinted in *Center and Periphery.*
25. Freyer's views were laid out in *The Theory of Objective Mind: An Introduction to the Philosophy of Culture* , edited and translated by Steven Grosby (Athens: Ohio University Press, 1998).
26. Edward Shils, *Tradition* (London: Faber & Faber, 1981).
27. *Movements of Knowledge* was the last major work undertaken by Shils, see the introduction to this book and note one above.
28. The essay appeared originally in Talcott Parsons and Edward Shils, eds., *Theories of Societies* (Glencoe, IL: The Free Press, 1961). However, a revised and longer version appears in the third volume of Shils' selected papers, *The Calling of Sociology* (Chicago: The University of Chicago Press, 1980). The careful reader will discover interesting differences between the two versions.
29. These essays appear in *The Virtue of Civility.*

Society, Collective Self-Consciousness and Collective Self-Consciousnesses

I

I intend to deal with a phenomenon with which neither Max Weber nor Emile Durkheim dealt explicitly, namely the constitution of society. In doing so, I shall draw upon certain ideas which they produced but which were not used by them to throw light on the character or constitution of societies. I shall concentrate my discussion on a subject they did not discus at all except by implication.

Professor Fredrich Tenbruck declares that Max Weber had no conception of society; he also asserts that there is no such thing. He is correct in the former statement; incorrect in the latter.

As far as Durkheim is concerned, he, like Weber, took the existence of society for granted. He spoke of types of societies and he directed attention to certain features of particular types of societies such as the division of labor and collective consciousness; but he did not have any explicit idea of society as *sui qeneris*.

I do not regard the constitution of society as tantamount to all the individuals, collectivities, strata, etc., existing within a territory, but rather as a phenomenon that comprises them in distinctive and coherent pattern. A society is a pattern or structure in the same way as that of a family or a party or a church. It has a coherence within boundaries just as do these institutions. One of my tasks here is to tell why societies cohere as societies, despite their large degree of internal differentiation into numerous strata and collectivities and despite the numerous and frequent conflicts among them.

I will begin by delineating the entity which I call society.

II

Society is a pattern of complex interactions of institutions within a division of labor extending over the various areas of a bounded territory; it is a site of a common market of goods and services as well as of numerous local and regional markets. It has a monetary system as part of the society wide market. It is the site of a national labor market, with internal migration between peripheries and centers. It has a distribution of possessions, powers and statuses. It has usually a central government with responsibility for laws that are valid throughout the society. (It might also have subordinate legal systems that enjoy a partial autonomy within the radius of their validity.) Finally, it has a collective self-consciousness of its own which has the society itself as its primary referent but which also has other constitutive properties such as nativity, territorial location, etc. as concurrent referents. This collective self-consciousness of society I will call the central or major collective self-consciousness. (This central collective self-consciousness coexists with numerous collective self-consciousnesses focused on or referring to their corresponding collectivities and aggregates and with individual self-consciousness almost as numerous as the living members of the society.)

The order of a society is a more or less stable recurrent pattern of coherence and consensus, hierarchy and equality and of variations in the direction of greater or less coherence, steeper or more gradual hierarchy, and of the concomitant variations in degrees of equality or inequality in the distribution of possessions, etc.

Coherence is the degree of interdependence of its various local and regional parts of the society within the bounded territory as compared with their degree of autonomy *vis-à-vis* each other. Consensus is the degree of participation of the population, within the boundaries of the territory, in the central (major) collective self-consciousness of the society. Hierarchy is the degree of inequality in the direction of the exercise of power or, to put it in opposite terms, the degree of unilaterality of power and authority.

The four categories of coherence, consensus, hierarchy and equality are useful for the description of the pattern of a society and changes in it. They may be seen as more differentiated manifestations of the relations between centers and peripheries. Centers are points—places, institutions, persons and ideals—about which coherence and consensus exist in variant forms or on which they are focused. The centers are the *loci* of the higher zones of the hierarchy that may be steep or gradual; they are the higher zones of the unequal distribution of income and health. Peripheries are the zones that lie at the outer limits of coherence and consensus; these peripheries are the objects of the power, authority and exemplariness or influence of the centers; they are the zones of the lower end of the unequal distribution of income and wealth.

Individuals and sectors of society are coherent with each other when they are interdependently engaged in exchanges with each other, and participate in a corresponding division of labor with each other; they are also coherent when they engage concertedly in a single task under the direction of authority. The coherence of a society does not mean its internal harmony. Coherence only refers to inclusion in a pattern of interaction, in this case, a society-wide pattern; its different parts might be in conflict with each other; but this is in reality possible only within some limits. Limits are phenomena of collective self-consciousness. The members of society are consensual when they participate in the central collective self-consciousness of the society. The consensus is never complete; there are too many competing collective self-consciousnesses to permit the attainment of such a condition; there is too much refusal to participate.

Even Marxists have had to recognize that the total dissolution of the central collective self-consciousness through class conflict, which they thought should in principle be universal throughout the length and breadth of society, never reached that condition. They acknowledged this by the self-serving term "false consciousness."

Consensus refers simply to the fact of agreement. Collective self-consciousness refers to the restraint on the scope of individual self-consciousness. Collective self-consciousness, too, is focused on a center that is central because of its power and its authority. Power refers to coercive capacity, the capacity to punish by ineluctable physical deprivation and constraint of those who refuse obedience to commands. Power as such does not in principle have anything to do with collective self-consciousness. Alongside of power at the center stands authority; authority is to a large extent sustained by the normative central collective self-consciousness that legitimates the commands and rules which issue from authority.

The collective self-consciousness is a pattern constituted by a plurality of minds oriented towards an image——of an objective symbolic configuration——of their own society and towards the individuals who participate in that objectivated symbolic configuration. The collective self-consciousness is oriented towards the image of the society, the members of which are in part constituted by their participation in that configuration. The collective self-consciousness is oriented towards the center of its society; and in doing so it is also oriented towards the transcendental center that legitimates the earthly center—-or denies its legitimacy. The transcendent center is a power—a deity or deities—or a body of norms inherent in the universe, for example, in nature disclosed by reason or revelation or some combination of them. The cognitive central collective self-consciousness contains accounts of the connections among the earthly centers and of the connection of the earthly and transcendental centers.

Hierarchy refers to the range of dispersion of the distribution of valued objects between the center and the peripheries as well as to the separateness of the center from the periphery; it refers to the degree of inaccessibility of the center to the desires, representations and interests of the periphery. No society is homogenous, not even a primordial society formed around a lineage or a kinship group and a narrow locality or village. A large society is inevitably heterogeneous, in spatial location, in the provenience of its members, in the distribution of wealth and income, in the distribution of deference, authority and power, in the extent of participation in the culture and language of the society and as well as in the degree of participation in the central collective self-consciousness.

All large societies exhibit combinations of consensus and dissensus among their individual members. In other words, individuals and aggregates of individuals and collectivities participate in unequal degrees in the central collective self-consciousness.

No center ever fully pervades and dominates its peripheries. No society-wide central collective self-consciousness is ever inclusive of all the members of society. It is unlikely to have equal or uniform participation by those who do participate in it. The divergent lines of attention and the diverse interests of individuals, collectivities, and strata ramify and truncate their participation in the central collective self-consciousness. They wish to realize their own individual interests and the interests of their sub-collectivities that are not represented in the central collective self-consciousness; they have no gratification in or do not care intensely about the valued objects of the central collective self-consciousness.

There are numerous collective self-consciousnesses in large, territorially extensive and differentiated societies. There, societies are differentiated by occupation, location, ideals, religious beliefs, historical memories, etc., and by the interests that are inherent in the situation of these aggregates and collectivities in the larger society. Each has its own collective self-consciousness.

Furthermore, the center is seldom entirely unitary. No ascendant center is entirely uncontested by counter- or rival centers. The ascendant center itself is internally differentiated by divergent interests and divergent emphases or interpretations of the ascendant central collective self-consciousness.

It should at the same time be said that the participation of any individual in the collective self-consciousness is often supported or reinforced by the action of that individual, when he acts from his individual self-consciousness and intends to maintain or enhance his own benefits. Collective self-consciousness is reinforced when the individual realizes his own individual ends through conformity with the rules, stipulations, or commands of the collective self-consciousness.

III

Central collective self-consciousness is, then, with ecological and economic interdependence through the division of labor, territorial boundaries, nativity and residence, the jurisdiction of power, authority and law and the distribution of income and wealth, a constitutive element in the ordered pattern of society.

Collective self-consciousness must now be analyzed in greater detail. But since collective self-consciousness is above all to be distinguished from individual self-consciousness, it will be helpful to say first what I mean by the latter. By individual self-consciousness I do not mean individual consciousness that is the consciousness within the individual about many things other than himself. Individual self-consciousness is nevertheless part of the individual's consciousness. It is his awareness of his own self, i.e., his own attainments, properties and dispositions; it includes his possession in his memory of his own actions and beliefs and of his experiences of the actions and judgments of others towards himself, and above all, his image of the interests, goals or objectives that he pursues with himself as the intended beneficiary of his own actions. An individual could not pursue his own interests if he did not have some consciousness of his own future condition as the beneficiary of the actions that he takes or intends to take on behalf of his interests.

The individual knows that he has a body separate from the bodies of others. When he thinks about future events, he often sees himself as a distinctive actor or participant in those events. He remembers his own experiences; of course, he remembers much else in addition to the things that have happened to him. His memory includes a great deal about things outside his own experiences. Memories are often faulty; experiences once recalled in memory fade from memory. Few, if any, individuals remember everything that happened to them; they sometimes attribute to themselves in recollection, experiences of events that happened to others. The fact that there are faults in the individual's recollections of his own experiences and his observations does not gainsay that individuals make a distinction between themselves and others. Only in rare and extreme cases does an individual cease to be aware that he is a separate organism, with memories of his experiences as a separate organism.

What is at issue is not the precision or the correctness of the image that the individual has of himself or whether his self-image is formed (as has sometimes been said) by the perception of the image that others have of him. The existence of individual self-consciousness is all that I wish to assert here; there is not likely to be much disagreement about this.

There are some important corollaries that are associated within individual self-consciousness. It means for one thing that an individual is capable of acting on his own behalf. He acts frequently to attain ends which entail benefits accruing to himself as he foresees himself in the proximate or remote future. The benefits that he seeks for himself are variegated. They include dermal, oral, gustatory, gastric states, states of sexual gratification, physical safety and physical well-being. They include the possession of property, the possession of wealth and income, the receipt of deference, the exercise of power and the receipt of love and solicitude, of protection of himself, etc. He acts to maintain or enhance his experience of these various physiological states and of the things that he receives through the actions of others; he acts to maintain or to increase the level of goods and services that he receives or obtains from others. The intended beneficiary recipient resulting from the attainment of the objective of actions performed by any particular individual is the individual himself in his future condition. Individual self-consciousness impels the individual to act to maintain or enhance the benefits of action with himself as their recipient. Actions to enhance his possessions of these valued states and objects are "self-interested" actions. Individual self-consciousness is the precondition of self-interested actions.

IV

Collective self-consciousness operates as a restraint on rational choice through its influence on individual self-consciousness. Collective self-consciousness can inhibit the rationality of choice because it prohibits self-benefiting actions under certain circumstances. A certain way of doing things might be rational but its rationality might not be the discovery of the individual actor even though he accepts and acts on the pattern presented to him through his participation in the collective self-consciousness of his collectivity. An actor might follow the path which is rational but which has been laid down by the tradition contained in the collective self-consciousness.

Certain ends might be laid down by membership in a collectivity and that membership is not rationally individually decided on. One becomes a member of the particular collectivity, not by any act of deliberation but by being born into it or by living within its locality or by entry into a particular occupation. An individual might become a member of a religious collectivity because he decided that the salvation is ultimately the most important objective in the world and that salvation could be acquired only through that membership in a particular church. But are these rational choices? They are rational choices if the choice of a church and ritual are rational means for the attainment of the end of salvation and if salvation is a rational means to the attainment of some other irreducibly valued end such as eternal bliss. The performance of ritual, the practice of prayer and the desire for salvation might be interpreted as rational means to an end but they are usually given as a result of participation in a collective self-consciousness and not usually deliberately or rationally chosen. Many ends, perhaps most ends, are given by the collective self-consciousness; certainly some are prohibited by collective self-consciousness.

The case of science—-the most rational of human activities—-provides an instructive example of the interplay between individual self-consciousness and collective self-consciousness. Scientific discovery is not the work of the collective self-consciousness. It is done by the individual, applying his own powers of observation and reasoning. He pursues a goal which, within certain limits, is his own decision; he pursues that goal which might be the testing of an hypotheses because he wishes to know and to have the gratification of knowing. His desire to be acclaimed as a discoverer, to be awarded some particular honor, or to be invited to fill a distinguished post, etc. might all add to the force of his motivation to discover whether the hypothesis he has formulated is true.

The objectivated symbolic configurations of scientific truth, its cognate rules for establishing truthfulness and the existing body of scientific knowledge is the one central referent of the scientists' collective self-consciousness. (This would have no significance for him if he were seeking rewards such as money and fame.) He orients himself towards other individual participants in the scientific collective consciousness with whom he forms a collectivity—-the scientific community—-to whose responses he is "responsive" because he recognizes that they, too, participate in the same scientific collective consciousness. They, too, are oriented towards the objectivated symbolic configurations of scientific truth, etc. and to him as a fellow participant in the same collective consciousness. The body of scientific knowledge is given, it is external to all the participants, it is the chief external referent—-objectivated symbolic configuration— of the scientific collective self-consciousness; the internal referents are the scientific community itself (or any particular specialized subdivision of it).

The participant scientist does not rationally choose his methods of research simply to gain individual gratification, monetary reward, social status, etc. He might well appreciate that the methods—-not the specific techniques used in his particular experiment—-are rational as means of testing hypotheses, but they are given to him as norms incumbent on him as a member of the scientific collective, i.e., the scientific community. If self-aggrandizement, increased monetary rewards, elevation of status, etc., were the objectives of the action of a scientist he ought to rationally discover certain "shortcuts" to spectacular results which would enhance his status. A few scientists—very few—use such "short cuts"; they break the rules which have been accepted and agreed that scientists should follow. These rules are rational rules; they can easily be justified rationally but they have acquired a nearly sacred quality. Adherence to them is a specification of the norms or obligations that are inherent in participation in the objectivated symbolic configurations of science, and by membership in the scientific community.

The example of the scientific community and the ways in which the individual self-consciousness of the individual scientist and the collective self-consciousness in which the individual scientist participates of which he is a part and which is a part of himself is useful. There are many other ways in which the individual and the collective self-consciousness interact, collide and conflict, coincide and reinforce each other.

V

It is appropriate to turn now to a consideration of the collective self-consciousness. This is not a notion that is easy to state very exactly. In its diverse versions it has long been dismissed. As the "group mind," it was laid to rest many years ago. As "collective consciousness," it has been viewed with skepticism and rejected. It has fallen into disregard as a "spook," as a metaphysical, empirically baseless conception. All this notwithstanding, it seems to me that it is indispensable. It is obvious that individuals act not only for themselves but also for others and for the collectivities of which they are members. Individuals know that they are individuals; they also know that they are parts of collectivities. Their use of the words "we," "us," "our" and "ours" is evidence of this. This too is obvious; its implications are less obvious. The existence and efficacy of collective self-consciousness should be acknowledged as necessary for the analysis of action by individuals on behalf of collectivities and other individuals. Innumerable problems are generated by the acknowledgement of the existence and efficacy of collective self-consciousness. Its constitution remains obscure, likewise the way in which it works.

By collective self-consciousness, I mean the awareness in the individual members of a collectivity of the existence of that collectivity as a trans-individual entity of which they and others are parts and that a corresponding belief is held by the others about other members of the collectivity including in certain cases themselves. I do not mean "collective consciousness" which is usually intended to refer to a belief or a set of beliefs possessed simultaneously by many individuals within a society. Collective consciousness is a frequently used term. (It is compatible with both methodological individualism and with substantive individualism.) Collective consciousness means only that all or most or many individual members of an aggregate or collectivity simultaneously hold certain cognitive and normative beliefs, about any particular topic or event or any class or cluster of topics or events.

The central collective self-consciousness is oriented towards an objective symbolic configuration in which the members participate as they would participate in a body of mathematical knowledge or of a body of historical knowledge or a body of theological beliefs. The mathematicians within a society and beyond the boundaries of society, the historians or the theologians are participants in their specialized, disciplinary collective self-consciousnesses. The collectivities are mathematical or historiographic or theological collectivities. Each of these has its own collective self-consciousness. The members of these collectivities, the participants, in their respective collective self-consciousnesses are also participants in many other collective self-consciousnesses.

Aristotle and Rousseau among others distinguished between small societies or states in which the members know each other and large ones in which they did not know each other. Practically all modern societies, even the smallest fall in the latter category.

Not many of the participants in a society-wide collective consciousness are concrete and particular individuals who are known personally by a large number of the participants in that collective self-consciousness. Most of participants in a collective self-consciousness are anonymous to most of the others. Most of the members of any large collectivity, which by definition is one in which most of the members do not know most of the other members, are unknown personally or concretely to most of the other members. They are, however, known as anonymous but through significant categories. They are significant because they have attributed to them properties such as residence in a common, bounded territory, nativity in that territory, speakers of a common language, subjects or citizens under a common body of laws enacted by that legitimate authority and intended to be and generally accepted as valid for all persons (or categories of persons) within the boundaries of that territory.

These individuals, very widely dispersed within the territory, are members of the same society, partly by the economic participation in a single society-wide division of labor and market for goods and services and labor, by intermarriage, by existence under a common authority and partly but equally important, by participation in the collective self-consciousness of the territorially bounded and extensive society.

When I use the word "participate," I do so with the specific intention of drawing notice to the phenomenon in the special sense used by Lévy-Bruhl. When Lucien Lévy-Bruhl spoke of the law of participation, he referred to the suspension or abrogation of the boundary between the individual acting subject and the physical, social and spiritual objects in which he stood in some relationship. "Participation" extends the idea of "sharing" to the point at which the individual acting subject and the objects of his attention and action become a single, unitary entity. The "participating" individual participates in his collectivity through the entry into his mind of the symbolic configurations presented by the traditions of his society and embodied in the actions and beliefs of his fellow countrymen. (I need not concern myself here with the validity of Lévy-Bruhl's assertion that thinking in accordance with the "law of participation" was characteristic of "primitive mentality"; he himself retracted that view towards the end of his life.)

When the object of that belief is the collectivity itself, of which those individuals are members, I would speak of collective self-consciousness. The word "self" refers both to the object of consciousness which is society and to the knowing or conscious acting individual subject. In collective self-consciousness the collectivity is both the knowing subject and the collectively known object.

What does it mean to say that the knowing subject is the collectivity? There is no physical locus in the collectivity, such as a brain or a neural system is in the individual, in which such collective consciousness can reside. When I say that collective self-consciousness exists, I also emphasize that it exists in the brains and neural system of the individuals who make up the collectivity. If that is so, then in what sense can we speak of the collectivity as a knowing subject knowing itself? The collective self-consciousness is an inter-individual structure of consciousness commonly aware of the membership in the collectivity.

If we look more closely at the phenomenon of "collective self-consciousness," we will see that there is more to it than simultaneity and widespreadness of the beliefs of many individuals in a single collectivity or outside it. In our usage of the term collective self-consciousness which acknowledges individual knowing subjects as the bearers of collective consciousness, the phenomenon of collective self-consciousness is not just the statistically frequent, more or less simultaneous acceptance of a belief by the numerous individual members of the aggregate or collectivity. There are important features of collective self-consciousness in addition to widespread and simultaneous acceptance of a given proposition. Mutual awareness is also entailed. The acceptance of the belief that is constitutive of collective consciousness is concurrent with consciousness that other members of the same collectivity also accept that belief and their acceptance of it is accompanied by the awareness that the others in their collectivity also accept it. Sometimes such a simultaneous plurality of a belief is referred to as a "shared" belief.

"Sharing" has pertinent connotations. It means that the object of the belief is not simply identical in each act of acceptance; it is a single object. It is an objectivated symbolic configuration that exists objectively outside the minds of the believers. The use of the terms "share" and "shared," which are very commonly used in the social sciences and in historical writings, accepts that there is an object which is shared. "Sharing" knowledge entails knowledge that others share the belief or knowledge about the same object. Once more it should be said that knowledge or belief has, for each of the knowers, an independent existence outside the knower. It implies that there is a "single" body of beliefs outside the believers that is available to be shared. The phenomenon or object that is shared, although having an external objective existence becomes internal to the collectivity through the widespread activity of believing or participation in it. The phenomenon of sharing should be added to widespreadness, simultaneity, and mutuality of awareness as features that have to be taken into account in our analysis of the beliefs that enter into the constitution of collective self-consciousness.

There are thus three major elements in collective self-consciousness. These are: (1) the knowing subjects; (2) the objects of knowledge or belief and the cognitive propositions and beliefs themselves about the objects; and (3) the knowledge, possessed by each—or rather most—of the knowing subjects in the collectivity of the other knowing subjects who constitute the collectivity.

Where the object of knowledge or belief is the society, we will speak of "collective self-consciousness." Where the object of belief is not the society, we will speak of "collective consciousness."

The knowing individual subjects know the object through the beliefs which each of them shares and they know that others in the collectivity accept or share that belief. I would call attention to the fact that the beliefs (cognitive and normative propositions) are not just states of mind of individuals. They are formed into an inter-individual, trans-individual pattern focused on certain objectivated symbolic configurations, such as the idea of "nation" or "nation-ality," "primordiality," "divinity," "class." The objectivated sym-bolic configurations used to be called "objective mind." Adapting the modern German terms (mainly those of Hans Freyer[1]), I have called them "symbolic objectivations" or "objectivated symbolic configurations." They are, what Karl Popper has called "World 3."[2]

I would like to say a little more about the lines of connection between (2) and (3) or the lines which connect the "idea" with the constitution of society. Individuals enter into or maintain a collec-tivity with other individuals when they see them as possessing certain relevant qualities. The qualities might be religious belief or membership in a religious community, political belief or member-ship in a political group, social status constituted by assessments of civil status, nationality, nativity, ethnicity, lineage, wealth, edu-cation, occupation, territorial location and provenience, etc. These qualities that may be possessed by individuals correspond to the ideas that are objectivated symbolic configurations. The percep-tion by a knowing subject of the former qualities in another hu-man being when it occurs, occurs simultaneously with recurrence to the idea—the abstract idea of which the quality perceived in an individual is a concrete instance or embodiment.

The perception of these properties in another person by a know-ing subject to whom these properties are significant maintains the collectivity or leads to the entry into it.

VI

That experience of being part of the collective self-consciousness is different from the individual's own self-consciousness. The indi-vidual perceives himself to be part of a trans-individual entity. He is part of "we"; this is different from his "I." The term "we" does not refer simply to a statistical aggregate. It refers to a whole of which the individual is a part. Yet, action as part of that "we" is action by an individual; but by an individual who is under the dominion of a collective self-consciousness is, by that token, under the dominion not of his own individual self-consciousness.

The collective self-consciousness is thus something that is largely "outside" each participating individual. By his participation in it, he is part of it. His participation in it has a corresponding precipitate within himself. Each individual member of a collectivity, insofar as he participates in the collective self-consciousness, has within himself, alongside his individual self-consciousness, his part or share of the collective self-consciousness. Usually, insofar as the individual has that part of the collective self-consciousness within him, his individual self-consciousness is confined and restricted. Usually, when he acts under the ascendancy of his participation in the collective self-consciousness, he is not acting as the individual guided by his individual self-consciousness but as a participant in the collectivity. Although he remains an individual, separate physiologically from other individuals, his own ends are not so prominent in his mind, he sees himself less as the acting subject. (He cannot escape completely from being an individual and having an individual self-consciousness because his organs—in this case, eyes—are part of his neurological organism.) In extreme cases, his image of himself as the acting subject and of himself as the beneficiary is greatly diminished. (It might even for a short time be almost entirely submerged. That is when the collective self-consciousness is at the height of the ascendancy.)

Thus far I have spoken only about some formal properties of collective self-consciousness *vis-à-vis* simultaneity, widespreadness, mutuality and sharing of a single objective symbolic configuration. I have said nothing about the subjective or experiential aspect, namely, what is meant by "participation in the collective self-consciousness." It is far more than apprehending or contemplating the "idea" of the society as an objectivated symbolic configuration; it is more than seeing in one's nearer environment individuals who possess in concrete form the properties possessed in abstract form by the idea and it is more than the awareness that other individuals have similar orientations towards the "idea" and towards the acting subject. Various writers in the past have written about the "fusion of selves," the "sense of 'we-ness,'" the "*Wir-Erlebnis*," the sense of "oneness," the transcendence of the individual and the formation of the collectivity. All these phrases are intended to describe what is entailed in the collective self-consciousness.

Now it is clear that there is no physical vessel for the collective self-consciousness such as there is for the individual self-consciousness. As I said earlier, the collective self-consciousness is an inter-individual phenomenon, a simultaneity of a plurality of persons with similar attachments to their society, sharing participation in the central objectivated symbolic configuration or "idea."

What happens to the individual self-consciousness under these conditions? It recedes. The individual remains; the consciousness of the individual remains but the self of the individual recedes and the part within the individual of the self that is a part of the collective self comes forward into great prominence and greater influence over the action of the individual. The individual self does not become completely inert except under extreme and relatively rare conditions. The individual nearly "forgets" that he is an individual; he is "possessed" by the collective self. He ceases to be conscious of himself or nearly so and acts almost entirely under the direction of the collective self. "We" suffuses his mind; he performs acts on behalf of, or under the influence of, the collectivity without rational calculation.

There are, in many other situations, a co-existence of the individual self-consciousness and the resident part of the collective consciousness. There is sometimes a tilt in one direction, sometimes a tilt in another direction. Sometimes the two selves are mutually complementary. Sometimes they are in conflict. And not infrequently the individual self-consciousness triumphs over the collective self-consciousness but seldom with a subsequent shift in the balance.

Just as the individual self-consciousness is scarcely ever wholly repressed and then for only short periods, so even when the individual self-consciousness seems to be in the ascendancy, it cannot remain without the considerable presence of the collective consciousness. An individual self-consciousness without the considerable presence of the collective consciousness would be without language. It would be without knowledge except for the small amount it could contrive for its own experience in its own lifetime. Its knowledge of technology would be negligible, consisting only of its inventions. In other words, the collective consciousness is ineluctable. The collective self-consciousness is perhaps more dispensable; but it, too, even in the most individualistic parts of society, cannot be suppressed. Every human being in order to survive for any length of time, and especially in infancy and childhood, cannot escape wholly from collective self-consciousness of one collectivity or another.

There are therefore usually two self-consciousnesses in the individual. One seems self evident, that is, the individual self-consciousness; the collective self-consciousness within the individual is more difficult to describe. It is a sort of state of possession by a power outside himself. We are not astonished when an individual is so absorbed in chess or mathematics that he cares for very little else. He has not ceased to be a neuro-physiological organism. He needs some food and some sleep; he might even have some vanity located in his individual self-consciousness, but his passion to live in chess or in mathematics, to envisage and to solve problems dominates everything else in his life. This being so in exceptional cases, with chess and mathematics, it should be easier for us to imagine a state of partial intermittent possession by the collective self-consciousness.

I know that this is no solution to a close analysis of selfhood, individual and collective. That urgently needs to be done.

The image or idea of society is a differentiated idea. An acting subject "places" another person or persons in his society in accordance with the criteria contained in the idea. A knowing subject might apply not only the criterion of nativity and territorial location; he might apply also criteria of lineage, status, education, etc. Hence the society is differentiated in its collective self-consciousness by its ecological, primordial and civil properties, etc. Not all of these properties are equally prominent in the central collective self-consciousness of the society. Territorial location and biological connections, e.g., nativity, are among the more important referents in the central collective self-consciousness of the society; other properties, place in the distribution of occupation, income, etc., might be more prominent in the peripheral collective self-consciousnesses within the society. The referent of territorial location defines who is to be included and who is to be excluded from the society. The territorial referent and derivative referents define the boundaries of the society. Activity in a single national market, a single national monetary system, a single national legal and governmental system, a single dominant or national language, a single nationality are further referents in the constitution of the collective self-consciousness. The collective self-consciousness unites and divides.

VII

The collective self-consciousness is a cognitive matter. The perception of the features or properties of each acting subject's own individual self and of the others who each faces or imagines are of great weight in the constitution of the collective self-consciousness. But the collective self-consciousness is not only a cognitive phenomenon. Participation in the collective self-consciousness generates the most fundamental norms which govern, in very general terms, the responses of members of the society to each other and to the members of other societies. The central collective self-consciousness is a source of the obligations which one member of the society has to the others. Of course, the norms in the general form emanating from the collective self-consciousness are not differentiated and specific enough to dominate the conduct of the members of society to each other. Participation in the central collective self-consciousness generates belief in the obligations of their members of society towards each other. These norms or obligations have to be and are further differentiated in legislation and the legal system, and particularly in the constitution. The central collective self-consciousness by its references to transcendental and earthly centers provide the legitimation which makes constitutions contain much more than that; they usually stipulate the pattern of governmental organization, but they also contain much regarding the rights and obligations of center and periphery that is drawn from the collective self-consciousness of society.

The elementary moral capacity of the human mind—the capacity to act in a self-transcendent way—is called forth by collective self-consciousness. It is the most elementary condition in which an individual human being transcends his own ends or desires and accepts the obligation to conform to a transcendent standard. The normativeness issues from the collective character of the knowing collective subject. The collective subject is accorded precedence over the individual as the beneficiary of the actions proposed or enjoined. It is in the nature of a collective self-consciousnesses to prescribe norms or rules which impose obligations on their participants *vis-à-vis* the other members of the collectivities which they help to constitute. Action as a participant in a particular collective self-consciousness entails renunciation of the objectives or desires of individual self-consciousness. The rules prescribe actions of which the collectivity is intended to be the beneficiary; these actions seek to protect or maintain the collectivity from damages arising from individual self-consciousness and from obligations to other collectivities. They invariably entail precedence for the ends or objectives of the particular collectivity over the objectives of other collectivities and individuals; they prescribe and proscribe certain kinds of actions. They require that actions towards members of their particular collectivity should be more beneficent than their actions towards persons who are not members of the collectivity.

Just as the actions originating in or guided by individual self-consciousness are intended to bring benefits to the individual actor, so actions originating in or guided by the collective self-consciousness are intended to bring benefits to the collectivity. The benefits are not exclusively benefits wrested from the environment or from external groups and individuals. They are also benefits of conformity internally with the norms of the collective self-consciousness itself. In many cases, the rules that prescribe the conduct of members of the collectivity within the collectivity maintain the collectivity, even though that is not necessarily the primary intention of the members in their actions towards each other. They act under the normative guidance or discipline of the collective self-consciousness of that collectivity. Familial collective self-consciousness demands actions that in the first instance maintain the family and confer benefits on it as a collectivity; ecclesiastical collective self-consciousness does the same for the church, etc.

Membership in the collectivity and participation in its collective self-consciousness impose the obligation to act on behalf of the collectivity against its external rivals. .

Each collectivity has one simple moral imperative that is the maintenance of the collectivity by adherence to its norms. The conflicts among the resultant moral imperatives of the different collective self-consciousnesses within the larger society generate the necessity of giving some moral imperatives precedence over others. Human beings often transcend their parochial collective self-consciousness in favor of a collective self-consciousness that stands higher, i.e., the norms of which are more imperative. By the exercise of their powers of ratiocination and imagination, the concrete demands impose by the imperative inherent in the collective self-consciousness are transcended on behalf of a moral universal ethic.

Moral philosophers seek to rationalize the plurality of moral imperatives. The moral imperatives of the collective self-consciousness are thought to be closer to sacrality and are accorded the highest precedence. Transcendence takes precedence over parochiality.

Within each collectivity, rules are assessed for their conformity or consistency with the higher moral imperative. The higher rules legitimate those that are derivative from them. Where there are intellectual and institutional procedures for making and asserting rules, these too must conform with the highest imperative. Their legitimacy lies in their conformity or consistency with the imperative. The requirement of legitimacy is a constitutive fact of collective self-consciousness. It is the precondition of the fundamental choice between "I" and "us," and between "we" and "them."

There are usually many collective self-consciousnesses in any large society. They coexist with the central collective self-consciousness. They may be at times in conflict with each other; but they can also coexist without utter and complete incompatibility. Thus, "class consciousness" can be more or less pervasive in large parts of the society; but this does not necessarily annul or extinguish the national or central self-consciousness. This is also true of other internally differentiating collective self-consciousnesses. The collective self-consciousness of occupational and professional collectivities, local and regional collectivities, familial and lineage collectivities, can coexist alongside each other, cutting across each other and even be in conflict with each other within the central collective self-consciousness of the national society. These reconciliations do not always occur. Some conflicts between collective self-consciousness are more readily assuaged than others.

Durkheim spoke of the affirmation of society that is necessarily entailed in the sacredness of the society itself. He did not attempt to proceed from this observation to an analysis of the relation of sacrality to the legitimacy of laws, rules and commands. Max Weber spoke of the legitimacy of the three main types of authority; but he did not, except fleetingly and infrequently, refer to the sacredness that underlies legitimacy. He did however, in several places, indicate that there was an ultimately sacred or charismatic part of the foundation of the rational-legal and traditional types of legitimate authority. At this point, Weber's and Durkheim's views implicitly complement each other. Some of these patterns of the relationship between individual and self- consciousness and collective self-consciousness were what Tönnies had in mind when he wrote about *Gemeinschaft* and *Gesellschaft* and emphasized the preponderance of the collectivity over the individual. It is what Henry Sumner Maine referred to when he wrote of "status and contract," meaning by "status," the ascendancy of role and participation in a collective self-consciousness in a collectivity over the individual as an independent actor with ends of his own. It was what Charles Cooley was discussing in his discussion of primary groups and the "fusion" of selves; it is what Robert Park in his discussion of "collective behavior" referred to when he distinguished the "crowd" from the "public." Max Scheler also deals with forms of the transcendence of the individual self into a collective self-consciousness and a cosmic self-consciousness. Psychoanalytic theory in its treatment of "identification" and the "super-ego" and the power of the super-ego on the action of the "ego" and the "id" was speaking about the same phenomenon. They were, in a variety of idioms, all discussing the ascendancy of the collective self-consciousness.

Georg Simmel and Émile Durkheim and those who follow them, in writing about modern societies, and in emphasizing the prominence of individualism, and later writers in discussing the disintegration of community, "mass society," and the "atomization" of the individual, touched on the reverse side of the phenomenon that I have been discussing here. They have dealt mainly with the recession of collective self-consciousness.

I am not in a position to say anything significant about how the collective self-consciousness works on an individual's individual self-consciousness so that he renounces objectives of gaining benefits for himself and gives precedence to objectives beneficial to the collectivity. It is difficult to find a language that is not metaphorical to describe the fundamental process of moral judgment and moral action. Physical, legal, and military metaphors are not uncommon in the accounts of the process of shifting ascendancy from the individual self-consciousness to the ascendancy of his share in the collective self-consciousness (and *vice-versa*). If the process were one of ratiocination, it would be easier to describe. Ordinarily, it is very little a matter of ratiocination. Nor is in a matter of affect. It is a phenomenon of the balance of the boundaries of the self, of what is included in the self or in the definition of the self. The constitution of the self is not one in which there is a helpful tradition of analysis.

It must be admitted that this is the weakest link in the analysis that I present here. Nevertheless, there can be no doubt about the fact that individuals are often—and not just illusiorily—participants in collective self-consciousnesses and that they act often on the basis of that participation. This is one of the most obvious facts of life.

The collective self-consciousness focuses on those properties or features of individuals which cause them to be seen as fellow-members of the individual's own collectivity, or which by their absence cause them to be seen as non-members of those collectivities. These features or properties I call the "referents" of collective self-consciousness. Kinship and lineage, ethnicity and ethnic connections, locality or residence, generations or age, nationality and territory of nativity and residence, occupation, skills, and status, income and wealth, power and authority, capacity to provide goods and services, religious beliefs and sacral qualities, knowledge and achievement, institutional connections, temperamental or affective qualities, moral qualities, etc., are among those properties.

Collectivities can be formed around any of these referents; but the most enduring collectivities in society (and those that arouse the most passion) are those formed around referents to the vital powers that affect the lives of individuals and societies. It is not the objects of reference that form collectivities directly by their own factual or empirical existence. It is rather their becoming the objects or referents of the collective consciousness. It is not the physical facts of kinship or blood ties or lineage or locality which form collectivities; it is only through their being taken up as referents of the collective self-consciousness that these primordial properties or qualities form a *Gemeinschaft*.

Tönnies failed to make this distinction between the primordial properties as such and the reference to them in the collective self-consciousness of the *Gemeinschaft*. It is only when they become referents of the collective consciousness that collective self-consciousness and hence collectivities around them are formed. Marxists were wrong to think that it was the hard fact of "position in the relations of production" which forms a class with a collective self-consciousness—"class consciousness." It is the reference to "class position" which forms a collectivity—a class—in the collective self-consciousness of the incumbent of those positions in the relations of production with its distinctive collective ("class" self-consciousness).

Likewise it is not pigmentation or physique or ancestry which forms a "race" or an ethnic group; it is rather its being a referent in the collective self-consciousness in consequence of which other persons who possess or are thought or seem to possess those qualities of pigmentation, or physique or type of ancestry that racial or ethnic collectivities are thereby formed.

Collective self-consciousnesses and hence collectivities are also formed about "interests." Some might be collectivities in which individuals come together and cooperate with each other, each acting only for the realization of his own individual ends. The collectivity for each of these individuals is entirely and solely a rational means for the attainment of benefits for himself that he could not otherwise obtain. Many collectivities that are formed about the interests of individuals also acquire a collective self-consciousness that often restrict the actions which could emerge from the individual's self-consciousness. (The solidarity of the members of a trade union is often of this sort. It is not just a consequence of the insight that each individual gains from conformity with the demands of the other members of the union; they are brought into "solidarity" with each other through their collective self-consciousness.)

A collective self-consciousness can contain plurality of referents at the same time. A national collective self-consciousness might be sustained at the same time by a racial and ethnic referent. The predominant referents might vary from one sector of the society to another and from one period within a given society to another period. The reference to status might be very pronounced or prominent in some societies and in some sections of a given society, but not in other societies or in some sectors of a particular society. Likewise religious or ecclesiastical collective self-consciousness might be prominent in one sector of a society but weak in others.

VIII

The legitimacy of any collectivity in the mind of its own members and the commands, rules, or laws asserted in its name flow ultimately from its ostensible proximity to or conformity with the transcendental (or charismatic or sacred) source of legitimacy. The transcendental source of legitimacy lies usually outside any existing institution. It was Durkheim's view that society itself is sacred; he regarded this sacredness as ultimate. It is my view that society, where it is regarded or accepted as sacred by its members, usually is so regarded or accepted because its participants regard it as in conformity with a sacred power which lies outside of, or which transcends, earthly existence.

Transcendental powers are not only transcendent; they also enter integrally into human societies. Transcendental powers exist of course within human societies. (In some cases, they might be thought to lie entirely with human societies, as Durkheim thought.) They lie in society as a whole or in particular institutions; they enter into every level of human society down to its individual members. It is in the nature of the mind to seek to connect itself with the transcendental realm, to legitimate itself, to give evidence of its worthiness or dignity. The completion (or "closure") sought by many human beings is conformity with or derivation from a norm in which sacrality is embodied.

Much of the ordering of human society is to be accounted for by the consensus of the central collective self-consciousness and the component collective self-consciousnesses about the relative superiority of rules that are thought to contain (or to be imbued with or to embody) a transcendental sacred element.

This does not gainsay that something like immanent sacrality is possible; it does indeed exist, although at first glance, it seems paradoxical. Wherever there is a high concentration of power to affect human life, there is a spontaneous tendency of those subject to it and those who exercise it to see that tremendous power as a locus of sacrality. Power, the power to coerce, has, when it is sufficiently effective, a tendency towards the generation of its own legitimacy. When it is reinforced by the sacrality that underlies legitimate authority, it is especially imposing on those over whom it is exercised. There are contrary tendencies at work, too. Great concentrations of power, like a very demanding collective self-consciousness, also arouse antinomian dispositions.

It was wrong of Durkheim to fail to see that human beings have really believed in the existence of deities who enunciate or exemplify commandments or norms. He was right in seeing that it is the power of society which gives rise to the attribution of sacredness to it. But he was wrong to be unwilling to accredit the belief among human beings that there are powers which transcend human existence, which are beyond society but which also enter into it, and into the rules which they lay down or which human minds derive from those powers (i.e., from the powers located in the transcendental realm).

This was a severe deficiency in Durkheim's understanding both of religion and of society. This is a point where Max Weber was much superior to Durkheim. He saw, in a much more profound way than did W.I. Thomas, that "if human beings define situations as real, they are real in their consequences." Weber saw the capacity of the human imagination to apprehend the transcendental sacred powers. Since Durkheim thought that the human mind was astray from truth when it conceived of the transcendental realm, why was he unwilling to believe that the views of divine powers, even if wrong, could be taken seriously? He was unfaithful to his own idea of seriousness (*la vie serieuse*). Of course, he was no less wrong when he derived the categories for understanding the universe from the simple and direct experience of the spatial configurations of the local settlement.

Durkheim himself imagined things which were not imagined by other scholars before him and which were not just "reflections" of the spatial pattern of society in which he lived. Why did he confine the imagination of the human race to the interpretation of its own immediate, local experiences?

In a more favorable interpretation of Durkheim's views on this matter, it could be said that he conceived only societies in which the charismatic power was immanent in society. He did not think that there could be societies in which the sacred was not immanent but was believed to be transcendent.

IX

Collective self-consciousness, in its usual usage, implies homogeneity. I think that this is correct, but not entirely correct. It implies homogeneity, insofar as membership in a collectivity implies the homogeneity of the quality of membership as such. But the members of a collectivity, beyond the most elementary fact of their bare membership, are not uniform. Societies, particularly large societies, have a very pronounced tendency towards internal differentiations; these differences arise partly from the division of labor from inequalities in the distribution of rewards, from ethnic heterogeneity of other diversity of proveniences, etc. They are not only different among themselves but they are also capable of seeing the differences among themselves.

The collective self-consciousness of a primordial collectivity, like a family or a kinship group or a lineage, contains within itself the awareness of the diversity of statuses of the members. Externally they may be thought to be homogenous and part of the whole so that one can be taken as representative of the entire collectivity, as for example, in the attribution of collective responsibility for the commission of a criminal action. A representative is imagined as acting for the whole. There can be a high degree of solidarity—not merely the mutual attachment of individuals to each other—among persons who are, nevertheless, very different from each other.

The internal heterogeneity of the membership of a collectivity can in part be accounted for by the coexistence in the same population of a multiplicity of collective self-consciousnesses. Even within a population which participates in a particular collective self-consciousness, and which is bound together by the attachment to that collectivity and hence to its individual members simply in their capacity as members, there are various collective self-consciousnesses. The latter collective self-consciousnesses might variously be in conflict with each other or they might be indifferent towards each other, within the context of a single, society-wide, central collective self-consciousness.

Simmel, in *Die Kreuzung sozialer Kreise*, discussed the closely related phenomenon of the multiple memberships of individuals in a plurality of collectivities. He spoke about the internal tensions of individuals who experience such multiple memberships; but, as I recall, he did not deal with the phenomenon in quite the way I attempt to do here. Simmel approached the phenomenon from an individualistic standpoint; he saw multiple memberships in the experience of individuals and in the patterns of face-to-face interaction. But what he touched upon has profound implications for the understanding of the cohesion of whole societies. Because he was not interested primarily in whole societies— rather in parts of society— he did not attend to the problem of the relationship between parochial or sectoral collective self-consciousness and the central collective self-consciousness of the whole society. That is the problem that I wish to explore.

It is common to observe that there are such phenomena as "conflicting loyalties," "conflicts of interest," etc. The emphasis is usually laid on the "conflicts" between the "loyalties" or "interests," not on the solidarities within each component collectivity in the conflict or the simultaneous participation of the conflict of individual or classes of individuals in the central collective self-consciousness. There could not, it is obvious, be a conflict of loyalties if there were not loyalty to begin with; and this being so, there are situations in which the loyalties coexist without being in conflict. Must the conflict necessarily reach resolution by the rupture of the attachment to one of the collectivities and re-affirmation of attachment to the other? Can they not coexist without culminating in a rupture?

Where the conflicts are between divergent interests of the same individual(s), let us say increasing one's income through private business activities while at the same time maintaining the security of tenure in a professorial post, cannot the conflict be contained by absenting oneself from the university as much as the loose terms of the contract of appointment permit but not to the point where the breach of contract would become scandalous? Why should it be any different in matters of conflicts of loyalties of individuals to their respective collectivities?

The question really can be reduced to the question of how individual self-consciousness and collective self-consciousness can co-exist in the same individual. We do not know much about the details of their coexistence within the mind of an individual; but we know, at the crudest levels of observation of others and oneself, that they do coexist and that sometimes one gains ascendancy over the other. We also know that many individuals maintain a bearable balance between their two kinds of self-consciousness. They develop certain conventions—consistent with a wider social convention—as to when it is reasonable to grant ascendancy to one and when it is reasonable or appropriate to grant ascendancy to the other. There are conventions in society, very vague ones, it is true, about how much to give to oneself, and how much to give to one or another collectivity or to the inclusive collectivity or society. These conventions sometimes have sanctions attached to them, where the breaches are very obvious and very extreme—usually in the direction of gratifying the demands of individual self-consciousness.

Why then cannot the society-wide central collective self-consciousness be co-existent with parochial collective self-consciousnesses? There are, it is true, situations in which their coexistence might turn into conflict between them. Collective class self-consciousness or ethnic collective self-consciousness might come into acute conflict with the central collective self-consciousness of the national society; on the other hand, it might become attenuated in the face of a heightened central collective self-consciousness.

It is obvious that various kinds of self-consciousness, collective and individual, can and do coexist. It is also obvious that there is some degree of society-wide or central collective self-consciousness. Society is not simply an ecological fact, or of a society-wide division of labor and a society-wide market, or a fiction of nationalistic doctrine. Society is not only ecological or territorial, it is not just an "internal market" within the legally defined boundaries of the political entity. It is also an object of collective self-consciousness. It is an object of collective self-consciousness that is created partly by its existence as an object of collective self-consciousness!

Does the society-wide central collective self-consciousness have an intense and continuous operation? It probably operates intermittently and at very varying degrees of intensity. It is a real task to discern how it remains effective in its half-life and just how it comes forward and takes precedence or recedes in the face of the demandingness or readiness to yield of the other coexistent sectoral collective self-consciousnesses or to the interests or ideals of individual self-consciousnesses.

The collective self-consciousness permits inequality of status of those who participate in it, just as it allows inequality of power and authority. It permits a picture of society as heterogeneous and a picture of the knowing subject as the incumbent of one of those roles or as a member specifically located in one of those diverse parts.

It is this differentiating property of the collective self-consciousness that permits the functioning of centers and peripheries. Centers might exist simply in consequence of differences in the power to elicit, coercively, obedience to commands. They might exist simply in consequence of the economic advantage of certain places that attract settlers as a result of the economic opportunities they offer. Centers could exist even if they were not the most convenient or profitable markets. They could exist simply by being the loci of courts, luxury, and the pomp of power and authority.

X

I would like to conclude with some reflections on the bearing of what I have said thus far on the understanding of modern societies. How does what I have said apply to the analysis of far-reachingly "secular" societies in which sacredness in general and the sacred element in the society-wide collective self-consciousness has evaporated and in which there is a powerful trend toward a very high degree of individualism? The answer is that modern societies are not as secularized as is often made out. Very large parts of the population of modern "secular" societies still believe in the reality of the transcendental realm and of the divine power that is thought to reside there. The large numbers of Christian and Jewish believers, the proliferation of sects and of fundamentalist religious movements in contemporary Western societies testify both to the readiness of many to affirm the Christian and Jewish traditions and to the unwillingness of many persons who have departed from the traditional churches to accept a strictly secular—unsacral—conception of the world and of society. To assert that these beliefs are archaic traditions, that they are the remnants, unthinkingly espoused, of traditional beliefs about the transcendental realm is to misunderstand the nature of tradition.

It is certainly true that many persons accept prevailing traditions uncritically. But that does not mean that they do not believe them to be true. Perhaps if they were to think about them critically, they would cease to believe them. Since, however, they do not assess their beliefs critically, they do think them to be true.

Traditions do not simply "live on." They live on because human beings believe them to contain what is true about the world or some small part of it. The human mind does not generally believe what it thinks is untrue. The task of students of society requires that they recognize that truth is important to human beings, even those alleged truths are not such as the students of society believe to be true.

Feuerbach thought the religious beliefs are fictions that are engendered by the unintelligibility of events of this world. But even if this world were intelligible to the minds of sociologists, which is not by any means wholly the case, would all existence, the existence of the cosmos and the place of human beings in it be completely and exhaustively intelligible? There are scientists who believe that the secret of life has been opened and dispelled by the discoveries made in recent years in molecular biology. Even if this were so, which is not at all likely, much of the human race knows little about molecular biology.

Human minds are different from each other, just as human bodies differ. There is no ground for believing that anyone who has been sufficiently trained and coached can become a great basketball player or a great sprinter or long distance runner. Similarly, there is no ground for believing that anyone, if sufficiently educated and disciplined, could become a great mathematician or a great logician or a great astrophysicist. It is in contemplation of these differences that I emphasize that sensibility to the sacred is also unequally distributed among all the adult members of any society. If the imaginative powers that permit the discovery, or the imagination, of the sacred were equally distributed, there would be no charismatic individuals, no prophets, no founders of the great world religions. The fact is that some human beings have had this charismatic gift, and it is possible that others will have it in the future, while others have it and will continue to have it to a smaller extent. Many others have only the capacity to appreciate or to respond to it in others or to attribute it to others, and finally there are many who not only do not have this gift but who do not recognize it when it is in their presence.

The realm of the sacred and the idea of the sacred belong to the category of objectivated symbolic configurations. They exist outside the individual mind; and individuals participate in them very unequally. Nor is the participation equally stable in all those who do participate in them. What is evident as sacred in some circumstances is not so evident in others. Charisma, as Max Weber pointed out, is unstable. Correspondingly, the need for it is also unstable.

There are therefore marked variations in society between sectors of the population and at various times in the evidentness of the sacrality of rules, commands, and institutions. Probably at no time in human history has any society ever been wholly saturated by participation in the sacral referent of the collective self-consciousness.

At the other pole from the sacred is the profane or more precisely, the secular—the sphere in which all objects are earthly states, conditions and things, in which all objectives are earthly objectives, and in which all norms and rules are matters of earthly convenience and convention and in which it is thought that all actions are matters of visible cause and effect. If we can imagine actions which are not in any way affected by collective self-consciousness, and in which individual (self-) consciousness is the sole source of initiated actions and of responses to the actions of others and in which conditions referred to in the just preceding sentence obtain, then there would be a wholly secular sphere of society. The economic sphere—and particularly the market—corresponds most closely to this pattern of action in society. This is the sphere of rational purposeful action. This is the sphere that is most rationalizable. The other spheres of society are less amenable to this interpretation. But, in fact, even the economic sphere, when it ceases to be coterminous with the market, is permeated by the effects of collective self-consciousness. Even the market is penetrated and hedged about by the repercussions of collective self-consciousness, manifested in the actions of government and the moral restraints and discipline of the participants in its transactions.

Modern and, above all, American society is marked by a very strong tendency towards individualism, and towards antinomianism which goes much further towards emancipation from authority and from cultural and moral traditions. Nevertheless, emancipationist and individualistic orientation still do not prevail throughout the length and breadth of American society, and even less, those other societies of Western and Eastern Europe or the great societies and civilizations of Asia, to say nothing of African societies.

There are numerous, very strong primordial attachments in modern societies. In the United States, there are strong ethnic and racial attachments—and the collective self-consciousnesses with very prominent racial and ethnic referents. Nationality remains a very powerful collective self-consciousness. We need here refer only in passing to the reunification of Germany, to say nothing of the strength of Jewish primordiality which is different from Jewish religious belief. In black Africa, primordiality of lineage, locality, region, tribe or nation is so prominent that it cannot be disregarded even by those who think that primordiality has disappeared from the collective self-consciousness. In other words, collective self-consciousness, not only primordial collective self-consciousness, but religious and national collective self-consciousness are very strong.

These numerous kinds of collective self-consciousnesses are very strong in contemporary societies. But what about the society-wide primordial collective self-consciousness? That sometimes seems to be very faint. Nevertheless, it is there and very strongly, too. Patriotism seems to have a very low status—especially in the minds of intellectuals but it remains very strong. Let me refer only to the reaction against the burning of the American flag in which the Supreme Court has declared itself not very long ago. The fact that the Supreme Court decided as it did testifies to an anti-patriotic belief in the American people; but we must also take notice of the very widespread and negative response to that belief.

There has been in recent years a revival of the idea of civil society, not just among Eastern-European intellectuals although they are the ones who write about it. The demand for a civil society in Eastern Europe, the demand for it in China, to say nothing of the great civil rights movement among American blacks which testifies to their desire to become "full citizens" of American society, show that modern societies not only have a place for various kinds of collective self-consciousnesses but that a central collective self-consciousness with its correspondent civil society still lives on in great vigor.

Notes

1.   See Hans Freyer, Theory of Objected Mind, trans. and ed. by Steven Grosby (Athens: University of Ohio Press, 1998).
2.   See Karl Popper, Objective Knowledge (Oxford: Oxford University Press, 1972).

Collective Self-Consciousness
and Rational Choice

A Note to the Reader

It is not my intention here to present my analysis of what I tentatively call "collective self-consciousness" as a refutation of *The Foundations of Social Theory* or as an alternative to it.[1] It is rather intended as a complement to it.

There is certainly much validity in the theory of "rational choice." It stands in an illustrious tradition of sociological analysis, an analysis in which most of the leading authors of the nineteenth and twentieth centuries have participated. *The Foundations of Social Theory* carries part of this tradition forward with unprecedented rigor. Its limitation lies however in its excessive inclusiveness and its disregard for what it is unable to include.

In what follows, I do not wish to give the impression of "refuting" or "replacing" *The Foundations of Social Theory*. I wish only to right the balance by bringing forward certain fundamental features of society that cannot be disregarded if we wish to understand why things are as they are.

The difference between the points of view implied by the two terms may be reduced to differences in the conceptions of certain features of the minds of individuals. The theory of rational choice conceives of the individual mind—hence forward to be called "the subject" or "the acting subject"—as focused primarily on perceiving the "interests" of the subject and on the assessment of the consequence of different arrangements for the fulfillment of those interests. The subject is moreover capable of calculating the costs and benefits of the different arrangements and then of rationally arranging his actions according to the criteria of maximal benefits and minimal costs.

I

The concept of interests is a complex one. It entails a prediction of advantages that are situated in certain determinate conditions. The interests are embedded in the conditions. The acting subject can act to realize them or he can disregard them by not acting in a way that realizes them. The interests are not a matter of choice. The only choice available to the individual is to act to realize them or to act against their realization. To disregard them is irrational. It is rational to seek to realize them. But the actions to realize them may be rational or irrational; rational action will realize them.

The following statements illustrate this definition: (1) "It is to my interests;" (2) "his interests lie in such and such"; (3) "the interests of the working class lie in a restriction of entry of foreign labor" (a future situation will be beneficial to the working class); (4)"there is a permanent clash of interests between working class and employers, between Canada and the United States, between Germany and Russia" (situations which are advantageous to the one will be disadvantageous to the other); (5) "he does not know his own interests" (he does not perceive or predict the situation which will be beneficial to him).

All of these usages imply that interests or interest situations— Max Weber spoke of *Interessenlage*—exist quite apart from the knowledge or desire of the acting subject; interests are a predetermined set of objects (advantages or benefits) which will exist in the future situations and which the individual or collectivity will have. The advantages corresponding to interests are self-evident; neither choice nor evaluation are part of this process.

The concept of interests is a predictive one. It asserts that certain advantages will accrue if certain causally efficacious actions are undertaken. It is a statement of the enduring and permanent distribution of scarce values, i.e., values for which the conflicting demands are inherent in the situation; the supply is fixed and there is a right way and wrong way to go about realizing the interests.

According to the theory of rational choice, the individual's actions are guided by his perception of his interests, i.e., his perception of the possibility or likelihood. His interests are combinations of his perceptions of the consequences for him of various courses of actions by others (including the attachments of these others to objects which they value and which are determinately distributed in accordance with their scarcity and the determinate actions and attachments of others to the same scarce objects). Interests are combinations of desires (i.e., desires for valued objects), norms of what is to be desired, and predictions regarding the consequences of the actions of the individual and of others for the individual's acquisition of those valued objects.

The theory of rational choice postulates that the desires of the individual for valued objects are desires for his own gratification or for his receipt of those valued objects. The beneficiary of actions taken for the realization (or satisfaction) of interests is the acting individual. The interest of the individual is the realization of a maximum of his own gratification.

Why does the individual think only of his own gratification as the right end of his actions? Why does he not think of the gratification of the ends of others? Why is his interest always defined as the enhancement of his own gratification, with the gratification of the interest of others being thought of only as a causal precondition for the realization of his own ends (i.e., the end of his own gratification)?

The whole collectivity can be affected by an action from within or outside; the whole collectivity can be a "participant." But can the whole collectivity be an actor? Only the individual participants in the collective self-consciousness can act as members of the collectivity; they act under the normative guidance that they receive as participants of their collective self-consciousness. They may act as "representatives" of the collectivity, by deliberate delegation or from an unspoken consensus that they should do so. They may be accepted as the legitimate interpreters of the ideas and norms of the collectivity or they might be chosen to do so by deliberate delegation or election. Representatives become the "bearers" of the collective self-consciousness, i.e., they have attributed to them or they can also claim responsibility for the maintenance and ideals of the collectivity and for the fulfillment of the interests of the individual members of the collectivity.

Representation may, hypothetically, be regarded as a condition in which the collective self-consciousness, shared by most of the members of the collectivity enters into and is expressed by the representatives. I know this sounds excessively Rousseauistic; but I think that it ought to be regarded as a real phenomenon. It is in fact no more than an extension of the elementary idea of shared collective self-consciousness of two individuals who use the word "we."

There can thus be a concerted action by a collectivity. It can be concerted fundamentally by the norms of the collective self-consciousness or it can be concerted by the deliberation of each individual in consultation with the others, each individual bearing in mind the increase in the benefits that he will receive as an individual from the concerted actions of the individual fellow-members.

There is a normative element in the concept of interest. The concept of interest asserts the determinative power of fundamental arrangements available for the individual's groups or classes which pursue them in accordance with the appropriate procedures which include rational calculation, self-adaptation, collaboration, manipulation and combativeness or even violence. Despite its "factuality," there is also something normative in the idea of interest. There is an overtone that more should be desired by one party or the other in the competition or conflict for advantages. "His own interests are to obtain more"; "that he does not want more is wrong because such a lack of desire is contrary to his real interests." In short, interests are given; the individual or the group should act in accordance with them. Failure to do so on the part of the "working class," is according to Marxism, a consequence of "false consciousness." ("False consciousness" is ordinarily regarded as a consequence of the manipulative intentions of the ruling class. Marxism did not concern itself with the "false consciousness" of individuals apart from their "responsibilities" as members of their class.)

Interests are almost invariably about wealth, income, power, to some extent, status and opportunities to increase the amount of such benefits. Ethical considerations are not, in principle, to be considered as factors in conduct according to the theory of rational choice. Ethical rules are restrictions on the rational pursuit of interests. Furthermore, they postulate the existence of a collectivity to the members of which certain obligations exist that restrict the pursuit of interest, i.e., the maximal advantage of the acting subject.

Now, it is certainly true that the theory of rational choice can be formulated in a manner that rational choice occurs within the setting of law and ethical judgments. That is certainly the case. That being so, it is necessary then to complement the theory of rational choice and of the exclusive pursuit of interests.

The complement to the theory of rational choice is what I tentatively call the theory of collective self-consciousness.

II

Although the subject can perceive others acting in their own interests, he cannot act in their interests unless he sees the satisfaction of their interests as a condition of the realization or frustration of his own interests. He can act for the frustration of their interests if it will prevent the frustration of his interests. The interests of others cannot be evaluated except as conditions of the realization or frustration of his interests.

The subject, in the view of the theory of rational choice, can act only with the intention of realizing his own interests. These are interests that are temporally bounded by his own demise when he will have ceased to be a subject with a self. It makes no sense to say that an individual acts for interests that will be realized—or which can be frustrated—only after his own demise. Because if he is capable of intending an act to confer benefits on other persons in the future when their receipt of these benefits can be of no benefit to him, this would indicate that he is capable of acting disinterestedly, i.e., that he can act for the realization of interests other than his own interests. But if an individual can act disinterestedly, i.e., without regard to the realization or frustration of his own interests, then the postulate of the theory of rational choice, namely, that the individual acts only with an intention to realize his own interests requires revision.

It could probably be argued that the theory of rational choice does not purport to be a universally valid description of how all individuals always act, but is rather a scheme for stating in general terms how individuals would act if they acted only with the intention of realizing their own interests (understood in the sense stated above). In that case, the theory of rational choice has real but limited descriptive or explanatory value. That is not what its proponents claim for it.

This limited applicability of the theory of rational choice reduces the range of its validity; it retains validity for a significant fraction of all human actions. In modern individualistic societies the class of actions for which the theory of rational choice is valid constitutes an even more substantial fraction of all human action than it does in less individualistic societies.

This is a very reasonable view and it commands agreement except for details. It must however be placed in the setting of a more comprehensive theory which can deal with the kinds of activity with which the theory of rational choice cannot deal. This would require some at least marginal adjustments to the theory of rational choice. It will require these adjustments because it will be necessary to deal with the interdependence between the two parts of the person—the part dealt with by the theory of rational choice and the theory that is to complement it.

The theory of rational choice defines the human being as a rational organism, while capable of perceiving the minds of others as entities like themselves, is capable of pursuing or acting on behalf of its own advantage only. But the knowledge that others seek their own advantage is also an acknowledgement that the individual is capable of knowing certain aspects of the minds of others. The acting subject, according to the theory of rational choice, does have the imaginative power to perceive that there are interests other than his own. Thus, he can understand that other minds have an independent existence, that they have rational powers, etc. This being so, he is also able to imagine human beings who will be alive after he is dead, and they will pursue their own life-time interests as he does in his life time. Since, however, their activities cannot affect the attainment of his own interests, he cannot assess them. He can have no interest in them.

Is there any room in the theory of rational choice for the acting individual to define the realization of the interests of others as an intrinsic interest of his own? If it is possible for an acting subject to attribute intrinsic value to the realization by others of their own interests, a different conception of interest is entailed. It is a definition that points to a collective interest focused on objects of intrinsic value to the acting subject. This definition of interest is radically divergent from the individualistic definition of interest that is, I think, the definition generally espoused by the proponents of the theory of rational choice. That definition which says that it is to my interest that the interest of other individuals be realized can be put forward to mean that there is a causal connection between their realization of their interests and my realization of my interests; in other words, the realization of their interests is instrumental to the realization of my interests. The alternative described above is a plausible one if a person says that the happiness of other persons, i.e., the realization of their interests—taking for granted for the moment the equivalence of happiness and the realization of interests—is one of his interests then he defines the beneficiary of a realized interest as a part of a single entity which includes himself. This is quite different from a conception of interest in which the acting subject is the only intended beneficiary.

So much for the self-containedness of the individual to his lifetime and himself (i.e., his self, bounded by the outer surface of his physical organism) as the ultimate beneficiary of interests.

III

The concept of the human mind that is postulated by the theory of collective self-consciousness may be contrasted with the conception of the mind in the theory of rational choice. According to the latter, the mind is homogenous (and susceptible to internal conflict only because it is of "two minds" when it is uncertain about the course of events in the future). There can be no moral dilemma in the theory of rational choice because the category of moral judgment does not exist within the theory of rational choice. The individual can have no divided loyalties because such collectivities to which the individual might belong according to the theory of rational choice hold their adherents only through their contribution to the maximization of the benefits of the individual. The individual alone can be the recipient of benefits; the collectivity of which he is perforce a "member" can be regarded as a legitimate beneficiary of actions if the receipt of those benefits by its other members are conducive to the acting subject's own receipt of those benefits.

The "self" is a rather unproblematic phenomenon in the theory of rational choice. It is the point at which cognitive activities occur and from which externally oriented activities originated. The acting subject has a memory; it consists of "generalized" cognitive propositions precipitated by particular experiences in the past. From this basis in remembered experiences, the acting subject can estimate the probable actions of different causes of action. His power of reason permits him to compare and weigh these outcomes, each against the other, and then to decide on which outcomes or combination of outcomes to choose to realize. The individual's mind is probably capable of calculating the optimal value that corresponds to his "interests."

When I said above that the mind of the individual according to the theory of rational choice is homogenous, I meant nothing more than that the individual acting subject does not seek a plurality of diverse objectives. The theory of rational choice posits the uniformity of the object sought. Income or wealth and values translatable into income and wealth are the main objects. Where the objectives that are resident in interests are of a single quality or can be reduced to a single quality (e.g., wealth and income), we are justified in saying that the mind of the acting subject is homogenous.

The theory of the collective self-consciousness postulates a multiplicity of spheres of life and their corresponding values. It does not postulate the translatability of these diverse values into a common value. It also admits the likelihood that they are in conflict with each other.

In the theory of rational choice the individual can certainly be a member of a plurality of collectivities or corporate bodies. He is however a member of these only to benefit from the increased benefits which the division of labor and the concerted action which these make possible and which increases his prospective benefits. He retains his internal unity and his boundedness *vis-à-vis* other individuals. If there is conflict, it is only transient; it lasts only until a maximizing resolution has been found. In the theory of collective self-consciousness, the individual is always internally dual or multiple. This means that within the individual there is always an individual self and a part of a collective self. There might be parts of many collective selves within a single individual.

IV

The most important feature of the human mind, as understood in the theory of collective consciousness, is its imaginative power to extend into the minds of other persons.

The mind of the acting subject approaches other individuals, not simply as actors whose actions can foster or interfere with his attainment of his own ends. It approaches them with openness to the possibility that they are like himself as responsive to symbolic objectivations (or configurations) and to transcendental aspects of life as he is.

The acting subject has a disposition to perceive in others any signs of their participation in the major symbolic configurations, i.e., to see in them signs of their nationality, religious community, ethnic group, social class, profession, linguistic community and to form, at least unilaterally, a collective self with them and therewith to become conscious of their being parts of a collectivity.

Many decades ago, Franklin Giddings used the term "consciousness of kind" to refer to this phenomenon. He was on the right track, but he did not persist on it. He never succeeded in differentiating his views or in seeing the phenomenon as having to do with the symbolic sphere. He conceived of it as an instinctive biological propensity.

There is a notable difference from the theory of rational choice. In that theory, there is no place for the formation of collectivities except for collaborative ones, i.e., collectivities formed by "contractual" arrangements among the participants each seeking thereby to maximize the ends of wealth, income, power, and status. The human mind as conceived by the theory of collective self-consciousness has a disposition to characterize the acting subject or the others by reference to primordial properties such as biological connection, place of nativity and place of residence, "territorial ancestry" (i.e., descent from persons born in a more or less bounded territory), duration of residence in a territory, or participation in a symbolic pattern of belief (e.g., scientific knowledge or religious belief), or participation in the same linguistic community. These characterizations of other individuals entail participation in the image of the collectivities formed around the common possession of those referential properties. That participation also precipitates a model of obligation towards fellow-participants, i.e., members of the same collectivities.

The theory of rational choice does admit that there is a "World-3" of symbolic configurations, made up of the image of the patterns of rational reasoning. Beyond that it contains nothing else.

V

At this point I should try to make clear what I mean by the words: "individual" and "self." Regarding the "individual," I mean the continuously functioning organism as the point from which actions are initiated. The point is a biological or neurophysiological organism. That point—the individual organism—is an emitting and receiving entity. It has the continuity of any physical object, i.e., identity through time, the physical or physiological properties enduring and being reproduced and only gradually replacing some of its substance by newly grown substance. The individual is recognized from the outside by others as the same individual in consequence of their recognitions of the similarity of features, size, color, shape, temperament, tone of voice, etc. over extended periods; the "others" share the image of the acting subject in their memories. The individual recalls from his memory his past experiences as his own, by having in his memory an image of himself as a physical object, which bears his name. The individual also forms knowledge about its properties or qualities from the responses of others to him. These responses are stored in his memory together with the images of the recent events that occurred to the individual in the presence of others or which were witnessed by the individual and by others or which were witnessed by himself alone.

From these memories of his experiences, from what he has been told by others or inferred from the actions and words of others, the self-image is formed within the individual. The self is a state of substantive, specific, and "telescoped" consciousness of the individual about himself. The self is an individual's state of consciousness of his own quality, propensity and desires. The self is the product of the individual's becoming an object of his own consciousness. It is a statement that "I am what I am." The self is not just a precipitate of memories of experiences and of previous states of the individual. It is not just a cognitive phenomenon. The self is a state of consciousness that initiates actions of the individual. It is the self-consciousness of the individual; it is individual self-consciousness. The collective self-consciousness is a state of consciousness of the individual as a participant in the collective self; there are as many collective self-consciousnesses as there are collectivities and collective selves of which the individual is a participant.

The collective self-consciousness is the outcome of the collectivity and the collective self, in which the individual participates, becomes the object of the individual's self-consciousness. Collective self-consciousness, unlike individual self-consciousness, does not have a memory of its own, outside the memories carried within the individual. They are however memories of the experiences of the collectivity. The collective self does not, unlike the individual self-consciousness, initiate actions of the collectivity; it does so through its influence on the individuals who bear it.

At this point, methodological individualism must be observed; but it is important, at the same time, to acknowledge its limitations: collectivity, the collective self and collective self-consciousness all have distinctive reality.

Can there be an interest of a collectivity? Of course, there can be! The theory of rational choice conceives of this collective interest as being the maximization of the ends of the individuals who make up the collectivity. The theory of collective self-consciousness conceives the collective interest as a statement regarding the determinate constellation or conditions furthering the well being (gratification?) of the collectivity as a whole. (This embraces the realization of the interests of individuals constituting the collectivity but not necessarily, e.g., a collectivity in wartime.)

Does the individual's collective self-consciousness exist as something entirely separate from his own individual self-consciousness? No, the collective self-consciousness and the collective self-consciousnesses are part of his "larger self"; but they are different from his individual self-consciousness. The individual self has two levels. On the one level, the individual sees himself as distinct from his collective self-consciousness; at this level the self is manifested in the individual self-consciousness, at the other—larger or more comprehensive self-consciousness—he includes his individual and his collective self-consciousness as the self.

Individual self-consciousness resembles closely the properties of the mind portrayed in the theory of rational choice. It shows the individual as having cognitive powers that include observations of present events and objects and prediction of the probability of future events set into motion by the individual's own actions and the actions of others. The knowledge used to estimate the likelihood of occurrence of events in the future is generalized knowledge, although very seldom explicit and formalized; it is based on experiences and perceptions of past events, stored in memory. Thus, the individual's cognitive powers are retrospective and prospective as well as in the present moment. Thus, the individual possesses memory and imagination, just as he does in the theory of rational choice.

How far does the imagination of the individual extend? Does it extend to events beyond the end of the individual's life span? It certainly can extend beyond the individual's life span, according to the theory of collective self-consciousness because the individual possesses the power to participate in collective selves. Collective selves may and often do include past individuals and past collectivities and they can include collective selves and individuals who will be participants in collective selves in the future.

The capacity to participate in a collective self is not among the capacities of the individual according to the theory of rational choice.

The theory of collective self-consciousness conceives of the individual as capable of, and, to some extent, regarding as valid the ends of other individuals and the ends of a collectivity of which he is a participant. The latter is possible because the individuals are simultaneously hosts to a collective self-consciousness as well as being the seats of their own individual self-consciousness.

The acting subject's perception of the other person might be multiple in focus. He might perceive the other person as simultaneously similar to himself in one reference, and different from himself in another reference. The acting subject might see in the other person the properties that he shares with him and the properties that he does not share with him. The acting subject might see the other person sharing with him nationality (nativity and territorial residence) and ethnicity (descent not from particular or direct ancestors but from ancestors of a particular territorial nativity and language); but he sees him as not sharing properties of class or states, etc., in any combination. This means that each individual might participate simultaneously in a number of collectivities and collective selves. Anyone of them might be more salient than the others to the individuals who participate in it. For some, nationality and ethnicity might be salient while class status is recessive (or secondary); in the case of others, the rank-order might be reversed.

Social stratification (i.e., rank or status or deference) is a function of perception and assessment of what I once called "status-relevant characteristics or properties." What I did not see was that these assessments were simultaneous assessments of the other person in comparison with oneself and that the assessment placed the other person within the same neighboring or remote category of deference. In doing so, it created a collective consciousness embracing that other person and often shared with him or them.

The theory of collective consciousness allows for a plurality of values (valued objects). In its conception, the mind is capable of multi-valence. Each of these values casts out a net which falls upon many known and unknown. It forms these covered by it into a "we"; it puts those outside it into a "they"; but both "we" and "they" may fall into a single "we" according to another, no less important referent. Not every separation of "we" from "they" is an unbridged cleavage, which is never attenuated or suspended by some other "we," i.e., by some other collective self.

The collective self entails consciousness of persons unknown to each acting subject who participate in it. The perception of the other person, seen or even known by name, animates or arouses the image of the collectivity. The image of the collectivity, unless it is a small and new one, always contains images of members, a small number known by name and face, a far larger number unknown but accepted cognitively as existing. In any such collectivity, dead members are included, some—the founders, the heroes, the benefactors— known by name, but of most all that is known is that they are said to have existed. All large collectivities embraced large numbers of persons most of whom are unknown to each other.

Even in such situations, however, there are differences in the intensity and comprehensiveness of the collective self-consciousness. Some individual selves are insensate to the referents that are very significant to others. Can an individual who is inimical to his own society participate in its collective self-consciousness?

Collective self-consciousness is very complex. It can engender solidarity and enmity. The solidarity is not unalloyed. It can be affirmative with respect to certain objects, negative or inimical with respect to other features of those objects. It is not unknown for criminals to be patriots! What this means is that collective self-consciousness is not always comprehensive and homogenous.

There are various modes of enmity towards a society on the part of those living in it. One, as in the case mentioned above, the enmity towards society is only partial; the collective self-consciousness prevails in most of the acting subject's life. Then there is the complete refusal of the collective self-consciousness. Perhaps it is an overstatement; even terrorists like the Russians of the 1880s and the Italians a century later do not refuse entirely all of the national collective self-consciousness. This is surely the case with many criminals, such as gangsters in the United States, in the past three quarters of a century.

Collectivities formed around a collective self-consciousness have ideals, but they also have interests. They may be concerned to increase the wealth, income, power and status of the collectivity. In some cases, these "interests" are justified logically or rhetorically by the ideals of the collectivity. But whatever their justifications, they are "interests" in the same sense as the interests of individuals are interests. They are in conflict with the interests of other collectivities.

With respect to ideals, too, collectivizes can be in conflict. Ideals seriously striven for, norms which are observed or for which observance is called for, may be in conflict with the ideals and norms of other collectivities and even in conflict within the same collectivity.

Collectivities might also have an interest in the maximization of the interests of their individual members. Within collectivities there can also be conflicts between the interests of individual members and the interests of other members as well as conflicts between the interests of various sectors or sub-groups within the collectivity.

This raises a necessary question. What is the relation of dissensus in the collective self-consciousness? I will say no more at this point than: consensus and collective self-consciousness may be regarded as in effect synonymous but only with the collectivity which shares the particular collective self-consciousness.

It must also be remembered that not everyone in a society is brought equally and completely into the collective self-consciousness. It must also be remembered that the collectivities that are formed have collective interests just as individuals have individual interests.

VI

The constitution of the collective self-consciousness within the individual and as an inter-individual (trans-individual) pattern is obscure. Its relationship to individual self-consciousness, i.e., how it affects and confines individual self-consciousness is no less obscure. It is possible however to say a little about its contents.

The collective self-consciousness contains an image of the particular society in which the individual is living, not simply as a collectivity made up of others but also containing the individual himself; or rather his image of himself as an individual with self-consciousness and as a participant in the collective self-consciousness. The collective self-consciousness is the consciousness that contains an image of the pattern of the society and its internal differentiation. It contains an image of the individual's relationship to the center, as a member of the center or as a member of the periphery; it contains the individual's image of his individual participation in that differentiated pattern of center and periphery.

The collective self-consciousness is probably never a highly and precisely differentiated image of society. Those who are closer to one sector have a relatively more differentiated image of that part while those who live in other parts have a more highly differentiated image of those parts. Nevertheless, most of the members of a society have an image of the major lineaments of the society.

At this point, I would like to take up a very difficult examination of some of the problems of the social structure of collective self-consciousness. We know that actions have a recurrent pattern or structure; we know that the actions are the actions of individuals articulated inter-individually so that they form a recurrent pattern. Are the individual experiences of (participations in) the collective self-consciousness susceptible to being seen as a single structure? By this I mean a single structure of the collective self-consciousness in its possession by individuals.

We speak easily of the structure or pattern of a national economy spread out over the national territory, its parts interacting with each other as an interdependent system. We speak of the national legal political and governmental system spread out over the national territory, all their respective institutions working and interdependent internally, and in mutual interdependence with the other systems. Can we do the same for the symbolic configurations that are the collective self-consciousness? They do, after all, have the spatial dispersion that is the dispersion of the individual human beings, of the individual consciousnesses in which they are contained.

Let us take a simple (!) case, that of scientific knowledge. We could, in principle, but not in fact, draw a map of the distribution of scientific knowledge in any particular society. I do not mean the body of validity, established and "certified" knowledge such as could be synthesized in a textbook, manual or treatise. I mean rather all the existing knowledge in human minds, its thinness and concentration, at various points in society (and in space).

If this were possible (in principle although not empirically since it is too complicated in our present state of knowledge and skill), we could speak of the spirit that "dominates" society. It is like public opinion, which is a simple thing, opinions spread over the area, and susceptible to cartographic representation. But to show all the collective self-consciousnesses (large and small) and their differentiated participations, that is impossible to carry out and very difficult even to conceive. Still, it is desirable to make some approximation to it.

VII

The knowledge of society possessed by sociologists and anthropologists, etc., is collective self-knowledge. The knowledge of the sociologist or anthropologist is a knowledge formed from the collective self-consciousness of numerous human beings. Even demography is ultimately that because it depends on the knowledge conveyed by individuals to registrars, census, enumerators, etc. The field work of sociologists and anthropologists, whether participant-observer, or sample surveys using questionnaires, is an assembly of existing knowledge from the persons interviewed, overheard or observed. In a sense, the sociologist-anthropologist becomes the custodian of the collective self-consciousness. (Unfortunately, given the prejudices of the social scientists, the collective self-consciousness so gathered and reconstructed is distorted in accordance with radical political prejudices.)

Objectivity requires that the individual see his society as truthfully as he can, i.e., without any of the parti-pris or any of the blindnesses for parts of his own society which a society of acting subjects might possess. Can a social scientist divest himself of the qualities which he possesses as a participant, whether loyal and patriotic or hostile?

It is not merely a matter of one's own society, the society in which the acting subject lives his life. It is also of concern to the historian who studies a society—if it is ancient or oriental—of which he is not an acting subject. The statement might need qualification with respect to ancient occidental societies; given the nature of society which amalgamates present and past, the disjunction between the society studied and the society in which the observed and acting subject lives is not unbridged. Even for the study of ancient or medieval Chinese societies, a Western scholar must acquire some of the collective self-consciousness of that society. He must read the primary literature, documents, accounts of officials about conditions in the provinces; he must use the knowledge which the people of that society acquired from others who possessed either through their own experience or who received it from others who, etc.

Objectivity must be attained by the assessment of the limits of the knowledge that those contemporaries had, correcting it by paleontological and archaeological evidence, inscriptions, etc. The observation of contemporary societies by a person who is an acting subject of such societies must be achieved by self-discipline—partly by divesting oneself of one's share in the collective self-consciousness but retaining enough fundamental knowledge of participation in collective self-consciousness that the phenomena of the ancient (or the contemporary) society can be understood. In other words, the historian like the sociologist must know: (a) what categories and varieties of collective self-consciousness can be understood; and (b) he must suspend or divest himself of the substantive collective self-consciousness of his own society—at least in doing his research.

VIII

The imaginative powers of the mind, according to the theory of collective self-consciousness, extend not just to the perception of others but to their inclusion in the collective self-consciousness in which the individual participates. There is something more there than the plain perception of others or even the knowledge of other (i.e., their) minds. Knowledge of the content of the mind of another is not a decisive thing. The decisive thing is taking the content of the other's mind and the content of one's own mind as part of the collective self-consciousness. This common participation when sufficiently intense binds the minds together into a single mind.

The imaginative expansion of the mind of the individual, according to the theory of collective self-consciousness, might embrace the ends of the other members (participants) to the point where their ends become the ends of the acting individual. He strives to realize their ends; he strives to realize ends that they hold in common because the acting subject and his fellow-members see themselves as the members of the same collectivity.

The imagination is a taking into the mind of things not there previously. Imagination goes beyond the perception of things and events immediately experienced; it is the perception of things, persons and events beyond the limits of the immediately experienced.

Imagination brings things, persons, and events not immediately perceived as present within the radius of the individual's perceptive attention. It is also bringing into one's consciousness images of things, persons, and events not previously part of it. Imagination can change both the individual's self and the collective self by adding to them the image of persons or parts of persons who were previously not parts of them. Yet, this imaginative incorporation into the self within the individual is not a delusion, like the delusion of the person who thinks that Napoleon dwells in him, that Napoleon has taken possession of him.

The Napoleonic delusion is the belief that Napoleon, once an external and real entity, has come into the person and dwells there—not his body but his spirit. Possession by spirits is much like this. Spirits, once outside, are thought to have entered into oneself, dwell there, perform the actions that are natural to or inherent in them while there.

What is the difference between the Napoleonic delusion, the delusion of possession, and the phenomenon that I am trying to delineate and comprehend? I am trying to deal with the phenomenon of acting on behalf of a collectivity for benefits of the collectivity and not of the action himself as an individual. A soldier sacrifices himself for his comrades or his "mates" or his "buddies"; he risks death for the survival of his unit or for the attainment by his unit of the objective assigned to it by its sergeant or lieutenant. A graduate of a college gives a gift to the college; a teacher works hard to improve a student's dissertation without thinking about whether the student will be grateful or whether the dean or the head of the department will take notice of his exertion and will increase his salary, raise his rank, and spread the "story" that he is a wonderful supervisor; an impecunious college or university teacher spends days writing without monetary compensation or any public acknowledgement a detailed report of a paper which has been submitted to a journal, the author of which he does not know and who does not know him. All of these persons are doing things which are costly to themselves in time, health, even life itself, money, energy and which bring no return to themselves as individuals to enjoy, aside from the enjoyment of the sense of having conformed with an ideal or norm, of having done something beneficial to others, or of having obeyed the order of a superior. They are acting on behalf of persons they do not know and who will know nothing about them and who, if they are grateful will be unable to convey their gratitude to their benefactors.

The culmination of the actions of the sort I have mentioned is very different from the culmination that the theory of rational choice asserts are the intended culmination of all actions of individuals, namely, the enhancement of the status, wealth, power, health, longevity, sensual pleasure, physical comfort, etc., of the acting subject.

What happens in the cases of "disinterested" or "selfless" action, of works of charity, of works on behalf of an ideal, of work on behalf of others whom one knows or does not know, which imposes costs on the individual, and which confer benefits on others, living and unborn. How are we to describe actions that fulfill or realize an ideal that conforms with a tradition.

Of course, the theory of rational choice will say that the individual does it in order to obtain the deference or esteem of his present contemporaries. This explanation might hold in some cases; but it disregards the fact that such "disinterested" conduct is sufficiently highly regarded that it is thought to merit award. And sociologists argued some years ago that scientists seek truth so that they can exchange it for prestige! In his book *The Scientific Community*, Professor Hagstrom said nothing about why the recipient scientists wished to have the truth. Did they wish to exchange these truths for prestige? But why is the acquisition and possession of scientific truth thought to merit prestige? But this looks differently if one says that a scientist produces the truth to be shared by others and their agreement is evidence that that proposition has now become a common possession. In contradiction to Professor Hagstrom, one could say that a scientist pursues a truth with the intention of enriching the body of knowledge and of participation in the community of those who have come to share that knowledge. The individual scientist is not exchanging his knowledge for prestige, although he might be granted prestige in acknowledgement of his contribution to knowledge. He is contributing to a trans-individual common culture in which he and his fellow scientists participate. As participants in that objective body of scientific knowledge, they form, when they are aware of the existence of such participants (even if not by sight or name) the collective self-consciousness of the scientific community.

Psychoanalytic theory speaks of incorporation of the qualities of the persons who exercise authority from its external performers into the individual mind. The incorporated authority became the super ego, dominating the ego, inhibiting it, and deforming it. Psychoanalytic theory does not ordinary speak of the super ego elevating ego. (The main activity of the super ego is repressing the id from its natural expression which is a progression from one sexual object to another, a movement towards maturity.)

This simplification of the psychoanalytic view has a considerable coherence but it leaves most of the problems unsettled. For example, what is "internalization"? It is an act of imagination. It entails perception of another person—the parent—and the imagination that the "self" of that person is within one's own body. It is different from the ego that might be parallel to the self of the individual; but, as I recall, Freud does not deal with memory except as a part of the super-ego. Freud also saw all relations with other persons as controlled by the superego. In contrast with this, the image of the collectivity ("World-3") does not represent only authority; it is an image of a collectivity in all dimensions, although, of course, vague and ambiguous to critical intelligence.

It is the superego, as conceived by psychoanalysis, that is of most interest to me. It certainly bears some relationship to the "collective self-consciousness": "internalization," dominion over the actions of individuals, the constriction of the sphere of the ego (the individual self-consciousness).

But the superego is the source of all collective selfness. It is the origin and chief constituent of any solidarity. The idea of the superego is that it is the fundamental experience of collective existence. All collective experience is derivative from it. This is an important difference between the psychoanalytic theory of "the social bond" and that of the theory of collective self-consciousness. In the former all relationships outside the primary relationship between parent and child are derivative from that primary relationship; in the latter, the relationship with authority, although it comes first in the history of the individual human being, becomes a part of a more primary relationship with human beings formed in accordance with the possession of certain primary properties, e.g., primordiality, lineage, locality, nativity, ethnicity, nationality, class (also a matter of nativity, etc.)

Now, looked at from the point of view of the theory of collective self-consciousness, the superego can be said to be a primordially oriented form of the self. It is an intra-familial phenomenon; it arises in the relationship between parent and child. It could, therefore, be said to be one narrow variant of a primordial phenomenon; but it collapses because it has no place for relationships to persons of the same locality and of nativity in the same locality (or territory). It is an event—the sole event—in the relationship of a child to its parents, having no place for any image of ancestors and very little to coevals. Even more striking among the omissions is the absence of the fact of nativity and of any image of the "tie of blood." It is simply a fact of the sexual possession of the mother (for the male child). It is a very constricted conception of the relationship of the child with the mother.

One problem that sometimes troubles me is: how does that part of the collective self, which resides within the individual, affect the individual self, e.g., how does it act through the individual self?

In psychoanalytic terms, the question would be: how does the superego act on the ego? The answer is simple. The psychoanalytic solution to this problem is metaphorical and undifferentiated. It is no solution at all.

Psychoanalytic theory has no place for solidarity, i.e., for the "collaboration" of a constellation of concurrent superegos in a plurality of individuals. I myself conceive of the collective self-consciousness as a fact of "co-presence": the more or less concurrent participation of a plurality of individuals, participating in a common image and responding to each other through those parts of the collective self-consciousness in which they participate. Psychoanalytic theory, in contrast, sees the superego as a deposit of subjective apprehension, actions and beliefs of another person, namely, the father. It is the product of what psychoanalysts used to call "a two-body relationship." My own idea of the collective self-consciousness refers to a plurality of bodies, in reciprocal relationship. In the psychoanalytic theorem, the father is a *deus absconditus*; he does not participate in the relationship once it has got underway. He need not be present. He might be dead; he often is. The relationship is not only a "two-body" relationship; it is also a two-generational relationship. Psychoanalysis shortens the duration of society to two generations. It has little or no idea of tradition that constitutes a society temporally.

It is not desirable to become too entangled into the criticism of the fundamental theorem of psychoanalysis. It is sufficient to show that it presents a very narrow treatment of primordiality and that its conception of the constitution and the process of the formation of the collective self-consciousness or of the superego is not at all illuminating—any more than is Durkheim's (or for that matter my own!)

In these fundamentals, the theory of rational choice and psychoanalytic theory have much in common. Both think that the individual should maximize his benefits by realistic cognition of the situation and by rational application of generalized realistic knowledge of the discovery of the best means to the maximal outcome. They part ways at the point where they analyze the failure of the individual to act rationally and realistically to maximize his benefits. The theory of rational choice attributes the failure to cognitive mistakes; the psychoanalytic theory attributes the failure to a fear of achievement or attainment of the beneficial outcome because the super ego forbids it. If the super ego could be weakened or abolished then individuals would be able to have a clearer, more correct idea of what is advantageous or beneficial to them and could pursue that benefit more rationally, more realistically and more fruitfully.

Note

1.   James Coleman, The Foundations of Social Theory (Cambridge: Harvard University Press, 1990)

Index